# The Evidence-Based Social Work Skills Book

## Barry R. Cournoyer

*Indiana University*

PEARSON

*Boston • New York • San Francisco*
*Mexico City • Montreal • Toronto • London • Madrid • Munich • Paris*
*Hong Kong • Singapore • Tokyo • Cape Town • Sydney*

**Series editor:**  *Patricia Quinlin*
**Editorial assistant:**  *Annemarie Kennedy*
**Marketing manager:**  *Taryn Wahlquist*
**Manufacturing buyer:**  *JoAnne Sweeney*
**Composition and prepress buyer:** *Linda Cox*
**Cover designer:**  *Kristina Mose-Libon*
**Editorial-production administrator:**  *Anna Socrates*
**Editorial-production service:**  *Chestnut Hill Enterprises, Inc.*
**Electronic composition:**  *Modern Graphics*

For related titles and support materials, visit our online catalog at www.ablongman.com.

Between the time Web site information is gathered and then published, it is not unusual for
some sites to have closed. Also, the transcription of URLs can result in unintended typo-
graphical errors. The publisher would appreciate notification where these errors occur so
that they may be corrected in subsequent editions.

**Library of Congress Cataloging-in-Publication Data**

Cournoyer, Barry.
   The evidence-based social work (EBSW) skills book / Barry R. Cournoyer.
      p. cm.
   Includes bibliographical references and index.
   ISBN 0-205-35862-4
   1. Social work education. 2. Social service  I. Title: EBSW skills book. II. Title


HV11.C782 2004
361.3'072—dc22

2003053685

Printed in the United States of America

10   9   8   7   6   5   4   3   2   1      07   06   05   04   03

# Contents

**Preface**   v

**1  Evidence-Based Social Work**   1

*What Is EBSW?*   3

*Practice Effectiveness*   4

*What Is Evidence?*   5
    Legal Evidence   6
    Medical Evidence   7
    Evidence in Psychology   9
    Evidence in Social Work   11

*Phases of Evidence-Based Social Work*   15
    Questioning   15
    Searching   16
    Analyzing   17
    Applying and Evaluating   17

*EBSW in Contemporary Practice*   18

**2  Questioning**   21

*Formulating a Practice-Effectiveness Question*   23
    Asking about Special Populations   23
    Asking about Social Problems   24
    Asking about Target Client Groups   27
    Asking about Assessment and Evaluation Tools   30
    Asking about Services   30

*Generating Synonyms and Keywords*   32

*Planning the Search*   41

**3  Searching**   49

*Searching: The Basics*   51
    Think Database   51

Boolean Logic    52
Documenting Search Activities    55

**Searching Library Resources**    63
Reference Works    64
Books    71
Dissertations    74
Professional and Scientific Journals    76

**Searching Bibliographic Databases**    85

**Searching Evidence-Based Collaborations and Government Resources**    101

**Searching the World Wide Web**    112

## 4    *Analyzing*    118

**Evaluating Evidence**    118
Source    121
Contents    130

**Assessing Authority-Based Evidence**    146

**Assessing Research-Based Evidence**    148
Validity and Reliability    148
Research Papers    154
Research Syntheses    161
Practice Guidelines    166

**Grading the Evidence**    168

**Synthesizing Evidence**    172

## 5    *Applying and Evaluating*    179

**Applying**    179
**Evaluating**    186

## *Epilogue*    194

**References**    198

**Index**    212

# Preface

I love social work. I have been a social worker for nearly thirty years and a social work professor for more than twenty. I love the profession's fundamental values, principles, and mission. The term "social worker" appeals to me much more than "psychologist," "sociologist," or the ever popular "psychotherapist." I would rather be a "worker" than a "therapist" any day.

Despite my continuing love affair with social work, I am concerned about the future of the profession, the nature of its education, and the quality of social work services. Universities graduate more than ten thousand social workers each year. However, only three hundred or so of them receive doctoral degrees (DSW or Ph.D.). Most doctoral students learn how to conduct research and analyze findings, while most BSW and MSW graduates learn how to serve people through other forms of practice. The social work profession has far too few researchers, and only a handful of those study the effectiveness of social work services. Moreover, an extremely low percentage of BSW and MSW practitioners regularly read research articles that pertain to practice effectiveness and use such evidence to inform their service to people in need.

In the contemporary world, social workers must be much more than well-intentioned, kind, and caring people who hold strong values of service and altruism. There are simply too many examples of harm done by people with good intentions (Gibbs, 2002; Kirk, 1999). Rather, we must become more active producers and better consumers of practice-effectiveness research (Hess & Mullen, 1995). As a social worker, you must read, critically analyze, and use findings from studies that pertain to service processes and outcomes. Social work educators must encourage professional-level scholarship among students, and instill a passion for providing clients with the highest quality services that are (1) supported by evidence of effectiveness, (2) informed by practice experience and critical thought, and (3) consistent with clients' personal and cultural values.

Although social workers conduct a small fraction of the total, the number of relevant practice-effectiveness research studies is growing at an increasingly rapid rate. The findings are often pertinent to social work and our clients. The researchers who conduct these studies often receive support from the U.S. federal government (the Departments of Health and Human Services, Justice, Education) or private foundations (Robert Wood Johnson, Pew Memorial Trust, Annie E. Casey). Many helping professionals and their associations are extremely interested in the findings of such studies, especially as they relate to service and treatment outcomes. Several years ago, through the Cochrane Collaboration, medical doctors initiated processes to collect, analyze, summarize, and publish systematic reviews of practice-relevant research studies to promote evidence-based medicine. During the 1990s the Clinical Psychology Division of the American Psychological Association began to review research studies that led to the identification of several empirically supported treatments.

Members of the social work profession have also recently begun to participate more actively in these endeavors. In today's real world of professional practice, social workers need to learn how to search for and analyze scholarly information that pertains to their clients, the problems and issues their clients address, and especially the effectiveness of services intended to help. During the twenty-first century, social workers will increasingly use evidence-based knowledge to plan, implement, and evaluate the quality of their own professional activities.

I prepared this book to help social work students develop the skills necessary to search for, discover, analyze, synthesize, and apply evidence of what works in service to people in need. I refer to these as evidence-based social work (EBSW) skills. Students who learn, practice, and apply them in service to others will almost certainly become more knowledgeable, compassionate, principled, and competent social workers, better able to help clients address issues, maximize strengths, resolve problems, and accomplish goals. Our clients and communities deserve at least this much—and a great deal more!

## Organization of the Book

*The Evidence-Based Social Work Skills Book* is primarily intended for students enrolled in one or more social work practice or research courses or seminars. It may serve as the primary text for practice courses that provide opportunities for individual learners or small groups of students to develop expertise about a certain target client group and the best or most effective practices for service to them. Typically, such courses also attempt to encourage students' development of scholarship and critical thinking abilities, and self-directed lifelong learning skills. *The Evidence-Based Social Work Skills Book* may also be used as a supplemental text for courses that address generalist practice, mental health practice, child welfare practice, ethnic-sensitive practice, practice with families, practice with individuals, practice with groups, policy, community organization, planning, program development, administration, or other courses that involve in-depth study about the effectiveness and outcomes of professional helping services.

Available free with this book is *Research Navigator for the Helping Professions* that contains an access code that will enable students to register with the Research Navigator on-line databases at http://www.researchnavigator.com. Once registered, they will be able to search bibliographic databases that contain citations, abstracts, and full-text articles from hundreds of professional journals in social work, sociology, psychology, education, medicine, anthropology, criminal justice, and other fields. Students may use Research Navigator and various other electronic sources to complete exercises throughout the book.

The book is organized as follows. Chapter 1 considers a working definition of evidence-based social work, the significance of the EBSW skills, and the phases and elements of EBSW. Students will learn about the assumptions, principles, values, and ethics that support the approach. At the end of this chapter, students will complete several introductory exercises.

Chapter 2 covers formulating an evidence-based practice-effectiveness question and developing a preliminary search plan. It discusses the tasks and functions associated with the questioning phase of EBSW, identifying and describing each of the relevant skills. At the end of the chapter are several exercises to practice the skills and strengthen learning. Importantly, students will select a target client group (members of special population group affected by or at risk of being affected by a contemporary social problem), formulate a practice-effectiveness question specific to the people they would most like to serve, and prepare a preliminary plan by which to pursue their search for evidence.

Chapter 3 demonstrates how to search for valid, reliable, and relevant evidence; document the activities; and compile information gained into an organized portfolio. It describes the purposes, tasks, and skills associated with the searching phase of EBSW and presents more learning exercises to develop proficiency in the searching skills. In particular, students will conduct and document a search and compile evidence of effectiveness for services to or for members of the target client group selected in Chapter 2.

In Chapter 4, students will learn how to analyze, evaluate, and synthesize evidence gained through their search and compilation. They will develop skills needed to identify a practice approach that is (1) supported by evidence, (2) consistent with professional expertise, and (3) compatible with the culture and values of the target client group. They will also learn how to synthesize the results of their analysis in the form of a practice effectiveness evidence report (PEER). The PEER may be submitted as a course or program requirement, shared with researchers, or disseminated to colleagues and practitioners.

Chapter 5, the final chapter, covers how to use the knowledge gained through the search and analysis and the preparation of the PEER to implement, if possible, an evidence-based approach and evaluate its effectiveness. It describes the purposes, tasks, and skills associated with the application phase of EBSW. Students will undertake more learning exercises to develop proficiency in the skills used to deliver evidence-based services to members of a target client group. In lieu of actually implementing the evidence-based approach with clients, they will prepare an abbreviated practice manual for service to members of the target client group.

## *The Author*

I am a professor at the Indiana University School of Social Work in Indianapolis, Indiana. I earned a masters degree in social work from the University of Tennessee and a doctorate in social work from the University of Utah. I have been with the Indiana University School of Social Work since 1979 and have enjoyed participating in its growth and development. Indiana University sponsors one of the oldest and largest schools of social work in the nation, offering accredited social work programs to nearly nine hundred students on five campuses.

I teach social work practice courses, usually to MSW and Ph.D. students, and sometimes to BSW students. I am author of *The Social Work Skills Workbook*, Third Edition (2000, Brooks/Cole-Wadsworth), coauthor of *The Social Work Portfolio: Planning, Assessing, and Documenting Lifelong Learning in a Dynamic Profession* (2002, Brooks/Cole-Wadsworth), and former editor of *Advances in Social Work: Linking Research, Education and Practice*—the professional journal of Indiana University School of Social Work. In addition to my faculty responsibilities, I continue to provide social work services on a part-time basis to individuals, couples, and families in the Indianapolis area.

## *Acknowledgments*

Many of the ideas and concepts presented in *The Evidence-Based Social Work Skills Book* derive from the work and publications of authors, professors, and researchers in the field of evidence-based medicine (EBM). The following have had a profound impact: David L. Sackett and colleagues (Sackett, Straus, Richardson, Rosenberg, & Haynes, 2000), Trisha Greenhalgh (1997), and Daniel J. Friedland (1998) and colleagues. In addition, several centers and institutes in Canada, Great Britain, and the United States have published resources related to evidence-based medicine, mental health, child health, and social services,[1] and a growing number of journals focus on evidence-based practice: Evidence Based Medicine, Evidence-Based Mental Health, Evidence-Based Nursing, and Clinical Evidence. These resources, along with those of the Cochrane Collaboration and its remarkable library[2] and the recently developed Campbell Collaboration,[3] have been inspirational in the process of completing *The Evidence-Based Social Work Skills Book.*

I also want to acknowledge the contributions of many social workers whose empirical and evidence-based work I routinely use in my research, teaching, and practice activities. The list of notables in empirical and evidence-based practice is substantial and, I fervently hope, growing rapidly. I will mention a few social workers whose research and publications have been available: Paula Allen-Meares, David Austin, Sharon Berlin, Scott Briar, Juliet Cheetham, Beulah Compton, Elaine Congress, Kevin Corcoran, Kathleen Ell, Joel Fischer, Eileen Gambrill, Burt Galaway, Charles Garvin, Len Gibbs, Dean Hepworth, Walter Hudson, Srinika Jayaratne, Al Kadushin, Laura Myers, William Nugent, Enola Proctor, William Reid, Sheldon Rose, Aaron Rosen, Bruce Thyer, Edwin Thomas, Ray Thomlinson, Jerome Wakefield, Janet Williams, and John Wodarski.

In addition, I wish to acknowledge my Indiana University faculty colleagues. Founded in 1911, Indiana University School of Social Work is the oldest program in the United States that has held continuous university affiliation since its origin. We have a superb faculty. I would like to express my personal gratitude to Margaret Adamek, Bill Barton, Bob Bennett, Carolyn Black, Lorraine Blackman, Katharine Byers, Valerie Chang, Gayle Cox, Linda Cummins, Jim Daley, Ed Fitzgerald, Gail Folaron, Sherry Gass, Carol Hostetter, Elsa Iverson, Kathy Lay, Brad Lighty, Eldon Marshall, Paul Newcomb, Phil Ouellette, Michael Patchner, Cathy Pike, Irene Queiro-Tajalli, Mary Stanley, Theresa Roberts, Carol Satre, Pat Sullivan, Denise Travis, Bob Vernon, Marion Wagner, Bob Weiler, and especially Jerry Powers for their active and generous support as friends and colleagues. I would also like to thank the following reviewers: Jacqueline Corcoran, Virginia Commonwealth University; Matthew Howard, Washington University; and Mary Ruffolo, University of Michigan.

I dedicate this book to the following special people in my personal life: Catherine, the social worker I love most of all—she has been my friend, partner, confidant, and spouse for nearly twenty-five years; John Paul and Michael—our wonderful teenage sons (yes, teenagers can be honest, honorable, moral, and generous); Marge and Armand——my mother and father, who remain constant internal companions; Cathy, Polly, Reed, Jane Ann, Jo Ann, Patrice, Eric, and James Patrick—my extraordinarily talented brothers and sisters; all past, current, and future clients who deserve the highest-quality services available; and all those social workers and social work students who actively seek to learn what works.

B. R. C.

## Notes

1. The Web site of the Centre for Evidence-Based Medicine (GB) may be accessed at http://cebm.jr2.ox.ac.uk/; the Centre for Evidence-Based Medicine (CA) at http://www.cebm.utoronto.ca/; the Centre for Evidence-Based Child Health at http://www.ich.bpmf.ac.uk/ebm/ebm.htm; the Centre for Evidence-Based Mental Health at http://cebmh.warne.ox.ac.uk/cebmh/; the Centre for Evidence-Based Social Services at http://www.ex.ac.uk/cebss/; and the Evidence-Based Medicine Resource Center at http://www.ebmny.org/.
2. The Web site of the Cochrane Collaboration may be accessed at http://hiru.mcmaster.ca/cochrane/.
3. The Web site of the Campbell Collaboration may be accessed at http://campbell.gse.upenn.edu/.

# 1

# *Evidence-Based Social Work*

Welcome to *The Evidence-Based Social Work Skills Book*. In this introductory chapter, you will learn about evidence-based social work (EBSW) and the assumptions, values, and principles that underlie its growing importance for contemporary professional practice. You will also become familiar with the phases and processes that characterize EBSW.

Some twenty years ago, Joel Fischer observed that the social work profession was undergoing a "quiet revolution" in progressing from services derived from "vague and haphazard formulations" to those that are "scientifically and empirically based" (Fischer, 1981). The notion that social workers should base their assessments, decisions, and actions on scientifically and empirically based evidence may not seem especially revolutionary. Indeed, the National Association of Social Workers (NASW)—the largest association of social workers in the world—clearly states in the *Code of Ethics* (NASW, 1999) that "Social workers should base practice on recognized knowledge, including empirically based knowledge, relevant to social work and social work ethics" (p. 22); "continually strive to increase their professional knowledge and skills and to apply them in practice" (p. 6); and "critically examine and keep current with emerging knowledge relevant to social work. Social workers should routinely review the professional literature and participate in continuing education relevant to social work practice and social work ethics" (p. 22).

The Council on Social Work Education (CSWE), the accreditation body for schools and departments of social work throughout the United States, has a similar expectation. In its Educational Policy and Accreditation Standards (EPAS), CSWE requires graduates of accredited school work programs to "use theoretical frameworks supported by empirical evidence to understand individual development and behavior across the life span and the interactions among individuals and between individuals and families, groups, organizations, and communities" and to "evaluate research studies, apply research findings to practice, and evaluate their own practice interventions" (CSWE, 2001, p. 9). Graduates are also expected to use "empirically based interventions designed to achieve client goals," to apply "empirical knowledge and technological advances," and to evaluate "program outcomes and practice effectiveness" (CSWE, 2001, p. 12).

Although the standards of NASW and CSWE clearly recognize the importance and relevance of research-based knowledge, several authors and organizations have advocated for even more explicit ethical principles (Klein, Bloom, & Chandler, 1994; Kutchins, 1998; Myers & Thyer, 1997; Tutty, 1990). For example, in arguing that clients have a right to effective treatment, Thyer and Myers (1999) ask social workers to imagine they are clients dealing with a particular psychosocial problem for which compelling evidence of the effectiveness of an appropriate intervention approach exists.

> Wouldn't you be comforted knowing that the social worker you were consulting had a professional and ethical obligation to provide such services? Wouldn't you be upset if your social worker were woefully ignorant of the latest science-based developments in helping people with problems like yours? Wouldn't you be calling your lawyer if your social worker did know about effective methods of helping but instead opted to provide you with untested therapies or interventions previously shown through empirical research to be ineffective? Suppose that our assertion is correct, and that science is slowly demonstrating that some psychosocial treatments really do work well and that others do not. One ethical implication is that social work clients should have the right to receive these effective treatments. (Thyer & Myers, 1999, p. 503)

Consumer groups have also advocated for service approaches that reflect a reasonable likelihood of effective outcomes. For example, the National Alliance for the Mentally Ill (NAMI) has vigorously advocated on behalf of persons experiencing mental illness for services that work (for example, Assertive Case Management [ACT or PACT]) (National Alliance for the Mentally Ill, 1998).

Despite these trends, relatively few social workers regularly read journal articles that contain the results of practice-effectiveness research studies and apply the findings in their service to clients. "Social work practitioners are unlikely to have the time, inclination, support, or resources to either read research or integrate it into their day-to-day practice" (Holosko & Leslie, 1998, pp. 436–437). Results of surveys of social workers (Gerdes & Edmonds, 1996; Kirk, Osmalov, & Fischer, 1976; Penka & Kirk, 1991; Richey, Blythe, & Berlin, 1987; Sheldon & Chilvers, 2000) suggest that practicing social workers rarely read research articles that might help them better serve their clients. This is especially disconcerting in light of the increasing production of research studies and other forms of evidence that directly relate to practice effectiveness and service outcomes (Thyer, 1996).

The expectation for high-quality, competent, ethical, skillful, responsible, and effective professional social work practice based upon recognized evidence-based knowledge is growing for other reasons as well (Cournoyer & Powers, 2002). Social workers are increasingly held accountable for the effectiveness of helping activities because of social, political, and economic factors such as the

1. Passage of legislation mandating greater professional accountability, including requirements for continuing education
2. Proliferation of managed health care systems that provide direct and indirect incentives for choosing service approaches supported by efficacy and effectiveness research

3. Emergence of strong consumer advocacy movements throughout the country, not only within the area of health and mental health services but also in social and educational systems
4. Growing trends toward performance-based or outcome-based funding strategies
5. Increasing number of malpractice lawsuits filed against helping professionals, including social workers
6. Court decisions that highlight helping professionals' legal responsibility for the nature, quality, and outcomes of their services

## What Is EBSW?

The term *evidence-based social work* is of relatively recent origin. EBSW is closely related to empirically based practice (EBP), which has a longer tradition. Indeed, *empirically based* and *evidence-based* are sometimes used interchangeably. This is understandable. The two perspectives share much in common. *Empirical* is an adjective that refers to phenomena that may be observed or experienced, or can be proved or disproved through experimentation or observation. Empiricists often recognize the utility of theories but do not view them as essential for the discovery of knowledge. The noun *empiricism* originally referred to a school of thought within medicine that emphasized experience, observation, or experimentation as means of establishing truth. The term currently retains its essential meaning by emphasizing information gained through scientific research.

The term *evidence* may refer to unobserved as well as observed phenomena if the former reflect signs or indications that support, substantiate, or prove their existence, accuracy, or truth. Perhaps because of its long association with legal proceedings, evidence may involve testimony of experts and witnesses, written documents, and other indications that aid in determining the truth or falsehood of a claim. The term *evidence* therefore, encompasses a somewhat broader range of phenomena than does the term *empirical.* In both evidence-based and empirically based perspectives, however, unobserved or unexamined phenomena are considered less valid, reliable, and pertinent than those subject to observation, experience, or experimentation.

The term *empirically based practice* is widely used within both psychology and social work, while *evidence-based* has gained substantial usage in medicine. In Canada and Great Britain, evidence-based medicine (EBM) is especially popular. Within social work, empirically based practice (EBP) reflects an impressive literature and a growing following (Blythe, 1992; Blythe & Briar, 1985; Briar, 1990; Fischer, 1993; Gambrill, 1994; Jayaratne & Levy, 1979; Myers & Thyer, 1997; Reid, 1992, 1994; D. Siegel, 1984, 1985; Thyer, 1996; Thyer & Wodarski, 1998). Blythe notes that "empirically-based practice is the integration of practice methods and knowledge with research methods and knowledge" (Blythe, 1992, p. 260). Of course, the relative value of research findings varies according to many factors, including the nature and quality of the studies, and their relevance for practice with a particular person, family, group, organization, or community.

Evidence-based social work shares many assumptions, values, and principles with empirically based practice. EBSW recognizes both *nomothetic* and *ideographic* dimensions of research-based evidence (Cournoyer & Powers, 2002) as well as selected authority-based information, values different epistemologies, and recognizes that all research studies and findings, various theories, and practice approaches have strengths as well as limitations. No single theoretical approach is universally applicable to all people at all times in all circumstances. Nor is any research study without flaw. EBSW also recognizes the importance of critical thought and logical analysis. Social workers must be able to evaluate the value, meaning, and relevance of practice effectiveness evidence; consider the fundamental values and ethics of the profession; recognize the worth of practice experience; and synthesize and apply evidence-based information in ways that respect clients' personal and cultural values.

In order to advance reflection and discussion about its meaning, consider the following as a proposed definition of evidence-based social work.

> Evidence-based social work is the mindful and systematic identification, analysis, evaluation, and synthesis of evidence of practice effectiveness as a primary part of an integrative and collaborative process concerning the selection and application of service to members of target client groups. The evidence-based decision-making process includes consideration of professional ethics and experience as well as the personal and cultural values and judgments of consumers.[1]

Some of the concepts included within the proposed definition deserve elaboration. For instance, what is "effectiveness" and what is "evidence"?

## *Practice Effectiveness*

Within social work, practice effectiveness refers to the extent to which services yield their intended results. When social work services lead to a favorable outcome (the accomplishment of goals jointly agreed upon by the social worker and members of the client system), we may reasonably conclude that they are effective. For example, suppose a social worker serves a client, Mr. Stevenson, who physically abused his longtime female partner. Together, the social worker and Mr. Stevenson develop and commit to the goal that he will "immediately discontinue the use of physical violence in any shape, form, or manner upon his partner and remain violence-free for a period of at least one year." You could reasonably consider the service effective if Mr. Stevenson remains violence-free toward his partner—as indicated by valid and reliable evidence—during the entire one-year period.

The concept of effectiveness applies to all phases and processes of social work service. It is not limited to intervention outcomes or goal achievement alone. Beginnings, assessments, contracts, evaluations, and endings can be effective, partially effective, or ineffective. For example, a beginning is effective when both client and worker reach clarity, consensus, and commitment concerning the general direction of their work together. An assessment may be considered effective when valid, relevant, and reliable information is collected, analyzed, and summarized and leads to the identification of pertinent goals and appropriate strategies by which to achieve those goals. An effective contract could involve full understanding and endorsement by the social worker and the members of the client system. An effective evaluation process might be reflected in the use of valid, relevant, and reliable indicators of progress toward goal achievement. An ending to the provision of professional services might be effective when both the consumer and the provider report that goals have been achieved and the client is satisfied with the quality of care. In an effective follow-up, a former client might report continued satisfaction with the results of service, and standardized instruments might also indicate that positive outcomes have been maintained for some months following the termination of services.

Effectiveness has both nomothetic and ideographic dimensions. For example, suppose a vast majority of practice outcome research studies published in professionally refereed journals indicate that cognitive behavioral strategies that involve exposure to the feared stimuli are effective for some 80 to 90 percent of all clients treated for specific phobias such as a fear of high places. Suppose the positive outcome rate is much higher than any other known intervention approach and that the National Institute of Mental Health, the American Psychiatric Association, the American Psychological Association, the Anxiety Disorders Association of America, and the National Alliance for the Mentally Ill all recommend a treatment approach that includes cognitive behavioral and exposure techniques. Under such circumstances, a social worker might reasonably conclude that such a practice approach would generally be effective for most clients struggling with an acrophobic condition. Because of the strong nomothetic evidence of effectiveness, the social worker would inform incoming clients who experience specific phobias about the approach and its generally favorable results. However, an individual client might be one of the relatively few people who do not respond favorably to the recommended protocol. The social worker would not usually know that in advance. Through regular monitoring of a client's progress during the intervention phase of service, the social worker gains ideographic information that the preferred approach is effective, partially effective, or ineffective in the particular client's case.

Social workers obtain evidence of effectiveness from research studies and expert opinions and, of course, from the feedback of clients and evaluations of services delivered to individuals, families, groups, organizations, and communities. Social workers benefit from both research-based and authority-based forms of evidence in efforts to provide effective services to others.

## What Is Evidence?

The social work profession does not reflect complete consensus about the nature of evidence for social work. Numerous epistemological and philosophical issues remain unresolved. Indeed, social work professors frequently engage in fascinating and sometimes heated debates about these topics (Cheetham, 1992; Davis, 1989; Fraser, Taylor, Jackson, & O'Jack, 1991; Ivanoff, Blythe, & Briar, 1987; Ivanoff, Robinson, & Blythe,

1987; Raw, 1998; Rosenberg & Holden, 1992; Schinke & Nugent, 1994; Thyer & Myers, 1999; Thyer & Strean, 1992; Weiberg, 1992; Witkin, 1992a, 1992b, 1993). Such exchanges have great potential value for social workers and the profession if the arguments and supporting documentation are considered in a fair, balanced, and reasonable manner. Unfortunately, many people, including some social workers, feel personally and perhaps emotionally defensive when challenged by opposing views or presented with confounding evidence. Defensiveness and closed-mindedness are, of course, anathema to professionalism and certainly to evidence-based social work.

Imagine what could happen if social workers genuinely listened to, reflected on, analyzed, and evaluated new information before reaching fixed conclusions or reaffirming prior convictions. The potential benefits of knowledge derived from rational analysis, civil discourse, and various forms of high-quality research for clients and practitioners alike seem difficult to overestimate. Quantitative and qualitative studies, action-research, single-system and case reports, practice wisdom, the stories of vulnerable and resilient people, and consumer reports are only some of the means by which practice-related knowledge could emerge. There are many ways of knowing, each of which may contribute to the body of evidence necessary to help practitioners provide competent and effective services. Evidence need not be limited to a single practice approach, one theoretical perspective, or a preferred research methodology. However, when different forms of evidence do exist, social workers need to determine which is more valid, more reliable, or more relevant. Openness to learning and critical thinking is required, as is a general commitment by students, professors, and practicing social workers to use evidence of effectiveness to guide and inform their professional services.

Social work, of course, is not the first profession to consider evidence as a legitimate basis for effective practice. Law, medicine, and clinical psychology have also explored this issue in various ways.

## Legal Evidence

Lawyers tend to think about evidence in terms of what might be presented within the context of a legal proceeding to substantiate or prove an argument or claim. Evidence may include documents, audio or video recordings, maps, photographs, and testimony. Only relevant information—evidence that is more likely than not to bear on the truth or falsity of the argument or claim—is considered. In some circumstances, even relevant evidence may be excluded when it is likely to lead to excessive confusion, misinterpretation, or unfair prejudice (Delaney, 1987).

Legal rules of evidence guide lawyers and judges in determining the admissibility and relative value of information (West Group, 1999). For example, information based upon hearsay usually is considered less valid and reliable than direct observation. Similarly, evidence not pertinent to the issue of concern may be deemed irrelevant, and evidence obtained through improper means may be judged inadmissible.

Within the context of legal proceedings, rival parties base arguments on direct evidence, logical analysis, references to precedents, expert testimony, and appeal to constitutional principles. There are, of course, certain risks and limitations associated with the use of legal rules of evidence. For instance, a person truly guilty of a crime may avoid prosecution or conviction because of various technical violations in the discovery, collection, handling, or storage of evidence. Ideally, however, these same rules help ensure that relatively few innocent people are convicted, even though a substantial number of guilty persons may go unpunished.

Rules imply values, and legal rules of evidence suggest that certain forms of information are more likely to be valid, relevant, or reliable than others. For example, a written, dated, and notarized contract signed by all parties is more compelling than the verbal statement of a self-interested person. Experienced social workers tend to adopt similar views about the relative value of information. For instance, when biological parents compete with each other for sole custody of a young child, allegations that the other partner is "unfit" tend to carry less weight—because of perceived self-interest—than when the stakes are not as high. Similarly, a social worker who observes and photographs deep bruises, welts, and cuts on a six-year-old child's legs, back, and buttocks would be likely to consider that information more convincing than a parent or guardian's statement that "The child is a liar. Those bruises are from falls in the playground."

Although both lawyers and social workers make judgments about the relative value of evidence, they tend to do so through different processes. Social workers tend to base their conclusions on personal and professional experience, theoretical perspectives, and the advice of colleagues. Lawyers also rely upon experience and advice. However, they do so within the context of legal statutes, precedents, and rules of evidence. These latter sources provide lawyers with published references and guidelines by which to assess the relative value of different forms of evidence. These are extremely useful for decision making. Social workers might do well to develop analogous guidelines and rules of evidence.

## Medical Evidence

Within the medical profession, information is generally considered more or less valid, reliable, and relevant to the extent to which it was discovered through research processes that conform to accepted scientific protocols. Perhaps because drugs and carefully defined surgical procedures represent major therapeutic tools of physicians, laboratory experiments and clinical trials are commonly used methods to determine treatment effectiveness. Of course, these scientific research processes reflect certain strengths and limitations.

During the last decade or two, the medical profession has invested heavily in the review and analysis of effectiveness research. Faculty in the medical school at McMaster University in Hamilton, Ontario, Canada, were among the first to emphasize and educate medical students in the principles and skills needed to search, discover, analyze, and apply evidence from scholarly research to practice with actual patients. The McMaster University Evidence-based Practice Center reflects the importance of the university's contributions to the development of evidence-based medicine. If you are new to evidence-based practice, an electronic visit to the center's

Web site at http://hiru.mcmaster.ca/epc will introduce you to many fundamental concepts and resources.[2]

Netting the Evidence and Turning Research into Practice (TRIP) are also organizations interested in collecting and disseminating evidence-based information. You may point your Internet browser to http://www.nettingtheevidence.org.uk and http://www.tripdatabase.com to review some of their valuable resources.

In the United States, one of the most important organizations contributing to evidence-based medicine is the Agency for Healthcare Quality and Research (AHQR). Sponsoring twelve Evidence-based Practice Centers (EPC) in the United States and Canada, the agency contributes in manifold ways to the development of evidence-based practice. The AHQR Web site at http://www.ahrq.gov contains documents and links to the evidence-based practice centers and to a large array of other invaluable resources. EPCs conduct research and publish evidence-based reports for use by health professionals. The Evidence-based Practice Centers include:

- Blue Cross and Blue Shield Association, Technical Evaluation Center (TEC), Chicago, Illinois (http://www.bcbs.com/healthprofessionals/tec.html)
- Duke University, Durham, North Carolina (http://www.clinpol.mc.duke.edu)
- ECRI, Plymouth Meeting, Pennsylvania (http://www.ecri.org)
- Johns Hopkins University, Baltimore, Maryland (http://www.med.jhu.edu/EPC)
- McMaster University, Hamilton, Ontario, Canada (http://hiru.mcmaster.ca/epc)
- MetaWorks, Inc., Boston, Massachusetts (http://www.metaworksinc.com)
- New England Medical Center, Boston, Massachusetts (http://www.nemc.org/dccr/Evidence-based%20Practice.htm)
- Oregon Health and Science University, Portland, Oregon (http://www.ohsu.edu/epc)
- Research Triangle Institute and University of North Carolina at Chapel Hill, North Carolina (http://www.rti.org/epc)
- Southern California Evidence-Based Practice Center—RAND, Santa Monica, California (http://www.rand.org/health/epc)
- University of California, San Francisco and Stanford University, Stanford, California (http://www.stanford.edu/group/epc)
- University of Texas Health Science Center, San Antonio, Texas (http://www.uthscsa.edu)

The United States Agency for Healthcare Research and Quality also sponsors the National Guideline Clearinghouse (NGC) (http://www.guidelines.gov) that houses approved practice guidelines. The NGC has adopted the definition of Clinical Practice Guideline promulgated by the Institute of Medicine (Institute of Medicine, 1990):

> Clinical practice guidelines are systematically developed statements to assist practitioner and patient decisions about appropriate health care for specific clinical circumstances. (p. 38)

The mission of the National Guideline Clearinghouse is

> to provide physicians, nurses, and other health professionals, health care providers, health plans, integrated delivery systems, purchasers and others an accessible mechanism for obtaining objective, detailed information on clinical practice guidelines and to further their dissemination, implementation and use. (National Guideline Clearinghouse, 2000a, About the National Guideline Clearinghouse section, para 2)

Among the key features of the NGC Web site are summaries and links to electronic versions of complete guidelines, or instructions on how to secure printed copies. There is also a tool to compare aspects of different guidelines. Guidelines published by the NGC typically refer to medical procedures and practices. However, medicine is such a large and resource-rich profession that some NGC guidelines could help social workers improve the quality of their service as well. Obviously, psychiatric practice guidelines can inform social workers who serve mental health clients. However, most social workers could also benefit from materials such as *Domestic Violence Health Care Guideline* (Institute for Clinical Systems Improvement, 2001), the *Substance Abuse Treatment for Persons with Child Abuse and Neglect Issues* (Substance Abuse and Mental Health Services Administration Center for Substance Abuse Treatment, 2000), and *Preventive Health Care, 2000 Update: Prevention of Child Maltreatment* (MacMillan & Canadian Task Force on Preventive Health Care, 2000).

The Cochrane Collaboration (http://www.cochrane.org)[3] and the Cochrane Library (http://www.update-software.com/cochrane) are important elements in the development of a comprehensive and international approach to the analysis of research studies related to medical effectiveness. As individuals, most physicians do not have the time or resources to plan, search, and analyze information related to the effectiveness of medical procedures for all illnesses or injuries. However, through collaboration, they generate synergetic resources to enable members of the medical profession to locate evidence of effectiveness. Groups of doctors interested in certain areas, issues, illnesses, or conditions carefully study and evaluate research studies for evidence of effectiveness. They follow systematic search and analysis procedures to produce summary reports of their results for inclusion in the Cochrane Library of systematic reviews.

Numerous other organizations are dedicated to evidence-based medicine. The Centre for Evidence-Based Medicine at the University of Toronto (http://www.cebm.utoronto.ca), the Centre for Evidence-Based Medicine at Oxford University (http://cebm.jr2.ox.ac.uk), the Centre for Health Evidence (http://www.cche.net), and the Evidence-Based Medicine Resource Center (http://www.ebmny.org) represent part of a lengthy and growing list of such organizations throughout the world.

## Evidence in Psychology

Like medicine, clinical psychology tends to use traditional scientific research methods to generate knowledge for use. However, this has not been an exclusive trend.

Theoretical and conceptual processes based upon personal observation, critical thought, and reflection play major roles as well.

During the last decade or so, the Society of Clinical Psychology of the American Psychology Association conducted reviews and analyses of evidence of the efficacy and effectiveness of various psychological treatments. The Division 12 Task Force on Psychological Interventions, under the leadership of Dianne Chambless and colleagues (Chambless et al., 1998), analyzed research-based evidence of the effectiveness of treatments for several significant psychological and psychosocial problems. The group has made remarkable progress in identifying efficacious and effective psychotherapeutic treatments for several psychological and some social disorders (Chambless et al., 1998; Chambless & Hollon, 1998; Chambless et al., 1996). The Task Force identified empirically supported treatments (ESTs) for problems such as anxiety disorders and stress, borderline personality disorder, childhood disorders, depression, drug and alcohol abuse, eating disorders, hair pulling, health-related problems, marital distress, schizophrenia and other severe mental illnesses, and sexual dysfunction (http://www.apa.org/divisions/div12/rev_est/index.shtml). The group organized the ESTs according to selected diagnostic categories (for example, anxiety and stress, depression, health problems, problems of childhood, marital discord, chemical abuse and dependence, and sexual dysfunction).

Members of the Task Force and their colleagues have also identified empirically supported treatment manuals (such as best practices, practice guidelines, and manualized treatments) for service to clients affected by psychological and psychosocial conditions (Sanderson & Woody, 1995; Woody & Sanderson, 1998). Among respected manuals are those that guide treatment for bulimia and binge-eating (Agras & Apple, 1999b; Fairburn, 1985; Fairburn & Brownell, 2002; Fairburn & Wilson, 1993; Garner & Garfinkel, 1997), chronic headaches (Blanchard & Andrasik, 1985) and chronic pain (Keefe, Beaupre, & Gil, 1997; Turk, Meichenbaum, & Genest, 1983), stressors (Meichenbaum, 1985), depression (Beck, Rush, Shaw, & Emery, 1979; Klerman, Weissman, Rounsaville, & Chevron, 1984; Weissman, Markowitz, & Klerman, 2000), conflicted couples (Baucom & Epstein, 1990; Gottman & DeClaire, 2001; Gottman & Silver, 1999; Jacobson & Margolin, 1979), enuresis (Azrin & Besalel, 1979; Foxx & Azrin, 1989; Liebert & Houts, 1985), generalized anxiety (Barlow, 2002; Brown, O'Leary, & Barlow, 1994, 2001; Craske, Barlow, & Meadows, 2000), obsessive-compulsive behavior (Foa & Franklin, 2001; Kozak & Foa, 1998a; Steketee, 1993), panic (Barlow & Cerny, 1988; Clark, 1989; Craske & Barlow, 2001; Craske et al., 2000; Hecker & Thorpe, 1992; Salkovskis & Clark, 1991), social phobia (Temple University Department of Psychology Social Phobia Program, n.d.; Turk, Heimberg, & Hope, 2001; Turner, Beidel, & Cooley, 1997), specific phobia (Craske, Antony, & Barlow, 1998; Craske et al., 2000), and children with oppositional behavior (Forehand & McMahon, 1981; Forgatch & Patterson, 1987; Kozloff, 1979; Patterson & Forgatch, 1987; Patterson, Reid, Jones, & Conger, 1975; Sanders & Dadds, 1993). There are, of course, numerous other practice manuals for psychological disorders, and more are published each year (Antony & Barlow, 2002; Barlow, 2001; Koocher, Norcross, & Hill, 1998; Nathan & Gorman, 1998).

## *Evidence in Social Work*

Perhaps because of the profession's broad and ambitious scope and mission, the emphasis on both person and environment, its inclusiveness and respect for diversity, the pursuit of social justice, the multiplicity of social work roles and functions, and the value of self-determination, social workers may find it more challenging to reach consensus concerning evidence than do professionals in law, medicine, and clinical psychology. Social workers serve individuals, couples, families, groups, and communities; help with psychological and social problems; advocate for social justice; and plan, implement, and administer social policies and programs of various kinds. In sum, social workers fill numerous roles and functions throughout a wide range of health, mental health, social, educational, and other systems, and do so within the context of various theoretical perspectives and service delivery approaches. Given the enormous complexity and variety of roles and functions, social workers are likely to need and use different kinds of evidence for various purposes.

In their search for evidence to support professional decisions and actions, social workers can benefit from the knowledge generated by and the experience of other professions. They can draw upon the growing practice-relevant and practice-effectiveness research literature both within and outside social work. There is more evidence upon which to base social services than ever before, and it is growing at an exponential rate. Of course, efficacious or effective services have yet to be determined for several psychosocial problems. Researchers and practitioners have published relatively few evidence-based best practice guidelines and manuals specifically for social workers. However, that should change in the near future. Indeed, you may contribute to their development!

Several collaborative efforts have recently emerged within the social work profession. The Institute for the Advancement of Social Work Research (IASWR), for example, has adopted the following mission statement.

> The mission of IASWR is to advance the scientific knowledge base of social work practice by enhancing the research capacity of the profession; to promote the use of research to improve practice, program development and policy; and to strengthen the voice of the profession in public education and public policy determinations by ensuring that social work is represented within the national scientific community. (Institute for the Advancement of Social Work Research, 2000, The Mission of IASWR section, para. 2)

During the 1990s the United States National Institute of Mental Health (NIMH) provided funding to create Social Work Research Development Centers (SWRDC). Several emerged and are likely to contribute significantly to the practice effectiveness research base. They are

- The Center on Poverty, Risk and Mental Health of the School of Social Work, University of Michigan (http://www.ssw.umich.edu/nimhcenter)
- The Children's Mental Health Services Research Center of the College of Social Work, University of Tennessee (http://utcmhsrc.csw.utk.edu)

- The Center for the Study of Mental Health Policy and Services of the Graduate School of Social Work, Portland Statue University (http://www.rri.pdx.edu)
- The Social Work Prevention Research Center of the School of Social Work, University of Washington
- Center for Mental Health Services Research of the George Warren Brown School of Social Work, Washington University (http://gwbweb.wustl.edu/Users/cmhsr)
- The Center for Mental Health Services Research of the School of Social Work, University of Pittsburgh (http://www.pitt.edu/mpittssw/cmhsr)
- The Center for Intervention Research on Adults with Severe Mental Illness of the School of Social Work, University of Pennsylvania (http://www.ssw .upenn.edu/SWMHRC/index.htm)
- The Comorbidity and Addictions Center of the George Warren Brown School of Social Work, Washington University (http://gwbweb.wustl.edu/Users/cac/)
- The Center for Hispanic Mental Health of the Graduate School of Social Services, Fordham University (http://www.fordham.edu/general/Graduate_Schools/Center_for_Hispanic_4163.html)

The Society for Social Work and Research (SSWR) is also interested in promoting research and evidence-based social work practice (http://sswr.org). In addition to sponsoring the journal *Research on Social Work Practice*, SSWR pursues the following goals.

- To foster a support and linkage network among social workers in research
- To encourage more social workers to become engaged in research activities
- To provide formal recognition of significant contributions to research by social workers
- To advocate for increased research funding and research training programs, including legislation to establish a federally-funded National Research Center for Social Work Research
- To promote advances in the knowledge base of the social work profession
- To promote the application of culturally-sensitive and culturally-relevant research
- To promote evidence-based social work practice. (Society for Social Work and Research, 2000, SSWR's Overall Goals section, para. 1)

In addition to its involvement in collaborative efforts with IASWR and SSWR, the National Association of Social Work (NASW) has formed a Practice Research Network (PRN) "to expand the research knowledge base about social workers and social work practice" (NASW, 2000, Purpose section, para. 1). The Web site for the NASW PRN may be accessed at http://www.socialworkers.org/naswprn/default.asp. NASW also publishes informative documents and standards about various aspects of professional practice. The Web page also contains links to NASW Standards and an array of clinical indicators. For example, the NASW Standards for Cultural Competence in Social Work Practice and the NASW Standards for School Social

Work are available to registered members of the association. These and other NASW standards represent important foundation material for social workers. Other practice-relevant materials may be found within the Practice Section at http://www .socialworkers.org/practice. For example, the NASW Practice Update entitled "Consent, Authorization, and Notice under HIPAA Privacy Regulations" contains vital information about confidential and privacy requirements contained in the Health Insurance Portability and Accountability Act of 1996 (HIPAA). "Minimizing Practice Risks with Suicidal Patients" is another useful document, as is a Practice Update about domestic violence entitled "Social Work Summit on Violence against Women."

Building upon the work of the Cochrane Collaboration in medicine, professionals in education, criminal justice, social work, and other related disciplines recently formed a Cochrane-like organization entitled the Campbell Collaboration or C-2 (http://www.campbellcollaboration.org). This international collaborative initiative hopes to contribute to improved decision making by facilitating access to scholarly and systematic reviews of research studies about the effectiveness of pertinent policies, programs, and services (Campbell Collaboration, 2001a).

The name of the collaboration reflects recognition of the work of Donald T. Campbell (Brewer & Collins, 1981; Campbell, Cook, & Cook, 1979; Campbell & Stanley, 1966; Heyes & Huyll, 2001), who vigorously advocated for the assessment and evaluation of the outcomes and effects of social policies and programs. He considered them social experiments and believed that effectiveness research was morally and ethically necessary as well as pragmatically useful. The subjects of various social policies and programs are often people involved in or affected by educational, criminal justice, health, mental health, alcohol and drug, and, of course, social service systems. As it evolves, the Campbell Collaboration will form review groups composed of interested professionals that conduct, disseminate, and update electronically accessible evidence-based reviews of what works within the social and educational sectors. Both the Cochrane and Campbell Collaborations base their work on nine key principles:

1. Collaboration, by internally and externally fostering good communications, open decision making, and teamwork.
2. Building on the enthusiasm of individuals, by involving and supporting people of different skills and backgrounds.
3. Avoiding unnecessary duplication, by good management and co-ordination to ensure economy of the effort.
4. Minimizing bias, through a variety of approaches such as abiding by high standards of scientific evidence, ensuring broad participation, and avoiding conflicts of interest.
5. Keeping up to date, by a commitment to ensure that Campbell Reviews are maintained through identification and incorporation of new evidence.
6. Striving for relevance, by promoting the assessment of policies and practices using outcomes that matter to people.
7. Promoting access, by wide dissemination of the outputs of the Collaboration, taking advantage of strategic alliances, and by promoting appropriate prices, content, and media to meet the needs of users worldwide.

8. Ensuring quality, by being open and responsive to criticism, applying advances in methodology, and developing systems for quality improvement.
9. Continuity, by ensuring that responsibility for reviews, editorial processes and key functions is maintained and renewed. (Campbell Collaboration, 2001, para 4)

The Campbell Collaboration is just a few years old. Nonetheless, the initiative reflects enormous potential and promise. A steering group, dissemination group, and methods group have been formed. Furthermore, education, crime and justice, and social work/social welfare review groups will coordinate systematic reviews within their respective domains. As time passes, many more social workers interested in what works will undoubtedly contribute their energy and expertise through the social work/social welfare review group of the Campbell Collaboration. Indeed, some social workers already collaborate with others in the preparation of systematic reviews "designed to meet the needs of those with a strong interest in high-quality evidence of 'what works'" (Campbell Collaboration, 2001, para. 2).

Organizations such as the Centre for Evidence Based Social Services (CEBSS) in Exeter, United Kingdom (http://www.ex.ac.uk/cebss/), represent the kind of initiative that may soon emerge in the United States. Such efforts reflect the increasing importance of service-related research studies about the effects and outcomes of a wide range of social policies and social service programs and practices. Within the next several years, individual social workers will be able to refer to sources such as the Campbell Collaboration, the Institute for the Advancement of Social Work Research, the Society for Social Work and Research, the NASW Practice Research Network, the Centre for Evidence Based Social Services, and perhaps a National Social Work Research Center for information concerning evidence-based policies and practices.[4] Despite these promising organizational and systemic developments, contemporary social workers and those in the future will always need to search, access, retrieve, and analyze information about the effectiveness of policies and practices for at least some of their own clients. Social workers cannot reasonably expect the effectiveness of all services provided to all populations affected by all social problems to be researched, reviewed, and reported in one of the collaborative efforts. Sometimes, individually or as a member of a journal club or a practice effectiveness review team, you will have to do the scholarly work yourself.

Within the context of this book, evidence of practice effectiveness includes research-based and authority-based information that is carefully considered on the basis of relevant criteria and yields documentary support for the conclusion that a practice or service has a reasonable probability of effectiveness when applied to or for members of a particular target client group. In effect, evidence constitutes the support for a claim that a practice or service works. That is, application of the evidence-based practice in service to clients is likely to lead to the resolution of the targeted problems and achievement of pertinent goals.

Such a view of evidence allows for the inclusion of information from both quantitative and qualitative research studies, expert opinion, and the results of your own practice evaluations. This conception of evidence is broader in scope than the usual view of empirical evidence. However, the use of classification and evaluation criteria lends credibility to the perspective.

## *Phases of Evidence-Based Social Work*

EBSW involves four phases or processes: (1) questioning, (2) searching, (3) analyzing, and (4) applying and evaluating. They will be explored in more depth in subsequent chapters.

### *Questioning*

The first step in EBSW is to formulate a practice-effectiveness question or query. The process often begins with an actual or prospective client (an individual, dyad, family, group, organization, or community). Many social work clients are members of a special population, and all are potentially or actually affected in some way by a contemporary social problem. As part of the process of questioning, clients are described in terms of both their individual and group characteristics.

Clients experience social problems, needs, or issues and reflect a corresponding set of explicit or implicit goals. The nature, extent, and dynamics of the social problem provide further clarification about the client-in-situation or person-in-environment. When you determine a relevant population group and a pertinent social problem, you have in effect identified a *target client group*. The term *target client group* refers to a clearly defined group of people social workers seek to understand and help. A target client group is characterized by two primary factors: (1) membership in a special population that is at-risk or vulnerable in some way, and (2) potential or actual experience with a contemporary social problem. The two factors overlap in that members of the target client group are vulnerable to or at-risk of experiencing the social problem (see Figure 1.1).

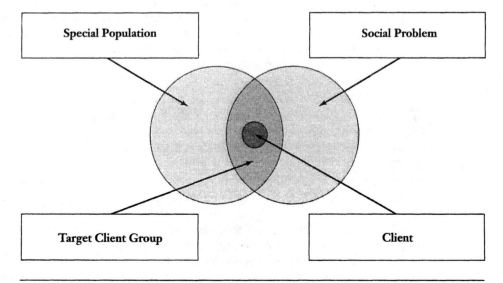

**FIGURE 1.1**   *Target Client Group*

Once you select a target client group by identifying a special population and a contemporary social problem, choose one or more aspects of service about which to seek evidence of practice effectiveness. You may need information about a particular phase of practice (preparing, beginning, exploring, assessing, contracting, working, evaluating, or ending) or you may be interested in the evidence of effectiveness of complete intervention or prevention programs, protocols, approaches, or models. For example, you might ask the following broad-based practice-effectiveness query: What intervention approach reflects the most compelling evidence of effectiveness in service to children who have been sexually abused? In other words, what services are most likely to help sexually abused children, or what works in helping sexually abused children? More commonly, you might generate a focused question, such as: What practice approach currently reflects the best effectiveness in helping sexually abused children overcome the symptoms of posttraumatic stress?

## *Searching*

Guided by the evidence-based practice effectiveness question, you clarify your terms and develop lists of relevant keywords, synonyms, terms, subjects, and descriptors to facilitate a comprehensive and scholarly search of relevant resources. You then use the synonyms and keywords to search for reference works, professional books, practice guidelines, relevant organizations (such as governmental or educational research or practice centers or institutes), experts, and, of course, research articles published in refereed journals. You identify and perhaps correspond with prominent practitioners and researchers in the field to obtain information and secure additional resources.

While searching, maintain a log of your search procedures and outcomes. Much as a chemist would keep track of chemicals used, amounts, temperatures, times, and processes applied in a laboratory experiment, a scholarly social worker also maintains a log of search processes and results. For example, you would identify the library and note the keywords used to search a library book catalog, the fields searched (such as title, author, subject, all keywords), and the results (such as an electronic copy of the bibliographic references obtained).

As you collect and begin to review relevant information, you also keep copies of relevant materials and summary notes—perhaps on traditional three-by-five cards or in an analogous electronic database, or with the aid of word-processing software—regarding both the sources of information (citations) and the contents that you find especially pertinent and credible. Collect electronic or printed copies of articles, reports, abstracts, bibliographies, and other forms of pertinent information. The search log, the source and content notes, and copies of original materials represent materials that you will compile, analyze, and synthesize.

Your search should generate relevant information about the problems, needs, symptoms, issues, concerns, and goals of members of a selected target client group and the services that may be helpful to them. As you review pertinent materials, keep track of the names of prominent authors and researchers, key effectiveness research studies, authoritative sources, and the titles and publishers of pertinent scales, questionnaires, or other assessment instruments and processes used by researchers. You will compile and organize the array of collected materials into a coherent portfolio. For example, you might include information related to the special population in one folder (electronic or actual), the social problem in another, measurement instruments in a third, and materials pertinent to the nature and effectiveness of services for members of the target client group in a fourth. One or more summary tables contribute to organizational coherence and ready reference.

## *Analyzing*

Information about the target client group and the effectiveness of services for them represents raw material. It does not yet represent evidence about how to best help clients. The raw material requires careful analysis, evaluation, and synthesis through sophisticated processes of critical thinking.

Defensible criteria are needed to guide the selection and critical analysis of information in terms of its validity, reliability, and relevance. In the course of your review and analysis, you determine the psychosocial service approach or model that reflects the best evidence and the highest probability of effectively helping members of the target client group address common needs, problems, or issues and accomplish goals.

Each client is unique. The individual people you serve undoubtedly differ in some ways from the descriptions provided by researchers, practitioners, and other experts. Some clients may not reflect characteristics commonly observed among members of the target group. Some may not respond favorably to service approaches that are usually effective. Therefore, as you locate information concerning effectiveness, remind yourself that you are interested in both nomothetic (group results) and ideographic (individual outcomes) research findings as well as high-quality authority-based (experts and professional organizations) recommendations.

Building upon careful analysis, you proceed to synthesize the evidence, reach conclusions, and formulate recommendations. You may do so in the form of a Practice Effectiveness Evidence Report (PEER) to share your findings with colleagues and other interested persons in a concise, coherent, and scholarly manner. The PEER might be presented at a professional conference as a poster or paper, or submitted to a professional journal as an article.

## *Applying and Evaluating*

Following careful analysis and synthesis of the evidence of practice effectiveness, social workers engage in a process of collaborative decision making with clients. Consistent with basic legal and ethical requirements of informed consent, social workers discuss appropriate service approaches and their relative advantages and disadvantages. You share information concerning outcome effectiveness and identify any risks or dangers that might be associated with particular practices. When your analysis of information yields evidence of a best practice, you describe it to relevant clients, explain and discuss pertinent pros and cons, and seek their consent to adopt or adapt it in providing service to them. Be sure to consider clients' personal and cultural values as a key aspect of the process.

If your clients consent to the proposed approach, you implement the evidence-based practice and evaluate its effectiveness. Recognize that each client is unique. Some clients may not respond as favorably as the nomothetic or authoritative evidence might lead you to expect. Because of the large number of factors that contribute to success or failure, usually effective services may not be so with a particular client. Therefore, continuous assessment and evaluation are imperative. Without ideographic processes to supplement nomothetic and authoritative information, services could not reasonably be considered evidence-based. The penultimate evidence appears in the improved lives and circumstances of clients—those individuals, families, groups, organizations, and communities that social workers serve.

In conjunction with your clients, develop a plan to assess the impact and outcomes of the practice application. Adopt or devise means and processes to evaluate progress toward goal achievement. Consider the relevance and appropriateness of using the assessment instruments adopted in research studies you examined, and implement single-system designs as you serve clients. During the work phase, conjointly assess progress and facilitate bidirectional feedback: Provide feedback to the client, and ask the client to provide feedback to you. Based upon the indications of progress, adapt, modify, or change the approach as needed, and continue to track indicators of progress toward goal achievement.

When your work with the client ends and you subsequently obtain follow-up information, summarize the results of the service and its effectiveness. Following relevant ethical guidelines (for example, obtaining the consent of your client and agency personnel), inform your professional colleagues about the approach and the ideographic results. As a supplement to the Practice Effectiveness Evidence Report, you might prepare a narrative description, case study, or single-system research report to share with interested stakeholders. If other professionals in your agency or colleagues in your practice-effectiveness network also serve similar clients from an evidence-based perspective, incorporate their ideographic results as well. Reflect upon the collected ideographic findings in light of the nomothetic evidence.

## EBSW in Contemporary Practice

Social workers proficient in the processes and skills of evidence-based social work are urgently needed to keep pace with the increasing demands and expectations associated with changing social and fiscal policies, the evolving demographic composition of the U.S. population, the nature of emerging and persistent social problems, evolving societal norms and mores, heightened competition, and ever-expanding knowledge and technology. Eileen Gambrill calls upon social workers to become less authority-based and more evidence-based (Gambrill, 1999, 2001) in order to provide the highest-quality services to people in need. Increasingly, contemporary social workers must document and account for the nature and outcomes of their service activities. Competent and consistent use of EBSW principles and skills not only helps social workers provide effective services to clients, but also serves to meet the accountability demands of contemporary practice.

Evidence-based social work skills include scholarly efforts to determine valid, reliable, and relevant nomothetic knowledge to guide practice decisions and actions that are, in turn, evaluated through ideographic research. Through use of EBSW skills, social workers attempt to provide high-quality services that are (1) supported by evidence of effectiveness, (2) informed by practice experience and critical thought, and (3) consistent with clients' personal and cultural values. The skills are applied during the questioning, searching, analyzing, and applying and evaluating phases.

Social workers in the twenty-first century are subject to heightened public and professional scrutiny. Greater expectations from employers, stakeholders, and consumers require social workers to base their professional decisions and actions on practice and ethical principles and on evidence of effectiveness. The form and strength of the supporting nomothetic and ideographic evidence necessarily varies according to contextual factors. In some instances, the best available evidence might be expert opinion, professional precedent, logical argument, or consumer satisfaction surveys. In others, numerous randomized controlled and several clinical trials may clearly support the effectiveness of a certain intervention strategy. Such strong evidence is certainly not always available. Nonetheless, while recognizing the natural limitations, contemporary social workers must be prepared to support their professional activities through rational reference to tangible evidence. Powerful feelings of compassion, sympathy, intuition, or good intentions are insufficient justification for professional decision making and action in the twenty-first century (Kirk, 1999).

Contemporary conditions require social workers to be scholarly and mindful in virtually all aspects of their professional activities. The knowledge and abilities introduced in this book can help you meet the demands of contemporary practice and improve your ability to provide effective services to current and future clients.

## *Introductory Exercises*

Now that you have read Chapter 1 and have a beginning understanding of evidence-based social work, prepare short-essay responses to the following exercises. Use a word processing program and save your essays in a computer file labeled *EBSW Ch1 Exercises*.

1. During the twenty-first century, you may anticipate dramatic increases in the completion and publication of research related to the effectiveness of various practices, services, programs, and policies intended to help individuals, groups, and communities. What roles do you think professional social workers will assume in these initiatives?

2. How important is it for medical doctors to know about current research regarding the effectiveness of treatments (such as medicines and surgical procedures) that might be prescribed for you or members of your family? What would you think and feel if you discovered that your physician was ignorant about the latest discoveries? What would you do if a family member became permanently disabled because of the doctor's ignorance?

3. Suppose your daughter needs services from a social worker. What would you think and feel if you learned that the social worker did not read research studies about the safety and effectiveness of practices and services that might benefit her? What would you do if the social worker's ignorance of an effective practice cost your daughter more than $1,000 and a year in needless counseling sessions? What if the consequences were even worse?

4. In two or three paragraphs, explore the similarities and differences between medical doctors and professional social workers in terms of their respective responsibilities to know about current practice relevant research.

5. In one or two paragraphs, evaluate your ability to conduct a scholarly review and analysis of the professional research literature and prepare a formal paper on a topic of relevance to contemporary social work. As part of the essay, use a traditional academic grading scale (A = Excellent, B = Good, C = Satisfactory, D = Poor, F = Unsatisfactory) to rate your ability to (a) use on-line library catalogs and bibliographic databases to locate research studies about the outcomes and effectiveness of one or more practice approaches, (b) understand and analyze the quality of research articles published in a professional journal, (c) locate valid and reliable assessment instruments (scales, questionnaires) for possible use in social work practice, and (d) incorporate single-system designs to evaluate the effectiveness of your service to clients.

## *Notes*

1. I am indebted to authors such as David L. Sackett et al. (2000) and Daniel J. Friedland (1998) for their conceptions of evidence-based medicine. Their thoughtful work served as a useful foundation in efforts to formulate the proposed definition of evidence-based social work.

2. When you get to http://hiru.mcmaster.ca/epc, click on the FAQ's (Frequently Asked Questions) button to access more than a dozen articles and reviews related to evidence-based practice.

3. Note: You may search abstracts of the Cochrane effectiveness reviews free of charge at http://www.update-software.com/cochrane/cochrane-frame.html. You may be able to gain full access to the entire Cochrane Library if your college or university has subscribed. Otherwise you may wish to consider an individual or departmental subscription (see http://www.cochrane.org for information).

4. Go to the http://thomas.loc.gov/ Web site and enter the phrase "National Center for Social Work Research Act" for information about the current status of the proposed center.

# 2

# *Questioning*

The first phase of evidence-based social work involves the formulation of a searchable question and the development of a preliminary search plan. The words *question* and *query* are derived from the Latin *quaere*, meaning to seek, search, ask, or inquire. In the context of evidence-based social work, questions refer to interrogative sentences that you create and the activities you undertake as you prepare to search for practice-relevant information. Clearly conceptualized questions and well-designed plans contribute to productive searches and improve the probability that the information you obtain will relate and contribute to better-quality services.

In this chapter, you will explore the tasks and functions, and become familiar with the EBSW skills commonly used during the questioning phase. You will learn to formulate an evidence-based practice-effectiveness question, generate synonyms and keywords for the central concepts of your query, identify sources and resources for relevant information, and prepare a preliminary search plan. In practice exercises, you will select a target client group, formulate an evidence-based practice effectiveness question, and prepare a preliminary plan to search for pertinent evidence.

The goals of the search are, of course, to help you understand current or future clients and provide the best possible service to them. In essence, you hope to locate valid, reliable, and relevant evidence to improve practice quality and enhance the probability that your professional efforts will be effective. Carefully worded queries, along with arrays of related synonyms and keywords, guide the development of your plan to search for knowledge about the population groups to which your clients belong, the problems or issues they experience, the programs and practices that might help, and evidence about their effectiveness.

The nature of the question varies according to your informational needs. For example, you might know a great deal about child abuse—its epidemiology, incidence, and prevalence; the factors associated with its occurrence; and the best practices for service to or for childhood victims. You may have comprehensively reviewed the relevant research literature and provided service to dozens of abused children and their families over the course of several years. However, suppose you never became truly knowledgeable about valid and reliable procedures or instruments (interview protocols, scales, questionnaires, inventories) for assessing the degree of psychosocial damage to childhood victims of abuse. In this instance, you might formulate a relatively specific practice effectiveness question such as: What are the most valid and reliable means and measures for assessing the nature and extent of psychosocial trauma among childhood victims of abuse?

Perhaps you have primarily served childhood victims of abuse and have not seriously considered the nature and characteristics of adults who have perpetrated child abuse. You might be unfamiliar with the nature and outcomes of services for abusive adults. Suppose you are about to begin work with a thirty-two-year-old man who abused his stepchildren. In such a case, you might prepare an effectiveness query such as: What are the most effective intervention practices or programs for men who abuse children? Additional questions provide further guidance. For instance, you might ask: What are the common characteristics of men who abuse children? Where are the major treatment facilities for men who abuse children? What are the most popular current treatment approaches for service to abusive adults? What practice guidelines or treatment manuals are available to guide service to men who abuse children? Where are the centers or institutes for research that study the effectiveness of services to men who abuse children? Who are the preeminent researchers in the study of the treatment of adults who abuse children? What professional, consumer advocacy, or self-help organizations might provide information or support to men who abuse children? How are the outcomes of services to abusive men evaluated or determined? What legal and ethical issues commonly arise while providing professional service to men who abuse children?[1]

You may conceptualize effectiveness queries on a continuum from general to specific or broad to narrow. Frame the questions according to factors such as the amount of foundational knowledge you need or the nature and extent of available information. For instance, if you know very little about a subject you would probably prepare a broad query to gain as much information as possible and acquire a general understanding. In this context, breadth is more important than depth because you need to become familiar with the scope of the topic. Similarly, if an issue is obscure or new (a recent social phenomenon, as was HIV/AIDS before people became aware of the virus), pertinent information may be difficult to locate. Therefore, a broad query would probably be more productive. An example of a general question is: What are the symptoms of trichotillomania and the characteristics of people who engage in compulsive hair-pulling? Other examples are: What drugs are popular among young people who attend raves? What factors are associated with sudden infant death syndrome (SIDS)?

Very specific questions are helpful when searching for information in areas that have been heavily researched over a number of years. For example, since the use of various medications and psychotherapies to treat depression has been studied extensively, a specific query such as What does the evidence suggest about the effectiveness of cognitive and cognitive-behavioral practices for the treatment of mild to moderately depressed, middle-aged African American women? may be more useful than a general question.

You might be interested in information about women, Latinos, or adolescents; homelessness, poverty, or drug abuse; and the effectiveness of outreach, diagnosis, or assessment procedures, contracting, planning, intervention or prevention strategies or techniques, evaluation tools, ending processes, or follow-up methods. The questions may be organized in flowchart fashion according to the sequence in which they will be explored.

During the questioning phase, social workers tend to use the following EBSW skills: (1) formulating a practice-effectiveness question, (2) generating arrays of synonyms and keywords, (3) identifying relevant sources and resources, and (4) planning the search.

# Formulating a Practice-Effectiveness Question

The nature of the needed practice-relevant information depends on several factors. Your social work role and function, the agency or program mission, your current knowledge level, and, of course, the needs of your clients all affect question formulation. If you serve as a social worker for a prevention program, you would probably ask about preventive approaches and models of service and their relative effectiveness. If you serve as a social worker within a mental health center, you might ask about the effectiveness of counseling, psychotherapeutic, advocacy, or case management interventions. If you are a manager responsible for the design and implementation of a new program for the agency, you would probably prepare queries to guide your search for effective programs whose missions and goals are similar to yours. You would look for evidence of favorable outcomes (effectiveness) as well as information that certain practices might increase the risk of harm.

For example, you might ask questions such as: What is the current best evidence regarding the effectiveness of psychological or social services for adult men who sexually abuse children? Which prevention programs are most effective in reducing the mortality rate of infants born to young African American women? What services are most helpful to adolescent girls who have experienced date rape? What programs effectively reduce the high school dropout rate among Latino males?

Depending on your needs, you may require information about one or more phases of practice (preparing, beginning, exploring, assessing, contracting, working, evaluating, ending, or following up) or about the effectiveness of an intervention approach or a prevention program. Social workers often seek evidence about the safety and effectiveness of a particular treatment model or approach for service to members of a particular client group.

## Asking about Special Populations

Social work clients are nearly always vulnerable, at-risk, or special in some way. People who need social work services are often members of groups that include a large number of disenfranchised or alienated people (such as undocumented workers, refugees, children in foster care, homeless persons). Of course, some clients are members of majority groups not usually considered at-risk, although they may be very much so at certain times. Indeed, most clients feel vulnerable in some way when they seek or receive social work services.

In essence, group membership serves as a lens through which to search for information about the sociological and demographic characteristics of actual or prospective clients. You might imagine the large array of possible dimensions by recalling that sociology is the study of human social behavior, including the description and analysis of social systems such as communities, organizations, institutions, and societies. Similarly, demography is the study of the vital statistics and characteristics of human populations. Age is one such dimension. The term *child* might refer to humans who are two to twelve 12 years of age. *Elderly* might include an eighty-five-year-old gentleman. The term *infant* might include newborns and babies up to two years of age.

Sex or gender is also a dimension. Female members of the human population might be categorized as "females," "women," or "girls." Males might be referred to as "males," "men," or "boys." Race (Caucasian, Asian, African), ethnic origin (Mandarin, Latino, Navajo, Zulu), nationality (French, Chinese, Argentine, Turkish), religion (Muslim, Catholic, Hindu, Baptist, Buddhist, Jewish, Mormon), sexual orientation (bisexual, heterosexual, homosexual), and physical or mental ability (able-bodied, disabled, hard-of-hearing, visually impaired, mentally impaired, attractive) are common descriptive characteristics. Socioeconomic status (unemployed, working, middle-class, upper-income), education (completed ninth grade, college-educated, graduate degree), military status (active, veteran), occupation (factory worker, medical doctor), family composition (single-parent, empty-nester, blended), relationship status (single, married, exclusive-relationship, living-together, divorced), residence (inner city, urban, suburban, rural), geography (mountainous, river, coastal), and region (northern, northeastern, southern, midwestern) may also be used as descriptors. Birthrates and mortality rates may contribute to the understanding of at-risk or vulnerable population groups.

As a social worker, you often need information about special, at-risk, or vulnerable populations because your clients are members of such groups. In your search for relevant information, you might formulate questions such as: What are the characteristics, strengths, attributes, and aspirations of African American men? What are the numbers and demographics of adult women who drop out of high school? What are the characteristics, needs, and concerns of children who live in single-parent households?

## *Asking about Social Problems*

One of the more common practice effectiveness queries involves asking about problems, issues, or goals that a social worker and client might jointly identify as the focus of their work together. Most active or prospective clients—whether voluntary, quasi-voluntary, or involuntary—seek or need social work services because they are dealing with one or more social problems. Some goals flow naturally from the problems. Others do not and must emerge through consultation and conversation with clients and perhaps other members of primary social systems.

Social workers commonly use sociological, psychological, legal, medical, and epidemiological concepts to capture the characteristics of the problems or issues of concern. At times, you might use terminology from other disciplines as well (such as from economics, biology, criminal justice, education, philosophy, religion, or spirituality). Most of the time, however, the concerns reflect one or more social problems.

In asking about a social problem, you might generate questions such as: What is the incidence and prevalence of alcohol dependency and addiction? What is the nature and extent of child abuse in the United States? What are the characteristics of persons who sexually abuse children? What does the evidence suggest about the factors that lead or cause persons to sexually abuse children?

Sociologists view social problems as conditions within a society that endanger life or its quality, threaten core societal values, and generate a sense that something ought to change. Social and behavioral scientists study social problems of all kinds, and social workers often refer to their findings to understand the nature and extent of issues affecting their clients. You may refer to theories, conceptual models, and research studies to help explain the origin, maintenance, or remediation of social problems.

*Epidemiology* refers to "the study of the distribution and determinants of health-related states or events in specified populations, and the application of this study to control of health problems" (Last, 2001, p. 62). It is the "study of the frequency and distribution of a specified phenomenon, such as a disease, that occurs in a population group during a given period. Usually this is expressed in terms of an incidence rate and prevalence rate. Other commonly used terms in epidemiology are . . . morbidity risk . . . (and) morbidity rate" (Barker, 1997). *Incidence rate* refers to the number of new instances or cases of a phenomenon—usually a disease, injury, social problem, or illness—within a particular population (such as residents of the United States) during a specific time frame (such as one year) (Last, 2001). *Prevalence rates* refer to the overall number of instances or cases of a particular phenomenon within a population during a given time frame. That is, *incidence* refers to new cases while *prevalence* refers to all cases.

*Morbidity risk* refers to the probability that a member of a population will experience the phenomenon (e.g., social problem) at some point during his or her lifetime. *Morbidity rate* reflects the proportion, often expressed as a percentage or ratio, of members of a population affected by the phenomenon during a particular period of time.

In recent years, the concept of health and the nature of epidemiology have expanded to include social factors and problems that affect the well-being of affected population groups. For example, the Centers for Disease Control (CDC) now studies violence—traditionally conceptualized as a social problem—because of its obvious relationship to life and health. Epidemiological and public health research studies can provide a great deal of relevant information about various problems affecting clients and can help you understand clients' situations from a person-in-environment perspective.

Social workers tend to serve people affected by a social problem within the context of their social world (families, friends, colleagues, neighborhood, school, work, organization, community, institution). Certain social problems tend to be associated with one or more professions and one or more service delivery systems. For instance, medical problems tend to be associated with the profession of medicine, legal problems with law, and educational problems with teaching. Similarly, crime tend to be associated with the criminal justice system, learning problems with school systems, health concerns with hospitals, psychiatric problems with mental health clinics, poverty with the social welfare system, and abuse of children with child and family service systems. Social problems are not the exclusive domain of sociologists or social workers. Members of numerous other professions and disciplines and many other interested persons and groups actively seek to understand and improve the lives of persons affected by social problems.

You may gain a sense of the vast range of social problems in the United States through a review of reports published by the Department of Health and Human Services and other federal or state departments, universities, research centers, service organizations, and professional, consumer, and advocacy groups. Quick review of the contents of the dozens of sociology textbooks that contain the term *social problems* in their titles is also revealing. Although organized in different ways (Mooney, Knox, & Schacht, 1997; Parrillo, 2002), authors identify contemporary social problems such as those reflected in Table 2.1.

**TABLE 2.1   *Contemporary Social Problems and Issues***

| *Health and Well-Being* | *Human Difference and Diversity* | *Injustice, Inequality, Stratification, and Power* | *Modernization* |
| --- | --- | --- | --- |
| Health and Mental Health Issues | Youth, Aging, and Ageism | Poverty, Deprivation, Hunger, Malnutrition, | Science and Technology |
| Ability and Disability Issues | Gender Inequality and Sexism | Socioeconomic Class, Status, and Inequality | Mass Media and Communication |
| Alcohol and Drugs | Race and Ethnic Relations, Majority-Minority Interaction, Prejudice, Racism, Discrimination | Work, Unemployment, Underemployment; Education, Under-education, Indoctrination | Alienation, Anomie, Isolation, Narcissism |
| Sexuality Issues | Sexual Orientation, Heterosexism, and Homophobia | Shelter and Housing, Inadequate Housing, and Homelessness | Population Growth and Decline |
| Crime, Delinquency, Violence (including abuse of children and other vulnerable persons), Suicide, Self-destructive Behavior | Appearance, Attractiveness, and Lookism | Access to Transportation, Communication, and Information: Inequities | Environmental and Ecological Issues; Urbanization |
| Death and Dying | Language and Culture; Egocentrism, Ethnocentrism, Xenophobia | Exploitation and Oppression of Children and Vulnerable People | Conflict, War, and Terrorism; Natural and Other Disasters |
| Family and Relational Issues and Transitions | Religious, Spiritual, and Philosophical Perspectives; Political Views | Justice and Injustice; Police and Criminal Justice/Legal System Issues; Civil Proceedings | Migration, Immigration, Resettlement; Refugee Processes |

Any effort to identify the entire range of contemporary social problems would end in failure. The potential array is virtually limitless and extremely dynamic. New social problems emerge as culture and society change. Could anyone living before the late twentieth century imagine problems such as "Internet addiction" and "cyber crime"? Could most Americans have imagined that reasonably affluent, adult men would hijack commercial passenger planes and willingly crash them into the World Trade Center and the Pentagon on September 11, 2001, knowing that they would die in the process? Prior to those acts of terror, how many Americans would have predicted that terrorism would become a primary concern of the U.S. population?

Several professional associations emphasize the study of social problems. They include the Society for the Psychological Study of Social Issues (SPSSI), the Society for the Study of Social Problems (SSSP), and the American Sociological Association (ASA). Numerous scholarly journals also focus on social problems, including *The Journal of Social Issues, Social Forces, Social Problems, Social Services Review, Analyses of Social Issues and Public Policy, American Sociological Review, Contemporary Sociology,* and *Journal of Health and Social Behavior.* In addition, several societies, organizations, and institutes concentrate on the development and implementation of policies and services to ameliorate or resolve specific social problems. An abbreviated list of centers and institutes that address issues related to poverty includes the Joint Center for Poverty Research, the Institute for Research on Poverty, the Institute for the Study of Homelessness and Poverty, the Poverty and Race Research Action Council, the Institute for Policy Research, the Synergos Institute, the Institute for Women's Policy Research, the Center on Hunger and Poverty, the Center on Urban Poverty and Social Change, the Poverty Institute, the National Center for Children in Poverty, the Institute on Race and Poverty, the National Law Center on Homelessness and Poverty, the United Nations Development Program, PovertyNet, the Southern Poverty Law Center, the Virginia Poverty Law Center, the Congressional Hunger Center, and the U.S. Department of Health and Human Services.

### Asking about Target Client Groups

Members of a special population actually or potentially affected by a social problem constitute a *target client group.* Social workers seek information about such groups in order to make inferences about how to best serve those who are or might become clients. A graphic depiction of the core aspects of target client groups is presented in Figure 2.1.

Questions about target client groups tend to be more narrowly focused than those about special populations or social problems. Social workers often follow general queries about a population and a problem with specific queries about a particular target client group. The greater specificity provides precision and clarity, and contributes to depth of understanding. In effect, such questions convey respect for the unique qualities and characteristics of clients. The more precise and focused a query, the greater the likelihood that the knowledge gained will enhance your understanding and appreciation of the clients you actually serve.

In asking about a target client group, you might create questions such as: What is the nature and extent, and what are the causes and effects, of alcohol abuse (the

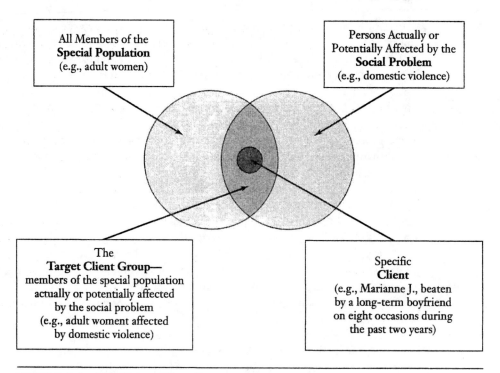

**FIGURE 2.1**    *The Target Client Group*

social problem) among adolescent boys (the special population)? How do preeminent scholars and researchers define and explain alcohol abuse among adolescent boys? What are the common treatment issues and goals of adolescent boys affected by alcohol misuse? A different set of questions might include: What is the incidence and prevalence, and what are the causes and effects, of sexual abuse (the social problem) of children (a special population) by older siblings (a special population)? How do preeminent scholars and researchers explain the sexual abuse of children by older siblings? What are the common problems and needs of children who have been sexually abused by older siblings? What are the common problems and needs of children who sexually abuse their younger siblings?

As mentioned earlier, a target client group includes those members of a special population affected by or at risk of being affected by a contemporary social problem. Typically, target client groups are identified for professional reasons. You might be reassigned within your agency and assume new functions and responsibilities with a different clientele. Or you might meet with a client who has problems and circumstances about which you possess limited knowledge. For example, you might think, "I've worked with hundreds of abused children and, I think, served them well. However, I really do not know much about the adults who inflict the damage. My new assignment will involve providing services to abusive adults. I'd better learn more about them and the nature and causes of the abusive behavior as part of my preparation for providing service to them." In this case, your target client group might be "adults who abuse children" (see Figure 2.2). The social problem is child abuse, and the population includes adults who abuse, have abused, or are at risk of abusing children.

In this instance, you plan to focus upon adults who do, have, or might abuse children rather than on the abused children themselves. You may narrow or expand your conception of the target client group according to your professional informational needs. For example, if you primarily serve parents who physically abuse their children, you could tailor the definition of the target client group accordingly.

Most of the time, you identify a target client group because you have already begun to serve or are about to initiate service to a particular client (individual, family, group, organization, or community). Obviously, you want to be as knowledgeable and as prepared to understand and help as possible. In pursuit of relevant information, you characterize clients through their membership in a target client group. For instance, suppose a middle-age woman going through a divorce seeks social work services. You might ask about the target client group in this fashion: How are middle-age women affected by divorce? Alternately, you may ask: What are the effects of divorce on middle-age women? The descriptors that characterize the target client group (divorce, middle-age, and women) guide the search for information that can you understand, assess, and help.

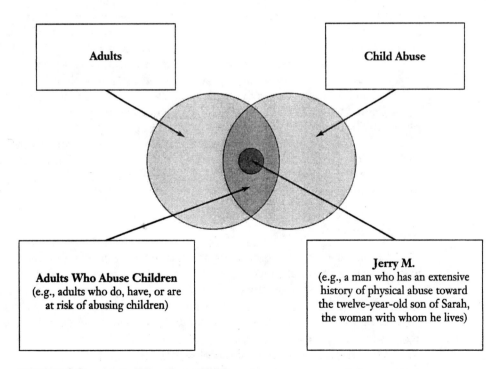

**FIGURE 2.2** *Adults Who Abuse Children*

## *Asking about Assessment and Evaluation Tools*

As you review pertinent research-based literature about services to members of target client groups, you will notice that scholars sometimes adopt different definitions of particular social problems. Consider, for example, the term *child abuse*. Some definitions emphasize physical violence inflicted upon a child but exclude neglect. Others incorporate emotional pain and personal neglect as well as sexual and physical abuse.

As definitions of social problems vary, so do the tools used to assess them and to evaluate service outcomes. Some tools for assessment and evaluation are standardized and commonly used in well-designed research studies. Such instruments typically have established levels of validity and reliability, and may have normative data (for example, average scores reflected by different groups). They may have "cutoff" or "clinical" scores that help identify persons in need of service. Articles based on research studies often include information about measures used for assessment and evaluation. Keep track of these measurement instruments used in pertinent research studies. They may help in literature searches, and you may be able to use them in service to clients.

Some assessment tools are informal. Although some unstructured interviews, general checklists, and assessment guidelines lack scientific validation, they may be appropriate in certain practice contexts. Some evaluation processes are idiosyncratic to particular clients. For example, a worker and client might determine that a self-reported daily log represents a useful measure of progress toward goal achievement.

Obviously, there are numerous types of assessment and evaluation tools. Asking about them is an important kind of practice-effectiveness question. You might, for example, formulate questions such as: What measurement instruments are used in research studies of persons affected by alcohol dependency and addiction? What tools and processes are available to assess the potential risk of child abuse? What assessment tools might identify school-age youth at risk of engaging in violent behavior?

In addition to regularly updated resource collections such as *Mental Measurements Yearbook* (Plake & Impara, 2001) and *Tests in Print* (Murphy, Impara, & Plake, 2002), there are invaluable books (for example, Corcoran & Fischer, 1987; Fischer & Corcoran, 1994) that provide summary reviews of instruments especially pertinent for social workers. There is also a resource rich on-line source (http://www.ericae.net) that facilitates access to information about assessment and evaluation tools and processes.

## *Asking about Services*

Although understanding of special populations and social problems is necessary, social workers—as agents of change—are most interested in services that might help individuals, families, groups, organizations, communities, and societies. Commonly, social workers seek to identify a range of relevant services that might be applicable to a target client group. In addition, they hope to determine which services are effective, ineffective, or dangerous.

The nature, format, and context of services vary widely. As you formulate questions, be aware of the enormous range of practices, and keep in mind the primary purposes for the services you hope to provide. They may be preventive, supportive, or interventive, and they may be delivered through one-to-one relationships, in small groups, in large groups, or indirectly through communities or through public or private programs. Services may emphasize education, habilitation or rehabilitation, therapy or counseling. They may focus on changes within, between, or among individuals, groups, or communities, or within the social or physical environment.

The nature, breadth, and depth of various practices or services provided to consumers vary enormously from setting to setting, profession to profession, and time to time. Standard acceptable practices in hospitals tend to differ markedly from those in community outreach centers. Services provided by medical doctors vary from those delivered by social workers. Practices and approaches that were popular thirty or forty years ago may be recognized as ludicrous or perhaps even dangerous today.

In asking about practices, you might prepare questions such as: What are the contemporary programs and professional practices used to serve persons affected by alcohol dependency and addiction? What rehabilitative or therapeutic services are commonly provided to persons at risk of sexually abusing children? What programs have been offered in attempts to prevent violence among youth in school settings?

Once a range of relevant services has been identified, you may seek to learn about the principles, strategies, and processes used in particular programs and practices. Questions such as: What are the essential components of Families and Schools Together (FAST) programs? What are the key characteristics and processes of Multisystemic Therapy (MST)? How would social workers implement a strengths-based case management approach in service to persons affected by severe mental illness? In effect, you hope to learn about the nature and characteristics of the practice. Ideally, your question leads to the discovery of books, articles, or manuals that provide detailed descriptions of the program or practice so that you and your client might genuinely understand how it works and, if appropriate, apply it.

Detailed understanding of services naturally leads to questions about how well they work. How effective is the Drug Abuse Resistance Education (DARE) program? How well does Life Skills Training (LST) work in reducing alcohol, drug, and tobacco use among middle-school children? When compared to traditional case management services, how effective are family and multifamily group services for persons affected by severe mental illness? Questions about what services work best are among the most common practice-effectiveness queries.

## *Formulating a Practice-Effectiveness Question: Exercises*

Unless the evidence-based practice-effectiveness question is clear, precise, meaningful, and relevant, it is unlikely to serve as an especially useful guide in your search for evidence. The following exercises are intended to help you gain experience in formulating practice-effectiveness questions. Word-process your responses, and save the computer file, naming it *EBSW Ch2 Questioning Exercise*.

1. Suppose you are a school social worker interested in developing an ethical and effective program to prevent unwanted pregnancies among adolescent girls. You are new to the role and know relatively little about adolescents, the problem of teenage pregnancies, or programs used to address the issue. Therefore you hope to generate a series of practice-effectiveness questions to guide your search for information about several aspects of this topic. Write one or two practice-effectiveness questions about each of the following: (a) a special population, (b) a contemporary social problem, (c) a target client group, (d) assessment and evaluation tools, and (e) practices, programs, or services.

2. Formulate a query in which you integrate the essential components of the earlier questions to ask about evidence of practice effectiveness. Use the following format: What is the current best evidence regarding the effectiveness of [identify the kind, nature, or aspect of service] services to or for [identify the target client group]?

3. Identify a special population, a social problem, and a target client group about which you feel special concern and interest. Make sure the topic is professionally meaningful to you. Generate a series of practice-effectiveness questions to guide your search for information about several aspects of this topic. In particular, write evidence-based practice-effectiveness questions about (a) the special population, (b) the social problem, (c) the target client group, (d) assessment tools and processes, and (e) services.

4. Formulate a query in which you integrate the essential components of the earlier questions to ask about evidence of practice effectiveness. Use the following format: What is the current best evidence regarding the effectiveness of [identify the kind, nature, or aspect of service] services to or for [identify the target client group]?

## Generating Synonyms and Keywords

A clearly stated query represents the fundamental skill in the questioning phase. The question guides the search for evidence. However, different scholars often use different terms to refer to similar or identical phenomena. If you do not incorporate the right terms in your search, you may fail to identify important information. This is probably the most common reason students report that they cannot find anything about the topic. A comprehensive search requires the use of multiple terms. You need to generate arrays of synonyms, keywords, and subject headings for each significant element of your evidence-based practice-effectiveness question. The lists enable you to use alternate terms in your search for information and evidence. A search of a library catalog using the term *abuse* obviously produces a different set of results from a search using the term *maltreatment*. Generating synonyms and keywords serves two primary purposes. First, it helps clarify your effectiveness question. Second, it represents a vital step leading to the search for evidence.

Social workers begin the process by carefully examining the effectiveness question and identifying the important terms. This process tends to yield several central dimensions that you may organize as columns of a table. They include (1) special population, (2) contemporary social problem, (3) practice or service, (4) setting, and (5) evidence. A sixth column allows you to identify the names of experts as you undertake the search.

You may incorporate more than one dimension in a column when, for example, you address more than one population (for example, African Americans in urban areas), problem (such as sexual abuse and emotional abuse), service (prevention and intervention), or setting (health and criminal justice and school). You may also need to increase the number of columns to accommodate additional aspects of your evidence-based practice-effectiveness question.

Once you prepare a blank table with the central terms as column headings, begin to brainstorm. Ask yourself or your colleagues: What words are synonymous with the special population I've identified? What subject headings are associated with the social problem I've selected? What keywords best capture the kind or aspect of service or practice I've chosen? What terms are synonymous with the setting or context I've selected? What keywords are associated with the words evidence and effectiveness? Address each of these questions through brainstorming in a totally free and open manner—no censorship here! Record your results in the appropriate columns.

Following the brainstorming session, consult a high-quality thesaurus or perhaps a specialized dictionary to generate additional synonyms. Do not limit yourself to the terms from your initial effectiveness question. Rather, use all the words that emerged in the brainstorming session in order to yield the greatest number of synonyms. Add the new terms to the lists within the appropriate columns.

Suppose, for example, you formulate the following query: What is the current best evidence regarding the effectiveness of services to or for children who exhibit behaviors consistent with the diagnosis of attention deficit hyperactive disorder (ADHD)? You would generate synonyms for each of the key themes. Table 2.2 lists the synonyms and keywords for central concepts in the effectiveness question.[2]

A review of Table 2.2 quickly reveals other dimensions than those reflected in the question. The special population (children), the social problem (ADHD), the practice or service (services), and evidence (effectiveness) are all explicitly mentioned in the query. Two other dimensions are implicit: setting and experts. Social workers are often interested in services provided within a certain organizational context such as a school, clinic, hospital, agency, or residential setting such as foster care or family home. If setting is vital to your search, be sure to include it in the question. Otherwise, identify general terms to capture the settings in which services might be delivered.

The experts' dimension is almost always an implicit theme. Social workers would only rarely be interested in evidence produced by a single scholar. Therefore, an expert's name is typically not included as part of the practice-effectiveness question. However, as you gain familiarity with topics of interest, the identities of the expert authorities emerge—often because their names recur so frequently. The foremost experts tend to be cited again and again by authors and researchers in the field. As they appear, add their names to the experts' column. The names can then be used as keywords to enrich your search. Also add synonyms to other columns as your initial searches reveal them. For example, you may want to learn about effective services for victims of "wife beating" or "spouse abuse." As you generate several synonyms and

**TABLE 2.2**  *Synonyms and Keywords*

What is the current best evidence regarding the effectiveness of services to or for children who exhibit behaviors consistent with the diagnosis of attention deficit hyperactive disorder (ADHD)?

| | Special Population | Social Problem | Practice or Service | Setting | Evidence | Experts |
|---|---|---|---|---|---|---|
| 1 | Child or Children | Attention Deficit Hyperactive Disorder, ADHD; ADD | Psychotherapy, Therapy | School, Education | Effective, Effectiveness | Barkley, R. A. |
| 2 | Student | Hyperactive | Counseling | Mental Health | Outcome | Rief, S. F. |
| 3 | Boy | Attention Deficit | Intervention | Health | Research | Koziol, L. F. |
| 4 | Girl | Learning | Approach | Family Service | Clinical | Spadafore, G. J. |
| 5 | Family | Academic Difficulty | Model | Child Welfare | Trial | Hall, A. S. |
| 6 | Son | Behavioral | Treatment | Juvenile Justice | Efficacy | Pelham, W. E. |
| 7 | Daughter | Cognitive | Strategy | | Study | Amen, D. G. |
| 8 | Brother | Concentration | Technique | | Best Practice | Hartmann, T. |
| 9 | Sister | Focus | Protocol | | Evidence | |
| 10 | Sibling | | Manual | | Meta-analysis | |
| 11 | Neighbor | | Guideline | | Empirical | |
| 12 | | | Education | | Consensus Statement | |
| 13 | | | | | Standard | |

begin the search, you may notice that some authors refer to "partner violence" or "intimate partner violence." At that point, you may add those terms to your table of synonyms and keywords for use in subsequent searches.

Keywords are special kinds of synonyms. Synonyms are words or phrases that have identical or similar meanings. Keywords are a few precise words that capture the essential content of a larger document. For example, most articles published in professional journals contain both an abstract (a brief summary) and a list of five or so keywords. The keywords associated with the article title, author, and other identifying characteristics go into a databank or database so that researchers may easily locate materials related to the keyword topics. For example, in a chapter entitled "Adolescents: Direct Practice" (Singer & Hussey, 1995), the authors and editors have included the following keywords: *adolescence, childhood, direct practice,* and *human development.* Each term is associated with and leads to other chapters in *The Encyclopedia of Social Work* (Edwards, 1995).

Keywords are also used to conduct searches of the Internet, on-line library catalogs, and other electronic databases. The keyword is entered into the search query box. Journal article abstracts often use the term *keyword* in a broader sense to refer to any substantive word in the title, author list, abstract, text, or bibliography of the entire article.

A "search string" or "string" is a group of keywords. The words may be entered independently or may be connected by Boolean operators (AND, OR, NOT). They may sometimes be enclosed in quotation marks ("urban youth violence") so that the entire phrase is sought.

In some contexts, *subject headings, subject, subject guide, and subject directory* refer to major keywords that encompass several minor ones. The subject headings are reflected in various classification systems, such as the Library of Congress Subject Headings (LCSH), the Medical Subject Headings (MeSH), and the Dewey Decimal Classification (DDC) system. Each classification scheme operates in a logical and coherent manner. For example, the DDC system is organized into ten classes that are subdivided into ten divisions, which are in turn subdivided into ten sections. Therefore, the first three digits reflect the class, division of the class, and section of the division.

The ten current major classes within the Dewey system are the following.

| | |
|---|---|
| 000 | Computers, information, and general reference |
| 100 | Philosophy and psychology |
| 200 | Religion |
| 300 | Social sciences |
| 400 | Language |
| 500 | Science |
| 600 | Technology |
| 700 | Arts and recreation |
| 800 | Literature |
| 900 | History and geography |

As a social worker, you might be interested in the contents of several of these classes. The social sciences (300) class in particular may contain works of considerable relevance. There are ten divisions within the 300 level class.

| | |
|---|---|
| 300 | Social sciences, sociology, and anthropology |
| 310 | Statistics |
| 320 | Political science |
| 330 | Economics |
| 340 | Law |
| 350 | Public administration and military science |
| 360 | Social problems and social services |
| 370 | Education |
| 380 | Commerce, communications, and transportation |
| 390 | Customs, etiquette, and folklore |

Social workers might explore works in several of these divisions. For illustrative purposes, consider the social problems and social services division (360), which is subdivided into the following ten sections.

| | |
|---|---|
| 360 | Social problems and services; association |
| 361 | General social problems and welfare |

| | |
|---|---|
| 362 | Social welfare problems and services |
| 363 | Other social problems and services |
| 364 | Criminology |
| 365 | Penal and related institutions |
| 366 | Associations |
| 367 | General clubs |
| 368 | Insurance |
| 369 | Miscellaneous kinds of associations |

Suppose you are interested in child welfare services to children in foster care. You would probably look within the social welfare problems and services section (362). A decimal point follows the first three digits. Following the decimal point, additional subdivisions reflect increasingly greater subject focus and specificity. Shorter numbers (three digits) reflect general subjects, and longer numbers (seven or eight digits) indicate highly specialized subjects.

The Library of Congress Classification (LCC) system has become even more widely used than the DDC. The LCC uses a combination of letters and numbers (such as HV8079.2 or B100.2). These identifiers are recognized by the term *call numbers*. Currently, there are twenty-one main or general classes.

| | |
|---|---|
| A | General works |
| B | Philosophy, psychology, religion |
| C | Auxiliary sciences of history |
| D | History: general and old world |
| E | History: America |
| F | History: America |
| G | Geography, anthropology, recreation |
| H | Social sciences |
| J | Political science |
| K | Law |
| L | Education |
| M | Music and books on music |
| N | Fine arts |
| P | Language and literature |
| Q | Science |
| R | Medicine |
| S | Agriculture |
| T | Technology |
| U | Military science |
| V | Naval science |
| Z | Bibliography, library science, information resources (general) |

Social workers might commonly find pertinent works within several of these major classes (for example, A—General works; B—Philosophy, psychology, religion; G—Geography, anthropology, recreation; H—Social sciences; J—Political science; K—Law; L—Education; Q—Science; R—Medicine; T—Technology; or Z—

Bibliography, library science, information resources). For instance, the call number "H1890" includes materials about health and mental health. Each class is divided into several subclasses. The following subclasses are currently included within the social sciences (H) class.

| | |
|---|---|
| HA | Statistics |
| HB | Economic theory, demography |
| HD | Industries, land use, labor |
| HE | Transportation and communications |
| HF | Commerce |
| HG | Finance |
| HJ | Public finance |
| HM | Sociology (general) |
| HN | Social history and conditions, social problems, social reform |
| HQ | The family, marriage, woman |
| HS | Societies: secret, benevolent, etc. |
| HT | Communities, classes, races |
| HV | Social pathology, social and public welfare, criminology |
| HX | Socialism, communism, anarchism |

Within the H class, social workers might explore sociological works in the HM subclass; family and marriage in the HQ subclass; and communities, classes, and races in the HT subclass. The HV subclass contains a great deal of information about social work itself. In particular, the HV40—HV69 range contains information about social service, social work, and charities. Additional numbers reflect greater specificity. For example, HV544.4 refers to international social work.

The Library of Congress Subject Headings (LCSH) comprise a controlled vocabulary for use by the Library of Congress and by other libraries throughout the nation and the world. They are related to but not identical with the Library of Congress Classification system and aid in search processes.

The main LCSH headings may represent general topics, forms, or proper names. For example, the terms *welfare*, *sociology*, *economy*, and *medicine* are topics; *encyclopedia*, *dictionary*, *atlas*, and *film* are forms; and *Jane Addams*, *Harry Hopkins*, *Dorothea Dix*, *Hull House*, and *Massachusetts General Hospital* are names. Your library may have a recent list of Library of Congress subject headings in print, CD-ROM, or on-line versions. Although it may help to know the relevant Library of Congress subject headings before you being to search, you may also use the 'basic search" and "subject browse" features of the LOC on-line library catalog, which is accessible on-line at http://catalog.loc.gov. A "subject browse" search using the term *child maltreatment* revealed that *child abuse* is a subject heading but *child maltreatment* is not. Obviously, a search containing the term *child abuse* is likely to be more productive than one containing the term *child maltreatment*.

The MeSH system serves the same functions as the LCSH and is widely used in medical libraries (such as the National Medical Library) and medical databases (such as MEDLINE®).

MeSH is the National Library of Medicine's controlled vocabulary thesaurus. Thesauri are carefully constructed sets of terms often connected by "broader-than," narrower-than," and "related" links. These links show the relationship between related terms and provide a hierarchical structure that permits searching at various levels of specificity from narrower to broader. Thesauri are also known as "classification structures," "controlled vocabularies," and "ordering systems."

MeSH consists of a set of terms or subject headings that are arranged in both an alphabetic and a hierarchical structure. At the most general level of the hierarchical structure are very broad headings such as "Anatomy," "Mental Disorders," and "Enzymes, Coenzymes, and Enzyme Inhibitors." At more narrow levels are found more specific headings such as "Ankle", "Conduct Disorder," and "Calcineurin." (United States National Library of Medicine, 2000, paras. 1–2)

The "MeSH vocabulary is used for indexing journal articles for *Index Medicus*® and MEDLINE® and is also used for cataloging books and audiovisuals" (National Library of Medicine, 2000, para. 1). "The MeSH controlled vocabulary is a distinctive feature of MEDLINE. It imposes uniformity and consistency to the indexing of biomedical literature. MeSH terms are arranged in a hierarchical categorized manner called MeSH Tree Structures and are updated annually" (National Library of Medicine, 2000, para. 2).

The term *child abuse* may be used to illustrate the MeSH system. An electronic visit to http://www.nlm.nih.gov/mesh/2002/MBrowser.html reveals a MeSH Browser search page. When the term *child abuse* is entered in the search window and the **Go** button is activated, a page emerges that contains a brief definition of the term ("Abuse of children in a family, institutional, or other setting") and its source (APA, *Thesaurus of Psychological Index Terms*, 1994). The page also displays where the subject heading *child abuse* is located within various MeSH tree structures (National Library of Medicine, 2000).

A tree structure illustrates where in the hierarchical scheme of the database the subject is positioned. In a kind of outline, child abuse appears in one tree structure just below "Child Welfare" and above "Battered Child Syndrome," "Child Abuse, Sexual," and "Munchausen Syndrome by Proxy." The MeSH tree structure might appear as follows.

- All MeSH Categories
  - Anthropology, Education, Sociology, and Social Phenomena Category
    - Social Sciences
      - Sociology
        - Social Welfare
          - Child Welfare
            - **Child Abuse**
              - Battered Child Syndrome
              - Child Abuse, Sexual
              - Munchausen Syndrome by Proxy

You may add LCSH or MeSH subject headings to your table of keywords and synonyms to facilitate searches for information about your practice-effectiveness question. Many on-line catalogs and modern electronic databases use subject headings as part of their classification system. As you search for evidence, you will see reference to Machine-Readable Cataloging (MARC) (http://www.loc.gov/marc). Developed and refined by the Library of Congress over the course of the past two decades, the MARC system reflects the standards by which networks and computers format bibliographic information for on-line cataloging. Most library catalogs and many bibliographic database services use the MARC system. Data information and its data elements make up the foundation of most library catalogs used today. Many university on-line library catalogs permit users to display citations in different forms (for example, brief, long, MARC). Table 2.3 shows information about a book (Cournoyer & Stanley, 2002) displayed in MARC format.

The MARC system provides standardization and facilitates data exchange across computers and networks. This is especially important for libraries. The system also helps scholars maintain bibliographic information in their own personal databases or bibliographic software programs (for example, EndNote®, ProCite®).

**TABLE 2.3**   *MARC-Formatted Entry*

| | |
|---|---|
| Leader: | am8a |
| Fixed field data: | 010523s2002 cau b 001 0 eng |
| LCCN: | 01035977 |
| Local system #: | (OCoLC)ocm47023564 |
| Cataloging source: | DLC DLC IUP |
| ISBN: | 0534343058 |
| Authentication code: | pcc |
| LC Call Number: | HV11 .C784 2002 |
| Dewey class number: | 361.3/2/071/5 21 |
| Author: | Cournoyer, Barry. |
| Title: | The social work portfolio: Planning, assessing, and documenting lifelong learning in a dynamic profession / Barry R. Cournoyer, Mary J. Stanley. |
| Published: | Pacific Grove, CA: Brooks/Cole-Thomson Learning, c2002. |
| Description: | xiii, 130 p. ; 28 cm. |
| Notes: | Includes bibliographical references and index. |
| Subject headings: | Social work education. |
| | Continuing education. |
| | Portfolios in education. |
| Other contributors: | Stanley, Mary J. |

## *Generating Synonyms and Keywords: Exercises*

The following exercises are intended to help you practice generating synonyms, keywords, and subject headings to use in searching for evidence in addressing evidence-based effectiveness questions. Word process your responses, and label the computer file *EBSW Ch2 Keywords Exercise*.

1. Suppose you formulated the following effectiveness question: What is the current best evidence regarding the effectiveness of school-based programs designed to prevent unwanted pregnancy among adolescent girls? Use a word-processing program to create a table of synonyms and keywords (see Table 2.2 for an example). Enter the important terms contained in the evidence-based effectiveness question in the first open row of the table. Go to a good quality thesaurus or a specialized dictionary to generate at least five additional synonyms for each important term. Enter them into the appropriate vacant cells.

2. Go to the Library of Congress on-line catalog at http://catalog.loc.gov. Use the "basic search" and "subject browse" features to locate the subject headings for key terms associated with the topic of "preventing unwanted teenage pregnancy." Enter the subject headings in the appropriate cells of your table of synonyms and keywords.

3. Proceed to the National Library of Medicine's MeSH browser at http://www.nlm.nih.gov/mesh/2003/MBrowser.html. Enter terms from the table of synonyms and keywords you created above to identify subject headings for use in subsequent searches. You might, for example, enter a phrase such as "teen pregnancy." Identify the MeSH heading associated with your terms (such as "pregnancy in adolescence"), and add the heading to your table of synonyms and keywords.

4. Create another table of synonyms and keywords with your word processor. Enter your own evidence-based practice-effectiveness question in the appropriate space. You may use the query you prepared earlier or identify a new one. Make sure that it is a question of genuine importance to you and to the people you most hope to serve as a social worker. Then enter the important terms contained in the effectiveness question in the first open row. Go to a good quality thesaurus or a specialized dictionary to identify at least five additional synonyms for each important term. Enter them into the appropriate vacant cells.

5. Go to the Library of Congress on-line catalog at http://catalog.loc.gov. Use the "basic search" and "subject browse" features to locate the subject headings for key terms associated with the topic you selected in item 4. Enter the subject headings within the appropriate cells of the table of synonyms and keywords.

**6.** Proceed to the MeSH browser at http://www.nlm.nih.gov/mesh/2003/ MBrowser.html. Conduct separate searches on the basis of each term in the table of synonyms and keywords you created above to identify MeSH subject headings. Identify the MeSH heading associated with each term, and add the headings to your table of synonyms and keywords.

## *Planning the Search*

In addition to clarifying the subject of your search through the formulation of practice-effectiveness questions and the identification of keywords and synonyms, you also need to determine where and how you will search. The plan for your search builds upon the practice-effectiveness question; the synonyms, keywords, and subject headings you generated; and the range of possible information resources. Review and reflect upon what you have thus far prepared and then consider the following issues.

- With which part of the effectiveness question should I begin? In other words, should I first search for information concerning the special population, the social problem, the service, the practice setting, or the evidence of effectiveness?
- What types of sources and resources should I access, and in what sequence should I pursue them?
- How might I document my plan and the search activities?
- How will I know that I have conducted a comprehensive and scholarly search for evidence?

When there is a large base of research about the topics reflected in your practice-effectiveness question, you may appropriately identify inclusion and exclusion criteria—as is commonly done in evidence-based medicine. In other words, you may include within your search only those research studies that meet a specific set of criteria (such as randomized control trial or clinical trial) and exclude from consideration other kinds of studies (such as case report, consumer satisfaction survey, expert opinion). Social workers often address problems, populations, and services that have not been widely researched. Therefore, establishing inclusion and exclusion criteria prior to the search may sometimes be premature. Recognizing the risk of selective bias, you may need to search for multiple forms of evidence and apply selection criteria during analysis rather than in the search planning phase.

In planning the search, take advantage of the resources available through your university library. Contemporary libraries are as much information gateways as they are buildings. Understanding common library organizational structures, departments, and services helps to identify the kinds of sources and resources needed to locate relevant information (Bolner, Dantin, & Murray, 1991). Once you prepare a practice-effectiveness question and identify synonyms, keywords, and subject headings, pay a visit to your library. University libraries possess truly incredible resources, including access to computer and on-line services that would cost thousands of dollars each year if purchased on an individual basis.

Libraries organize their resources in various ways, but virtually all of them maintain a catalog. Historically called a card catalog, this is now likely to be an electronic database containing records of holdings. The catalog may be housed in one or more locations within the library or accessed through the World Wide Web. Within the building itself, you may expect to find certain kinds of resources in distinct areas. There is usually a reference section that is typically overseen by reference librarians. Within this section, you may access encyclopedias, dictionaries, handbooks, directories, indexes, abstracts, annuals, and a host of other materials needed by serious scholars. The reference section may contain printed, microfiche, audiovisual, or computerized copies of government documents and other materials. A "reserves" section contains materials placed in a special status by librarians or professors so that students may have ready access. Some libraries have special sections to house archival documents (archives), rare books, and special collections. Dissertations or theses may be placed separately or within the general stacks along with other books and materials. Periodicals (journals and magazines) may be placed among the stacks or in a distinct location.

The circulation desk is a central hub in all libraries. This is where books are checked in and out. It may be the place to locate books held on reserve and often serves as the place to ask general questions about library usage.

The materials housed within libraries buildings are, of course, rich sources of relevant information. Reference librarians tend to be extraordinary individuals who tender advice and support to scholars. Modern libraries, however, provide more than people and products. They also offer invaluable services. Most university libraries belong to cooperatives through which they loan books and other materials to one another. Interlibrary loan enables scholars to borrow books and other materials that are unavailable in their own library.

In addition, most university libraries offer faculty and students access to assorted on-line services. Electronic access to bibliographic databases, journals, reference works, and other Internet services has revolutionized the concept of the modern library and makes evidence-based practice a genuine possibility for most contemporary social workers.

Many university libraries allow scholars free access (typically through the use of their user name and account password) to fee-based electronic resources. These include *The Congressional Quarterly (CQ) Researcher, Bowker's Global Books-in-Print, Government Periodicals Universe, Ulrich's International Periodicals Directory, Index to Legal Periodicals*, the on-line versions of numerous other journals, *The Oxford English Dictionary, Britannica Online Encyclopedia, Funk and Wagnall's New World Encyclopedia, A Matter of Fact (statistical information), STAT-USA/Internet, Electric Library, netLibrary, The Biography Resource Center, Marquis Who's Who: Current/Previous Biographies, Lexis-Nexis Universe*, and a plethora of commercial bibliographic databases. Collectively, electronic resources such as these would cost private individuals thousands of dollars per year in fees and subscriptions. As students, your college or university library provides them to you as part of your normal tuition and fees. It is an incredible bargain!

In addition to the fee-based electronic resources, there are thousands of scholarly resources freely available to everyone via the Internet and the World Wide Web. The Web pages of your library and those of other universities usually contain links to these materials. Contemporary social workers must become familiar with the resources available through their libraries. The virtual or electronic library is rapidly becoming just as important as the building that houses precious books and printed journals.

A categorical list of some types of sources and resources may provide organizational structure in the process of planning a search for evidence of practice effectiveness. Of course, all such lists are incomplete, and different searches warrant exploration of difference kinds of materials. Nonetheless, most evidence-based practice-effectiveness searches include consideration of some of the resources outlined in Table 2.4.

Use these categories to guide your efforts to identify general and specific resources that relate to your topics. By planning to explore resources within several categories, you ensure breadth of coverage—one of the hallmarks of scholarly endeavors.

For illustrative purposes, assume that you hope to locate evidence of effective services for members of a target client group about which you know very little. You would plan a comprehensive search that encompasses key dimensions of your effectiveness question: population, problem, service, setting, and evidence. If you already know some prominent researchers, include their names as well.

You might plan to search for information about the target clientele before you begin to explore effective service methods. Otherwise, you might underestimate or overlook an important aspect of the target client group's experience. It is entirely possible to search for and discover evidence for effective service to people struggling with

**TABLE 2.4    *Resource Categories***

---

Reference Works (Encyclopedias, Dictionaries, Bibliographies, Reference Guides)

Books (Scholarly Books, Book Chapters, Handbooks, Textbooks, Manuals, Guidelines)

Articles from Scholarly Journals

Government Publications

Dissertations

Materials from Other Sources (Professional Associations, Research Centers and Institutes, Experts, Advocacy and Consumer Organizations)

Summaries and Analyses from Evidence-Based Collaborations (Cochrane Collaboration, U.S. Agency on Healthcare Research, Evidence-Based Practice Centers)

Other Sources

---

**TABLE 2.5**  *Synonyms and Keywords—Sexually Abusive Youth*

What is the current best evidence regarding the effectiveness of services to or for youth who sexually abuse other children?

| | Special Population | Social Problem | Service | Setting | Evidence | Experts |
|---|---|---|---|---|---|---|
| 1 | Child or Children | Child Sexual Abuse | Psychotherapy, Therapy | Child Welfare | Effect(s), Effective, Effectiveness | Barbaree, H. E. |
| 2 | Youth, Adolescent | Sex Abuse, Abuser | Counseling | Mental Health | Outcome | Becker, J. V. |
| 3 | Friend | Sex Offender | Intervention | Health | Research | Berliner, L. |
| 4 | Boy | Sexual Offense | Approach | Family Service | Clinical | Coleman, E. |
| 5 | Girl | Molest, Molester | Model | Juvenile Justice | Trial | Halleck, S. |
| 6 | Son | Rape, Rapist | Treatment | School | Efficacy | Rasmussen, L. A. |
| 7 | Sibling | Violation, Violate | Strategy | Criminal Justice | Study | Saunders, E. |
| 8 | Neighbor | Pedophilia, Pedophile | Technique | | Best Practice | |
| 9 | Family | Paraphilia | Protocol | | Evidence | |
| 10 | Classmate | Sex Addiction | Education | | Promising | |
| 11 | | Child Abuse | Rehabilitation | | Empirical | |
| 12 | | Sibling Abuse Abused Children | Practice Prevention | | Manual Practice Guideline | |
| | | Sexual Behavior Problem | Service | | Statement, Consensus Statement | |
| | | | Program | | Handbook | |
| | | | | | Review | |
| | | | | | Meta-analysis, Meta-analytic | |

a particular social problem. However, unless you also appreciate and understand the members of that special population, you could easily apply the service in an insensitive manner that alienates clients. Therefore, conduct a reality check to determine your actual learning needs. In many circumstances, social workers require information about most or all dimensions of the effectiveness question.

Suppose you formulate a practice effectiveness question such as: What is the current best evidence regarding the effectiveness of services to or for youth who sexually abuse other children? Assume that you have generated the array of synonyms, keywords, and subject headings shown in Table 2.5.

**BOX 2.1** • *Narrative Search Plan—Sexually Abusive Youth*

I plan to address my practice-effectiveness question by conducting a thorough search of the professional literature. I will explore reference works such as encyclopedias, dictionaries, guides, bibliographies, indexes, catalogs; books and book sections; handbooks; manuals; practice guidelines; journal articles; governmental publications and reports; dissertations; and various credible documents accessible through the Internet to locate pertinent information. I will locate and review information from expert authorities, research centers, service organizations, professional associations, and consumer and advocacy groups interested in aspects of the question. In searching for evidence of practice effectiveness, I plan to use search strings derived from the terms included in my table of synonyms and keywords to search for relevant information about youth who sexually abuse other children. I will seek information about the demographics, qualities, characteristics, strengths, attributes, issues, needs, concerns, and aspirations of youth who sexually abuse other children. I will locate information about the definition, nature and extent, epidemiology, and causes and effects of the sexual abuse of children by other youth. I plan to identify standardized assessment and evaluation instruments used by researchers; learn about the common service (prevention, intervention, treatment) goals; find the current best evidence regarding the effectiveness of psychosocial services to or for youth who sexually abuse other children; and identify experts and authorities in the field.

You could then develop a plan that summarizes the major purposes of and goals for the search, and that includes the synonyms and keywords you intend to use to locate relevant materials within each resource category. The plan may be prepared in narrative fashion, such as in Box 2.1.

Search plans are subject to change as you add synonyms, keywords, and subject headings, and identify new kinds of resources as you actually conduct the search. The narrative plan may be supplemented with a tabular version (see Table 2.6) that contains greater detail and specificity.

The precise wording of the search plan varies according to the nature and focus of your practice-effectiveness question. Planning the search is not a technical or bureaucratic process. It is professional and scholarly, and it evolves over time. Think carefully and reflect upon the purposes and goals as well as the meaning and implications of your plan. For example, suppose you are interested in searching for evidence of effective prevention programs for the reduction of mortality rates among the infants of young African American women. You would need to recognize that your target client group includes young African American women who are or might become pregnant, and whose fetuses and infants could be at risk of mortality. If you were to focus exclusively upon at risk infants, you would miss vital information about young African American women and their circumstances. If you focused only on the young women, you might not learn about the characteristics of fetuses and newborns most susceptible to mortality.

**TABLE 2.6** *Search Planning Table*

Use the spaces below to describe how and what sources and resources you will explore in your search for information related to your practice-effectiveness question.

*Reference Works (Encyclopedias, Dictionaries, Bibliographies, Reference Guides)*
I plan to go to the reference section of the university library to locate pertinent reference works. I'll use the on-line catalog along with keywords and synonyms I've previously identified plus the terms *reference*, *encyclopedia*, *dictionary*, *bibliography*, and *annotated* to search for additional references. I'll also consult with the reference librarian to help me identify relevant source material.

*Books and Book Sections (Scholarly Books, Book Chapters, Handbooks, Textbooks, Manuals)*
I plan to use the on-line university and medical library catalogs in conjunction with the keywords, synonyms, and LCSH and MeSH subject headings to locate relevant books. I will also search the Library of Congress on-line catalog and Bowker's Global Books-in-Print service for books, handbooks, and manuals. I will record DCC, LCC, and ISBN numbers of materials. I will identify pertinent sections of the library and physically peruse works on the shelves in those areas. As part of the process, I will identify the titles of those professional journals most likely to contain pertinent information.

*Articles from Scholarly Journals*
I will use several bibliographic databases to search for relevant articles: Research Navigator, Social Work Abstracts, Social Service Abstracts, PsychINFO, MEDLINE/PubMed, PSYCLIT, SOCIOFILE, Sociological Abstracts, Social Science Citation Index, Science Citation Index Expanded, ingenta (formerly CARL uncover), Expanded Academic ASAP, Academic Search Elite, OVID, Emerald, MasterFILE Premier, Health Source: Scirus, Nursing/Academic Edition, Lexis/Nexis Academic Universe, ERIC, SIRS Knowledge Source, Infotrieve ArticleFinder, Infotrieve DocSource, and Project Muse. In my search, I will use the synonyms, keywords, and subject heading terms I have generated and incorporate the names of those authors who have published one or more scholarly books or book chapters, or key articles related to the topic. I will also incorporate in the search the names of those professional journals most likely to contain information.

*Government Publications*
I will use my synonyms, keywords, and subject headings to locate pertinent government materials, documents, and publications through Lexis/Nexis Government Periodicals Universe, the Government Printing Office (GPO) (http://www.gpo.gov/su_docs/), and the Catalog of U.S. Government Publications through the CPO Access Web site (http://www.access.gpo.gov/su_docs/locators/cgp/index.html). I will also use the main search engines of the U.S. federal government (http://www.firstgov.gov and http://www.fedstats.gov ) and the Web sites of the U.S. Department of Health and Human Services, National Institutes of Health, Department of Justice, and the Center for Disease Control (http://www.cdc.gov).

*Dissertations*
I will use my synonyms and keywords to search for relevant dissertations and theses through the services of ProQuest Digital Dissertations or Dissertation Abstracts.

*Materials from Other Sources (Professional Associations, Research Centers and Institutes, Experts, Advocacy and Consumer Organizations)*
I will search for relevant professional associations, research centers and institutes, experts, service delivery systems, and consumer and advocacy organizations that may have information by using several

**TABLE 2.6**   *Continued*

major Internet Search Engines: About.com, AllTheWeb, AltaVista, Beaucoup.com, Best Search Tools, Dogpile, Excite, Google, Infomine, Ixquick, LookSmart, Metacrawler, Northern Light, Oingo, Search.com, WebCrawler, Yahoo.

*Summaries and Analyses from Evidence-Based Collaborations (Cochrane Collaboration, U.S. Agency on Healthcare Research)*
I will search evidence-based collaborations that may contain systematic reviews or meta-analyses about my topic. In particular, I will search the Cochrane Library through OVID, Clinical Evidence (http://www.clinicalevidence.com), Turning Research into Practice (http://www.tripdatabase.com), Netting the Evidence (http://www.shef.ac.uk/~scharr/ir/netting), Bandolier (http://www.jr2.ox.ac.uk/bandolier), the U.S. Agency on Healthcare Research (http://www.ahrq.gov), the National Guidelines Center (http://www.guidelines.gov), and various other evidence-based organizations and journals (Centre for Evidence-Based Social Services, *Clinical Evidence, Research on Social Work Practice*).

*Additional Sources*
I will locate professors, practitioners, and consumers knowledgeable about the topic and correspond with experts in the field.

By reflecting upon the central meanings of and purposes for your search, you will be much more likely to discover what you really need. As is true for most professional activities, thinking is the most important aspect of planning a scholarly search for evidence of practice effectiveness.

## Planning the Search: Exercises

The following exercises are intended to help you practice planning a search for evidence of practice effectiveness. Word process your responses, and save them to a computer file. Label the file *EBSW Ch2 Search Planning Exercises.*

1. Refer to the practice-effectiveness question and the synonyms and keywords generated for the table you created earlier. After reviewing and, if needed, revising your table of synonyms and keywords, word process a narrative version of your search plan.

2. After you complete the narrative version, prepare a search planning table (see Table 2.6 for an example) to summarize your search plan.

3. In a word-processed file, indicate how and where you might locate general and specialized encyclopedias and dictionaries that might help address your practice-effectiveness question.

4. Describe how and where you might find specialized bibliographies and annotated bibliographies to address your practice-effectiveness question.

5. Discuss how and where you might locate authored and edited books—including handbooks, manuals, and practice guidelines—to address your practice-effectiveness question.

6. Describe how you might identify the names of relevant scholarly journals needed to address your practice-effectiveness question.

7. Outline how and where you might discover relevant articles published in scholarly journals to address your practice-effectiveness question.

8. Discuss how and where you might locate government materials and documents to address your practice-effectiveness question.

9. Describe how and where you might identify dissertations needed to address your practice-effectiveness question.

10. Indicate how and where you might determine the names and locations of professional associations that might possess information addressing your practice-effectiveness question.

11. Describe how and where you might identify the names and addresses of research centers and institutes that might possess information addressing your practice-effectiveness question.

12. Indicate how and where you might identify the names and affiliation of experts who might possess information addressing your practice-effectiveness question.

13. Describe how you might discover the names and locations of service delivery systems (agencies, clinics, hospitals, organizations that provide services to members of your target client group) that might possess information addressing your practice-effectiveness question.

14. Describe how and where you might identify the names and locations of advocacy and consumer organizations (such as National Alliance for the Mentally Ill) that might possess information addressing your practice-effectiveness question.

15. Describe how and where you might discover relevant evidence-based collaborations that might possess information addressing your practice-effectiveness question.

16. Indicate how and where you might identify other resources for information to address your practice-effectiveness question.

## Notes

1. Many social workers prefer "person-first" language to reduce the potential for bias and prejudice. The phrase *men who abuse children* appears in person-first form. The term *child abuser* is not person-first, and increases the probability of stereotyping.

2. Note: The special population, social problem, practice or service, setting, evidence, and experts are the six central dimensions of most effectiveness questions. Some questions require fewer and others need more dimensions. Adjust the table accordingly.

# 3

# *Searching*

The second phase of evidence-based social work involves seeking, locating, documenting and compiling information needed to address a carefully crafted practice-effectiveness question. In effect, you implement the search plan developed during the questioning phase. In this chapter, you will explore the tasks and functions and learn about the skills needed in the search phase of evidence-based social work. You will learn how to conduct a thorough search of reputable sources for evidence of practice effectiveness. You will develop techniques to log your search activities and results, and methods to record the sources and contents of the pertinent information you discover. Finally, you will conduct a search for evidence to address your own evidence-based practice-effectiveness question.

During the twenty-first century, searching for information is both easier and more difficult than ever before. You may access an enormous and continuously expanding body of information through modern computer and communications technologies such as the World Wide Web. However, the amount, complexity, and uneven quality of available information challenge you to be skeptical, critical, and analytical. Completion of a genuinely scholarly search for evidence requires implementing a carefully prepared search plan, documenting search activities, and compiling the information in a form that enables access and analysis. Sometimes, of course, the results of your search indicate that you must revise your plan.

The primary purposes of the search phase are to identify, locate, access, retrieve, and store relevant information needed to address your practice-effectiveness question. The search itself typically occurs via one or more university or research libraries and, of course, a variety of on-line services. Sometimes you may personally interview experts or consumers, or correspond with them by telephone, fax, e-mail, or old-fashioned mail. College and university students usually have access to an incredibly vast range of resources. Some resources may be accessed via the Internet through the use of student technology account identification numbers or usernames and passwords. Others may be found in the library building itself—perhaps at computer workstations. Libraries are changing and growing so rapidly that scholars should periodically request a tour and review of available resources.

In the search plan developed during the questioning phase, you described the general means by which to seek relevant information from reference works, books, book chapters, journal articles, and government publications. You incorporated synonyms and keywords, and identified potential resources as you outlined your plan to locate professional associations, research centers and institutes, experts in the field, service organizations, and relevant advocacy and consumer groups. You prepared tables and completed a narrative statement of your search plan. Writing and record-keeping are needed during the search phase as well.

Written documentation of activities is essential because the pursuit of evidence represents a form of research. Sometimes called "library research" or "literature reviews," the search plan is equivalent to the research design or methodology of a scientific study. Documentation of search activities is just as important as it would be for other kinds of research because it enables you and others to evaluate the quality of your search methods. In addition, compilation and storage of information is needed for subsequent retrieval, review, and analysis, and for actual use in service to clients in need.

The EBSW skills used in searching for evidence include (1) searching library resources, (2) searching bibliographic databases, (3) searching evidence-based collaborations, and (4) searching the World Wide Web. Documenting search activities and compiling information are, of course, essential aspects of these skills.

At some point during their formal education, most social work students prepare one or more library research papers. These projects are usually time-consuming and may be intellectually, emotionally, or even physically exhausting. However, if you are interested and passionate about the topic, the process can be one of the most satisfying learning experiences of your academic career. In many ways, searching for evidence of effectiveness is similar to the processes undertaken in preparing a scholarly library research paper (Badke, 1990; Beasley, 2000; Bolner et al., 1991; Fink, 1998; Mann, 1998). Some social work programs may require students to prepare scholarly papers that specifically addresses the question: What is the effectiveness of services to or for members of a target client group that you hope to serve? If your program does so, you are fortunate indeed. In conducting the library research and review of the literature to prepare the paper, you will probably learn more about your clients, the programs and practices used to serve them, and the effectiveness of those services than you possibly could any other way.

In conducting your search, reflect upon your question and plan, and consider possible search strategies. Just as there are various research designs (experimental, quasi-experimental, ethnographic, single-system), there are also various ways to search for information.

Easy access to the Internet may tempt you to log on to a major search engine such as Yahoo (http://www.yahoo.com) or Google (http://www.google.com) and simply type in a keyword to see what happens. Such an approach may, in fact, generate a good deal of information. You would almost certainly obtain many "hits," perhaps in the tens of thousands or even millions. However, the results of such a general search would probably be of extremely mixed value and quality. To be effective, the search process should be systematic and comprehensive to maximize validity, reliability, and relevance.

Most searches proceed from the general to the specific in both content and source. A search for and review of reference sources (encyclopedias, handbooks, dictionaries) typically precedes the attempt to locate books and book chapters, and that occurs before the search for professional journals, which takes place before seeking articles within those journals. Inevitably, however, there is a back-and-forth quality to the process. Often a chapter in an encyclopedia refers to key journal articles or the names of important researchers and authors. Scholarly books and book chapters contain reference lists and sometimes suggested readings. Similarly, the references included within journal articles often lead to important books, service organizations, experts, or research centers and institutes.

## Searching: The Basics

Physical exploration of pertinent sections of libraries and consultation with reference librarians are invaluable aspects of professional quality searches. In the contemporary world, however, most searches involve computers and electronic databases. Whether you access library catalogs, bibliographic services, governmental Web sites, or the entire World Wide Web, most searches reflect similar processes and procedures.

### Think Database

A systematic search for evidence of practice effectiveness involves exploration of several databases. Database systems are organized on the basis of "records" and "fields." A record is a single unit of information such as a book, book chapter, article, video, or perhaps a work of art or music. Each record contains a unique identifier that distinguishes it from others. Records are similar to clients' case files or students' academic records in that each one pertains to an individual person or thing.

Fields are the places where data are entered. For instance, suppose you were to identify a database field called "author." Within that field you might reasonably include the names of the authors of books, book chapters, articles, and reports. If you were to enter, say, a thousand authors' names, you would be able to search for any one of them by simply entering the name. All publications by that author would quickly be identified.

You may think of databases as large tables organized by rows and columns. The rows refer to records and the columns to fields. Table 3.1 is a template for a simple bibliographic database of a few journal articles. When you conduct a search, you essentially ask the computer to examine the data to see if there are matches between what you hope to find and the material contained within the fields you targeted for exploration. For instance, if you searched the author field of a bibliographic database using the string *child OR abuse*, you might identify authors named Child or perhaps Childers, but you would not retrieve much else. Data in the author field are irrelevant to such a search. However, if you searched for *child OR abuse* within the title, journal, keyword, subject, or all fields, you would return several pertinent records.

Most databases are organized in a fashion similar to that illustrated in Table 3.1, although they may contain different or additional fields. As you search, keep the database structure in mind. Since information is organized within categorical fields, whenever you enter a search term, the computer seeks out matches on the basis of data included within the fields you select. If you do not identify specific fields to examine, databases will automatically search the keyword field, the title field, or perhaps all of them. Sometimes that can lead to an enormous number of hits. For example, the MEDLINE®/PubMed® bibliographic database contains more than 12 million records. Each record holds data for fifty or more fields. Some of the MEDLINE® fields are abstract, address, author, call number, comments, country, date of entry, date of publication, ID number, issue/part/supplement, ISSN, journal title code, language, last revision date, MeSH heading, pagination, publication type, source, title abbreviation, title, unique identifier, volume issue, and year. These data, organized as they are within categorical fields, help scholars locate articles written by certain authors, published in specific journals or within a particular time frame, or containing particular words in the title, abstract, or text.

Obviously, the MEDLINE® fields and those included in Table 3.1 help organize information about journal articles. Other fields are needed to capture data about books, audiovisual media, and works of art. Libraries, such as the Library of Congress, use on-line catalog databases with sufficient fields to track different materials. Thus far, however, all libraries have yet to include within their catalogs the authors and titles of journal articles or those of chapters in edited books. Such integration will probably occur at some point in the future. Currently, however, you must search for book and journal titles in one kind of database (library catalogs) and the authors and titles of journal articles in another (bibliographic databases). Unfortunately, you must usually physically review the table of contents of edited books to locate chapter authors and titles.

Contemporary databases are extraordinarily sophisticated. They may include supplemental information such as keywords, subject headings, abstracts, and—like the Research Navigator databases (http://www.researchnavigator.com) you may access through the code included with this book—the complete text or "full-text" of contents (a complete article). Indeed, the full-text of some books may be viewed on the World Wide Web. Some databases contain links to other works by the author or publisher, or to other publications about the same topic. As their size expands and their artificial intelligence grows, databases increasingly permit searches for any word or word form in any field—including the full-text contents of published works.

## Boolean Logic

Sometimes called Boolean algebra or symbolic logic, Boolean logic guides the search operations of most contemporary databases. Scholars must understand certain Boolean principles and terms to conduct effective searches.

The most fundamental concepts are AND, OR, and NOT. The Boolean AND connects two or more search terms so that only records with both or all terms are returned. For example, if you enter the search string *child AND sex AND abuse* and

**TABLE 3.1    *Simple Bibliographic Database Template—Journal Articles***

| Unique Record Number | Author | Title | Journal | Year | Volume | Issue | Pages |
|---|---|---|---|---|---|---|---|
| 4389238 | Balk, David E. | The loss of personal power among women: Effects of child abuse | Death Studies | 2000 | 24 | 6 | 599–564 |
| 4389239 | Childers, Jane B., & Tomasello, Michael | The role of pronouns in young children's acquisition of the English transitive construction | Developmental Psychology | 2001 | 37 | 6 | 739–749 |
| 4389240 | Duncan, Renae D. | Childhood maltreatment and college drop-out rates: Implications for child abuse researchers | Journal of Interpersonal Violence | 2000 | 15 | 9 | 987–996 |
| 4389241 | Herman, Ellen | Child adoption in a therapeutic culture | Society | 2002 | 39 | 2 | 11–19 |
| 4389242 | Kinard, E. Milling | Services for maltreated children: Various by maltreatment characteristics | Child Welfare | 2002 | 81 | 4 | 617–646 |

search within the title field of a database, you will return a list of the records of works that contain all three terms in their titles. A title such as *Child Sex Abuse* would be identified, as would *The Abuse of the English Language: A Case Study of Sex Stereotypes in One Child*. The list would not include titles that contained only *child*, only *sex*, or only *abuse*. It would not include titles that contained only *child abuse* or only *sex abuse*. AND is the default Boolean process for many basic search operations. Unless otherwise specified, all search terms are usually presumed to be connected by AND.

In certain databases, the plus (+) sign serves about the same function as AND. Words that are immediately preceded by + must be returned. In those systems, the search string *+child +sex +abuse* would return the same list as would *child AND sex AND abuse*.

Use of the Boolean OR usually produces a greater number of returns because records containing any of the search terms are located. The search string *child* OR *sex* OR *abuse* would generate a list of records that include any one of the three terms. The OR operation is especially useful when you wish to make sure that all forms of a term are included in a search (*child OR children*). OR also enables you to use synonyms for an important concept (*fear OR phobia OR panic OR anxiety*) and even the same term in different languages (*male, macho, homme*) or a term with different spellings, often as occurs in British English and American English (*labor OR labour*).

The Boolean term NOT (or BUT NOT) excludes records containing certain words. For example, if you search the title field of a database with the phrase *phobia* NOT *anxiety*, you would obtain a list of all records containing the word *phobia* in the titles except for those that also include the word *anxiety*. This Boolean operation is especially useful when you wish to narrow your focus or when a term has multiple definitions or usages.

In several databases, the minus (–) sign serves a similar function as NOT. The search string *+substance +abuse –alcohol* returns the same results as *substance* AND *abuse* NOT *alcohol*. The Library of Congress (LOC) uses an exclamation point (!) instead of the minus sign to indicate NOT. In the LOC system, for instance, the search string *+substance +abuse !alcohol* would generate a search for *substance* AND *abuse* but NOT *alcohol*.

Another Boolean operator, NEAR, is used in a few databases to locate terms within a few words of one another. In such databases, the search string *child NEAR abuse* would produce a list of records in which the words *child* and *abuse* are present within a predetermined span of words.

In addition to these basic Boolean operators, several other search procedures are used in various databases—although there are modest differences from one to another. Quotation marks, for example, are commonly used to indicate that a specific phrase is sought. In other words, by placing quotation marks around the phrase *"child abuse,"* you would produce only records that contain the terms *child* and *abuse*, only when they occur in that sequence (where *child* precedes *abuse*) and are adjacent to each other (not separated by one or more other words). Where a search for *child AND abuse* returns works with the words *child* and *abuse* anywhere in the field, a search for *"child abuse"* yields only works that contain the specific phrase.

In a process called "nesting," parentheses are often used in algebraic form so that operations contained within them are considered distinct from outside and from those positioned inside another set of parentheses. For example, the following search string seeks to expand the search through the use of the OR operators and focus it through the parentheses, quotation marks, and the AND operator: *("child abuse" OR "child maltreatment") AND (sex OR sexual OR incest)*. Nesting is used to conduct complex searches.

An asterisk (*) usually serves as a substitute or wildcard for several undefined characters (letters or numbers). This process is sometimes called stemming or truncating. For example, in many databases, the search term *child\** would include any words that begin with the letters *C-H-I-L-D*, including *children, childhood, childless, child's, children's*, and so on. The question mark (?) is used instead of the asterisk in the Library of Congress catalog. In some other databases, however, the question mark is used to substitute a single character rather than many. For example, if you are certain of all but one or two digits in a numerical field (such as record number, ISBN, or ISSN), you could use question marks as substitutes for those unknown digits (for example, 342?62?10). Interestingly, the Library of Congress uses an asterisk to raise the relevance of a term. For instance, a keyword that is preceded by an asterisk (*abuse*) would receive greater attention in the LOC system than would *abuse* without the asterisk.

Certain databases are case sensitive, meaning that uppercase and lowercase letters are treated in a distinct manner. In those, the term *Maple* would not return *maple*, and *oak* would not produce *Oak*. Some systems require that Boolean operators be typed in uppercase (AND). However, case sensitivity is becoming less common as database managers recognize that its disadvantages outweigh the advantages.

Although most reflect many common features, each database contains its own idiosyncrasies. As a scholar, you should become familiar with those of the systems you commonly use. However, most have easily accessible help documents or FAQs that provide easy-to-understand explanations.

## Documenting Search Activities

As a social worker you are, of course, obligated to keep records about your professional activities as you serve individuals, families, groups, organizations, and communities. You maintain formal notes of your work with clients, contacts with collateral sources, services provided, and outcomes. Helping professionals are required by legal statute and ethical codes to keep records. It is a fundamental responsibility that reflects a minimal standard of performance.

Scholars and researchers also maintain records of their activities. As you search for information about practice effectiveness, you should do the same. Documentation serves several purposes. One of the most important is to maintain your focus on the practice-effectiveness question. So many intriguing materials emerge during each search that you may be tempted to explore irrelevant information. If you had unlimited time and energy, such explorations could be extremely valuable and enormously interesting. However, if you are searching for evidence of practice effectiveness needed to help one or more current clients, you need to work in an efficient manner. Documenting your search activities helps you focus on the task at hand.

In addition, writing represents a tangible manifestation of your thoughts and thought processes. Indeed, through a search activities log, you may improve both the quality of your thinking and the quality of your research methods. You may use a Search Activities Log (see Table 3.2) to record the date, time, and place of your search activity; the keyword search string and type of search; the sources searched; and a summary of your results. Scholars maintain such logs to ensure the integrity of their search processes and to save time. Unless you know how and what you have already done, it is quite likely that you will repeat search activities previously completed.

A log of search activities alone is an essential but incomplete reflection of all you think, do, and produce. You must keep track of other things as well. Notes about your ideas and hypotheses, reasons for the search, questions to explore, issues to resolve, to-do lists, summaries of documents you have reviewed, copies of selected articles or passages, references to assessment and evaluation instruments, and thoughts about findings must be retained and organized within an actual or electronic folder or portfolio.

Among the most critical forms of documentation are bibliographies and reference lists. A bibliography is a properly formatted list of materials identified or reviewed as part of a search for information about practice effectiveness. A reference list is similar to a bibliography in appearance. However, it includes only those references actually cited in a written document. Later, when you prepare a Practice Effectiveness

**TABLE 3.2    *EBSW Search Activities Log Format***

[Identify the effectiveness question here]

| Date, Time, and Location | Keyword Search String and Type of Search | Sources Searched | Results |
| --- | --- | --- | --- |
|  |  |  |  |
|  |  |  |  |
|  |  |  |  |

Evidence Report (PEER), you will create a reference list for materials actually cited in the body of the report. A bibliography of the other works you reviewed represents a valuable supplement, as does a specific list of recommended resources. Both bibliographies and reference lists are easily reproduced from information recorded in a search activities log, especially if the log is word processed.

Obviously, knowledge is of little use unless it can be retained and retrieved. As a professional, you need systems and processes for recording and organizing pertinent information. Historically, scholars have adopted various means to complete these tasks. The single most popular, or perhaps unpopular, method has been to write pertinent information on three-by-five or five-by-seven inch note cards. Two sets or boxes of cards are needed. One set is used to record reference information about the sources used. Refer to these as "source cards." The other set is for information gleaned or constructed from those sources. Call these "contents cards." Together, the two sets constitute a basic kind of database—even if they are handwritten.

Each card within the first set contains reference information about a single source. For example, books or book sections include the name of the author, title of the work, year and place of publication, publisher, and perhaps the ISBN or call number. Source cards about materials from periodicals include the titles of the article and the name of the publication, as well as the volume, issue, page numbers, and perhaps the ISSN number. Ideally, source information is formatted according to a standard style guide such as the *Publication Manual of the American Psychological Association* (APA) (American Psychological Association, 2001) or the *American Sociological Association Style Guide* (American Sociological Association, 1997). Many social workers prefer APA style because it is relatively easy to use and is commonly used by several social work journals. However, your school or department may prefer a different style guide, perhaps one published by the Modern Library Association (Gibaldi, 1999) or the University of Chicago Press (Chicago Editorial Staff, 1993), or Turabian (Turabian, Grossman, & Bennett, 1996).

Each source receives a unique number. The first citation receives the number 1, the second source number 2, and so forth. Since each source is identified on a single card, it becomes easy to identify and cross-reference. For example, if your third source is Stephen Toulmin's book *Return to Reason* (Toulmin, 2001), you would record the author's name, the book title, year, city, and publisher on source card number 3. Thereafter, the number 3 refers to *Return to Reason*.

The second set or box of cards contains information gleaned or derived from the numbered sources. If you wished to include a quoted passage from Toulmin's book, you would merely need to write 3 on a contents card to identify the source. Then you could copy the quoted material and identify the page numbers without rewriting or retyping the information already recorded on source card 3. The numbering system is especially helpful when an author has published several books and articles because each publication has a unique number and a separate source card.

You may use contents cards to record all kinds of information. You may include quoted, paraphrased, or summarized material from the source. You may also record your own thoughts about the source or perhaps ideas triggered by the original work. Obviously, whenever you quote the words or use the ideas of another person, you must properly credit the author and source. Short quoted passages should be enclosed within quotation marks. Long passages should be double-indented to clearly distinguish them from your own words, and the exact pages or paragraph numbers must be recorded as well. Paraphrased content should also reference the source and page numbers. Special care should be taken to avoid plagiarism. You must actually convert the meaning of the material into your own words. Substitution of a few words while retaining several of the author's words represents a form of intellectual theft. Therefore, it is usually better to summarize the meaning of the contents. Through summary, you capture the essence of the referenced material but do so completely in your own words. Of course, in doing so, you also lose some of the detail contained in quoted material or paraphrased notes. In all cases, however, authors must be cited. It also helps to note the page or paragraph numbers—even when you summarize rather than quote material—in case you need to refer back to the original source at a later time.

Box 3.1 shows a source card that contains reference information about an article from a professional journal. Observe that the reference is formatted in APA style so it may easily be reproduced in a report or bibliography. The number 24 in the upper left corner is the source identifier. Materials that come from that source (quoted, paraphrased, or summarized) are recorded on contents cards that also contain the number 24. Box 3.2 shows a contents card containing a quoted passage from source number 24.

The source card presented in Box 3.3 refers to a book chapter identified as source 25. Contents cards that contain information from that source include the number 25 as an easy form of cross-reference. Box 3.4 shows a contents card containing paraphrased information from source number 25.

Referencing material from electronic sources can be challenging. References and even full-text digitized copies of articles from printed professional journals may be accessible but sometimes lack original page numbers. How do you properly cite such electronic materials? Fortunately, the most recent editions of style manuals provide guidance in these matters. Most recommend the specification of section headings and paragraph numbers where the relevant passages appear.

The source card presented in Box 3.5 refers to an electronic source identified as source 32. Box 3.6 shows a contents card containing summarized information from source number 32. Annotated bibliographies represent a similar method for summarizing relevant information from sources. In essence, they are elaborate source and contents cards, usually integrated within a single document. The summaries, however, are expanded to reflect an accurate understanding of the contents of the book, book chapter, article, or report. Some scholars have formally published annotated bibliographies to facilitate further study and research by professional colleagues. Box 3.7 contains an example of a quoted passage from source number 32.

## BOX 3.1 • *Source Card—Journal Article in APA Format*

24.
Edleson, J. L. (1999). The overlap between child maltreatment and woman battering. *Violence against Women*, 5(2), 134–155.

**BOX 3.2 • *Contents Card—Quoted Material from Source #24***

24.
Edleson quote from page 136:
"The majority of studies reviewed indicate that in 30% to 60% of families where either child maltreatment or adult domestic violence is occurring one will find that the other form of violence is also being perpetrated. Seven studies that examined families with known or suspected cases of child maltreatment and also provided information on adult domestic violence were identified. These studies found that adult domestic violence also occurred in 26% (Child Welfare Partnership, 1996) to 73% (Truesdell, McNeil, & Deschner, 1986) of the families studied. Five of the studies fell in the range from a 30% to 60% overlap. Four of the seven studies specified the mother as being the target of the adult domestic violence." (p. 136)

"A far larger number of studies examining families with known spousal abuse have also identified child maltreatment. Twenty-five such studies were located. The co-occurrence of child maltreatment and adult domestic violence ranged from a low of 6.5% overlap (Dobash, 1976-1977) to a high of 97% (Kolbo, 1996). Twelve, or almost half of the studies, found the overlap to be in the range of 30% to 60% of families with children. The majority of studies identified the mother as the adult victim of domestic violence. Studies varied greatly on the type of child maltreatment reported although most studies reported some type of physical child abuse." (p. 136)

**BOX 3.3 • *Source Card—Book Chapter in APA Format***

25.
Cournoyer, B. R., & Powers, G. T. (2002). Evidence-based social work: The quiet revolution continues. In A. R. Roberts & G. J. Greene (Eds.), Social workers' desk reference (pp. 798-807). New York: Oxford University Press.

**BOX 3.4 • *Contents Card—Paraphrased Material from Source #25***

25.
Cournoyer and Powers argue that the technological revolution that accompanies the information age and the contemporary sociopolitical circumstances may lead social workers to become more scholarly, read the research literature about practice effectiveness, and apply evidence-based principles in their service to others. (paraphrased from para. 3, p. 798)

You may easily access and save electronic or photocopied versions of printed documents (articles, book chapters). The sheer volume of these raw materials requires a coherent organizational and retrieval system. You may use source cards with unique identification numbers (for example, 48) to reference these materials just as

**BOX 3.5 • *Source Card—Electronic Source in APA Format***

32.
NASW. (2001). NASW standards for cultural competence in social work practice. National Association of Social Workers. Retrieved July 8, 2002, from the World Wide Web: http://www.socialworkers.org/practice/standards/cultural_competence.asp

**BOX 3.6 • *Contents Card—Summarized Material from Source #32***

32.
The National Association of Social Workers' National Committee on Racial and Ethnic Diversity developed the "NASW Standards For Cultural Competence in Social Work Practice." The document outlines and describes 10 standards required for culturally competent practice.

you do for quoted or summarized contents. Then you may simply number the printed, electronic, photocopied versions of the relevant documents ("Reference Number 48").

Note cards may be computerized in the form of a database or spreadsheet, or in word-processed files. Several commercial software programs (EndNote®, ProCite®, Reference Manager®, BookEnds®, Citation®, Papyrus®, Biblioscape®, Bibliographica®, Biblogic®, Library Master®) may be used to facilitate the maintenance of bibliographic information. There are also a few freeware or shareware products (BiblioExpress, MedRefs, Scholar's Aid, Scribe) that may be downloaded at http://www.zdnet.com or http://www.cnet.com. Some of these products include features to maintain quoted material and research notes derived from reference sources.

Various word-processed tables facilitate the compilation of information. Building upon the "expert" column of your table of synonyms and keywords, you may prepare a separate table to include the foremost authorities in a field of study along with their titles or positions, affiliations, addresses, and contact information (e-mail address, telephone number). Knowledge of the genuinely expert scholars and researchers in an area is one of the hallmarks of professional expertise.

You might also prepare a table to record the names, addresses, point persons, and contact information for research centers or institutes that specialize in the study of certain social problems or provide services to people affected by them. Additional tables may be used to maintain lists of pertinent government departments or agencies, advocacy groups, consumer organizations, or professional associations.

A table may also be used to record or present a list of published research studies that pertain to the question of practice effectiveness. A fairly complex table (see Table 3.3) is needed to associate the studies with an accompanying set of source cards

**BOX 3.7** • *Contents Card—Quoted Material from Source #32*

32.

The NASW Standards on Cultural Competence outline the following 10 standards:

"Standard 1. Ethics and Values—Social workers shall function in accordance with the values, ethics, and standards of the profession, recognizing how personal and professional values may conflict with or accommodate the needs of diverse clients.

Standard 2. Self-Awareness—Social workers shall seek to develop an understanding of their own personal, cultural values and beliefs as one way of appreciating the importance of multicultural identities in the lives of people.

Standard 3. Cross-Cultural Knowledge—Social workers shall have and continue to develop specialized knowledge and understanding about the history, traditions, values, family systems, and artistic expressions of major client groups that they serve.

Standard 4. Cross-Cultural Skills—Social workers shall use appropriate methodological approaches, skills, and techniques that reflect the workers' understanding of the role of culture in the helping process.

Standard 5. Service Delivery—Social workers shall be knowledgeable about and skillful in the use of services available in the community and broader society and be able to make appropriate referrals for their diverse clients.

Standard 6. Empowerment and Advocacy—Social workers shall be aware of the effect of social policies and programs on diverse client populations, advocating for and with clients whenever appropriate.

Standard 7. Diverse Workforce—Social workers shall support and advocate for recruitment, admissions and hiring, and retention efforts in social work programs and agencies that ensure diversity within the profession.

Standard 8. Professional Education—Social workers shall advocate for and participate in educational and training programs that help advance cultural competence within the profession.

Standard 9. Language Diversity—Social workers shall seek to provide or advocate for the provision of information, referrals, and services in the language appropriate to the client, which may include use of interpreters.

Standard 10. Cross-Cultural Leadership—Social workers shall be able to communicate information about diverse client groups to other professionals." (NASW, 2001, *Standards for Cultural Competence in Social Work Practice*, paras. 1–10)

or a bibliographic reference list. As you prepare such a table, try to include information about the practice approach or intervention, client population and target problem, the research questions, research design and sample size, measures used, and the findings.

Note cards and tables—whether handwritten, typed, or computerized—are fundamental aspects of the documentation needed for evidence-based social work. So are search activity logs, bibliographies and reference lists, and copies of essential raw materials (articles, book chapters). In effect, these documents constitute evidence that you are trying to be evidence-based.

**TABLE 3.3     Table of Practice-Effectiveness Research Studies—Sample Format**

| Authors, Year | Practice Approach | Client Population and Problem Addressed | Research Questions or Hypotheses | Research Design and Sample Size | Assessment Instruments and Processes | Findings |
|---|---|---|---|---|---|---|
| | | | | | | |
| | | | | | | |
| | | | | | | |

In the search for evidence of practice effectiveness, use your research note cards, electronic or photocopied documents, or annotated bibliographic references to compile an organized portfolio of relevant materials. The practice-effectiveness portfolio may be prepared as one or more actual or electronic folders that contain sections such as the following:

1. Evidence-Based Practice-Effectiveness Search Question
2. Table of Synonyms and Keywords
3. Search Plan and Strategy
4. Search Activities Log
5. Bibliography
6. Note Cards or Database Containing Source and Content Information
7. Printed, Electronic, or Photocopied Versions of Significant Raw Materials (numbered and cross-referenced with source cards or database)
8. Table of Expert Authorities
9. Table of Research Institutes or Practice Centers
10. Table of Relevant Professional and Consumer Organizations, and Governmental Agencies or Departments
11. Table of Practice-Effectiveness Research Studies

Compiling information is not a particularly difficult task if you maintain a search activities log, a set of paper or electronic note cards to keep track of sources and contents, and copies of important documents. It is primarily a matter of organizing materials already created or collected. If you fail to keep track of your search activities and the proper citations of source materials, however, it can be an organizational nightmare. You may even have to repeat processes previously completed to document them and the results. In the long run, it saves time and effort to record as you go.

## Searching Library Resources

Modern university libraries are incredibly rich resources. In effect, they are information castles. They are typically where you begin your search. Although most university libraries allow electronic access to their catalogs and some other materials, an actual visit to the library building itself is best. There are several reasons for this. First, the environment and atmosphere of libraries contribute to a sense of serious scholarship. Second, some resources housed in the library are not electronically accessible, and some cannot be checked out. Third, university library computer workstations often allow patrons access to electronic resources that are inaccessible off-site. Fourth, electronic searches alone may produce incomplete results. Hand searches of tables of contents of edited books and issues of especially relevant journals may be needed. Finally, reference librarians—actual human beings—can provide expert advice about how best to implement your search and locate pertinent resources.

Gather up your five-by-seven cards, your laptop, or, if computers are available in the library, your floppy or Zip disk. Once in the library, pursue your search in the logical and organized sequence reflected in your plan. Use the library catalog, computer workstations, and other resources, including reference librarians, to locate places where the following materials are housed or accessed.

- Reference works
- Books
- Dissertations
- Professional and scientific journals

Make notes on the location or means to access these kinds of materials. You might even do so on five-by-seven cards or, better yet, use your word processor to record the information in a computer file.

## Reference Works

Reference works tend to provide general but credible overviews of topics suggested by your practice-effectiveness questions. If you already have a solid foundation in the fundamental knowledge associated with your topics, you may be able to move quickly to search for more sophisticated, advanced, or focused information.

Reference works include encyclopedias, dictionaries, reference guides, annotated bibliographies, annual reviews, directories, and other materials usually contained in the reference section of libraries. Most are designated exclusively for on-site use. Some reference materials are also available via computer workstations or the World Wide Web.

Numerous encyclopedias are available to help in the preliminary phases of your search for evidence about the target client group and the effectiveness of services. Encyclopedias may be general (*Encyclopaedia Britannica, Encyclopedia Americana, World Book Encyclopedia*) or specialized (*The Encyclopedia of Social Work*). Box 3.8 lists selected specialized encyclopedias that may apply to social workers.

Dictionaries also come in both general (*Oxford English Dictionary, Webster's Dictionary, Merriam Webster's Colleagiate Dictionary*) and specialized forms (*The Social Work Dictionary*). Box 3.9 includes several specialized dictionaries that may prove useful. Such dictionaries are often especially helpful in generating synonyms for the central terms in evidence-based queries.

Various subject or reference guides, directories, indexes, and bibliographies also help scholars in their search. Consider, for example, the reference works presented in Box 3.10.

Suppose you want to pursue a question such as: What does the evidence suggest about the effectiveness of services to adult couples affected by domestic violence? You would prepare a table of synonyms and keywords, develop a preliminary search plan, and then begin to seek relevant information. You might first visit the reference section of the university library to familiarize yourself with the kinds of materials available. As you browse the reference works, you might notice some works of potential relevance. You would make note of their titles and call numbers so that you could examine them more carefully later. Then you might examine the *Encyclopaedia*

**BOX 3.8 • *Selected List of Specialized Encyclopedic Reference Works***

Adolescence in America

African-American Encyclopedia

American Educators' Encyclopedia

Audiologists' Desk Reference

Blackwell Companion to Social Work

Blackwell Encyclopaedia of Social Work

Blackwell Encyclopedia of Social Psychology

Blackwell Encyclopedic Dictionary of Organizational Behavior

Cambridge Encyclopedia of Human Growth and Development

Corsini Encyclopedia of Psychology and Behavioral Science

Encyclopedia of African-American Culture and History

Encyclopedia of African-American Education

Encyclopedia of Aging

Encyclopedia of AIDS: A Social, Political, Cultural, and Scientific Record of the HIV Epidemic

Encyclopedia of American Education

Encyclopedia of American Prisons

Encyclopedia of Associations

Encyclopedia of Bilingualism and Bilingual Education

Encyclopedia of Blindness and Vision Impairment

Encyclopedia of Child Abuse

Encyclopedia of Conflict Resolution

Encyclopedia of Creativity

Encyclopedia of Crime and Justice

Encyclopedia of Criminology and Deviant Behavior

Encyclopedia of Cultural Anthropology

Encyclopedia of Deafness and Hearing Disorders

Encyclopedia of Disability and Rehabilitation

Encyclopedia of Drugs, Alcohol, and Addictive Behavior

Encyclopedia of Education

Encyclopedia of Educational Research

Encyclopedia of Empiricism

Encyclopedia of English Studies and Language Arts

Encyclopedia of Family Life

Encyclopedia of Higher Education

Encyclopedia of Human Behavior

Encyclopedia of Human Biology

Encyclopedia of Human Emotion

Encyclopedia of Human Intelligence

Encyclopedia of Human Nutrition

Encyclopedia of Learning and Memory

Encyclopedia of Mental Health

Encyclopedia of Multicultural Education

Encyclopedia of Native American Shamanism: Sacred Ceremonies of North America

Encyclopedia of North American Indians

Encyclopedia of Nursing Research

Encyclopedia of Obesity and Eating Disorders

Encyclopedia of Parenting Theory and Research

Encyclopedia of Psychiatry, Psychology, and Psychoanalysis

Encyclopedia of Psychology

Encyclopedia of Relationships across the Lifespan

Encyclopedia of Social Work

Encyclopedia of Sociology

Encyclopedia of Student and Youth Movements

Encyclopedia of Women and Sport in America

Encyclopedia of Women and Sports

*(continued)*

**BOX 3.8     Continued**

Gale Encyclopedia of Childhood and
Adolescence

Gale Encyclopedia of Medicine

Gale Encyclopedia of Multicultural America

Gale Encyclopedia of Psychology

Historical Encyclopedia of School
Psychology

International Encyclopedia of Adult Education
and Training

International Encyclopedia of Developmental
and Instructional Psychology

International Encyclopedia of Educational
Evaluation

International Encyclopedia of Educational
Technology

International Encyclopedia of Teaching and
Teacher Education

International Encyclopedia of Women and
Sports

Kister's Best Encyclopedias: A Comparative
Guide to General and Specialized
Encyclopedias

Macmillan Encyclopedia of World Slavery

MIT Encyclopedia of the Cognitive Sciences

Social Science Encyclopedia

Violence in America: An Encyclopedia

**BOX 3.9 • *Selected List of Dictionary Reference Works***

The AIDS Dictionary

Biographical Dictionary of Psychology

Biographical Dictionary of Social Welfare
in America

Blackwell Dictionary of Cognitive
Psychology

Blackwell Dictionary of Sociology: A User's
Guide to Sociological Language

Dictionary of American Social Change

Dictionary of Chicano Folklore

Dictionary of Childhood Health Problems

Dictionary of Cultural Theorists

Dictionary of Epidemiology

Dictionary of Family Psychology and
Family Therapy

Dictionary of Global Culture

Dictionary of Key Words in Psychology

Dictionary of Medical Syndromes

Dictionary of Personality and
Social Psychology

Dictionary of Psychology

Dictionary of Social Science Methods

Dictionary of Social Welfare

Dictionary of Sociology

Dictionary of Statistics and Methodology: A
Nontechnical Guide for the Social Sciences

Dictionary of Theories, Laws, and Concepts
in Psychology

Encyclopedic Dictionary of AIDS-related
Terminology

Encyclopedic Dictionary of Sociology

Family Mental Health Encyclopedia

Lexicon of Psychiatry, Neurology, and the
Neurosciences

Longman Dictionary of Psychology and
Psychiatry

Mosby's Medical, Nursing, & Allied
Health Dictionary

Psychiatric Dictionary

Social Work Dictionary

**BOX 3.10 • *Selected List of Other Reference Works***

Abuse of the Elderly: Issues and Annotated Bibliography

Allyn and Bacon Quick Guide to the Internet for Social Work

ARBA Guide to Subject Encyclopedias and Dictionaries

Author's Guide to Social Work Journals

Bibliography for Training in Child and Adolescent Mental Health: For Training in Child Psychiatry, Child Psychology, Social Work, and Child and Adolescent Psychiatric Nursing

Bibliography of European Studies in Social Work

Chicorel Index to Abstracting and Indexing Services: Periodicals in Humanities and the Social Sciences

Child Abuse and Neglect: An Information and Reference Guide

Cultural Anthropology: A Guide to Reference and Information Sources

Cumulative Index of Sociology Journals

Directory of Social Welfare Research Capabilities: A Working Guide to Organizations Engaged in Social Work and Social Welfare Research

Female Offenders: An Annotated Bibliography

Finding the Source in Sociology and Anthropology: A Thesaurus-Index to the Reference Collection

Gerontological Social Work: An Annotated Bibliography

Guide to Information Sources for Social Work and the Human Services

Guide to Reference Books

Guide to Selecting and Applying to Master of Social Work Programs

Humanities Index

KWIC (keyword-in-context) Index— Publications of the National Conference on Social Welfare

Lesbian, Gay, Bisexual and Transgender Issues

in Social Work: A Comprehensive Bibliography with Annotations

Occupational Social Work: An Annotated Bibliography

Reference Sources in Social Work: An Annotated Bibliography

Resources for Nursing Research: An Annotated Bibliography,

Social Sciences Citation Index

Social Sciences Index

Social Service Organizations and Agencies Directory: A Reference Guide to National and Regional Social Service Organizations, Including Advocacy Groups, Voluntary Associations, Professional Societies, Federal and State Agencies, Clearinghouses, and Information Centers

Social Work and Health Science: Medical Analysis Index with Reference Bibliography

Social Work Abstracts

Social Work as a Profession: A Bibliography

Social Work with the First Nations: A Comprehensive Bibliography with Annotations

Social Workers' Desk Reference

Sociology: A Guide to Reference and Information Sources

Spiritual Diversity and Social Work: A Comprehensive Bibliography with Annotations

Studies of Research on Social Work Practice: A Bibliography

Subject Guide to U.S. Government Reference Sources

Testing Children: A Reference Guide for Effective Clinical and Psychoeducational Assessments

User's Guide to Social Work Abstracts

Users' Guides to the Medical Literature: A Manual for Evidence-Based Clinical Practice

Women and Health: An Annotated Bibliography

Work-Family Research: An Annotated Bibliography

*Britannica* and locate a chapter about domestic violence. You might review that section and record some information (source, page numbers, significant concepts or terms, and perhaps some citations from the reference list). If you examined *Funk and Wagnall's New World Encyclopedia*, you might not find much of value to your search. However, the *World Book Standard Edition* (CD-ROM Version) contains useful material, and you might record a few notes from that source as well.

You might then turn to the *Encyclopedia of Social Work* (Edwards, 1995, 1997)—a three-volume set (plus a supplemental volume)—to see what might relate to your topic. If you scanned the table of contents, you would quickly find chapters on the topics of violence (Fraser, 1995), domestic violence (Davis, 1995), legal issues related to domestic violence (Saunders, 1995), and domestic violence among gay men and lesbian couples (Carlson & Maciol, 1997), along with others that relate to the topic.

You could then examine the *Social Workers' Desk Reference* (Roberts & Greene, 2002). The table of contents would reveal several pertinent chapters, including "A Community Capacity Response to Family Violence in the Military" (Bowen, Martin, & Nelson, 2002), "Children Exposed to Domestic Violence: Assessment and Treatment Protocols" (Lehmann & Rabenstein, 2002), "Domestic Violence and Child Protective Services: Risk Assessments" (Friend & Mills, 2002), "Group Intervention Models with Domestic Violence Offenders" (Buttell, 2002). You might note the authors, titles, and page numbers of those chapters.

The *Blackwell Encyclopedia of Social Work* (Davies, 2000) and the *Blackwell Companion to Social Work* (Davies, 2002) also contain valuable sections. Within the *Companion*, for example, there is a chapter entitled "Domestic Violence" (Humphreys, 2002). Each chapter from these works contains a pertinent reference list. Review the lists and note relevant works. Begin to track the names of authors that recur (for example, Davis, Edleson, Finkelhor, Gelles, Gondolf, Humphreys, Levinson, Roberts, Saunders, Steinmetz, Straus, and Tolman). You could add their names to your synonyms and keywords list. As you begin to read these chapters, you might notice and make note of pertinent federal policies and laws such as the Family Violence Prevention and Services Act, the Victims of Crime Act, Trafficking Victims Protection Act, and the Violence against Women Act. You would probably also make note of the names and sources of scales and assessment or evaluation instruments that have been or could be used in nomothetic or ideographic research. For instance, you might notice references to partner abuse scales (Hudson, 1990), severity of violence against women scales (Marshall, 1992), wife abuse inventory (Lewis, 1985), and conflict tactics scales (Straus, 1979, 1990; Straus, Hamby, Boney-McCoy, & Sugarman, 1996).

You might use five-by-seven source cards to record pertinent bibliographic information in the American Psychological Association (APA) format (American Psychological Association, 2001). Box 3.11 presents a selection of APA-formatted references. In addition, you would probably use contents cards to make notes about relevant information as you reviewed each chapter. A word-processing or bibliographic program such as EndNote® or BiblioExpress facilitates the process of recording sources and page numbers associated with each notation, and of distinguishing quoted passages from summary notes and your own ideas.

You might then go to a computer workstation and log onto the on-line university library catalog to search for additional reference works that might relate to the topic of domestic violence. You could search for works that contained search strings such as *("domestic violence" OR "family violence" OR "wife battering" OR "spouse abuse" OR "intimate partner violence") AND (encyclopedia OR dictionary OR guide OR bibliography OR handbook OR reference OR manual OR index).*

If you did, you might find several reference works that were not on your earlier list. For example, you might identify the *Domestic Violence and Child Abuse Sourcebook* (Henderson, 2000), *Domestic Violence: A Reference Handbook* (McCue, 1995), *Family Violence: A Clinical and Legal Guide* (Kaplan, 1996), *Foundations for Violence-Free Living: A Step-By-Step Guide to Facilitating Men's Domestic Abuse Groups* (Mathews, 1995), *A Professional's Guide to Understanding Gay and Lesbian Domestic Violence: Understanding Practice Interventions* (McClennen & Gunther, 1999), *Growing Free: A Manual for Survivors of Domestic Violence* (Deaton & Hertica, 2001a), *A Therapist's Guide to Growing Free: A Manual for Survivors of Domestic Violence* (Deaton & Hertica, 2001b), *When Violence Begins at Home: A Comprehensive Guide to Understanding and Ending Domestic Abuse* (Wilson, 1997), *Handbook of Violence* (Rapp-Paglicci, Roberts, & Wodarski,

## BOX 3.11 • *Formatted Bibliographic References*

Bowen, G. L., Martin, B. R., & Nelson, J. P. (2002). A community capacity response to family violence in the military. In A. R. Roberts & G. J. Greene (Eds.), *Social workers' desk reference* (pp. 551–557). New York: Oxford University Press.

Buttell, F. (2002). Group intervention models with domestic violence offenders. In A. R. Roberts & G. J. Greene (Eds.), *Social workers' desk reference* (pp. 714–717). New York: Oxford University Press.

Carlson, B. E., & Maciol, K. (1997). Domestic violence: Gay men and lesbians. In R. L. Edwards (Ed.), *Encyclopedia of social work* (19th, 1997 Supplement ed., pp. 101–111). Washington, DC: NASW Press.

Davis, L. V. (1995). Domestic violence. In R. L. Edwards (Ed.), *Encyclopedia of social work* (19th ed., Vol. 1, pp. 780–789). Washington, DC: NASW Press.

Fraser, M. (1995). Violence overview. In R. L. Edwards (Ed.), *Encyclopedia of social work* (19th ed., Vol. 3, pp. 2453–2460). Washington, DC: NASW Press.

Friend, C., & Mills, L. G. (2002). Domestic violence and child protective services: Risk assessments. In A. R. Roberts & G. J. Greene (Eds.), *Social workers' desk reference* (pp. 679–684). New York: Oxford University Press.

Garrison, M. E. B., & Keresman, M. A. (1998). Marital conflict, domestic violence, and family preservation. In J. S. Wodarski & B. A. Thyer (Eds.), *Handbook of empirical social work practice* (Vol. 2, pp. 225–240). New York: Wiley.

Lehmann, P., & Rabenstein, S. (2002). Children exposed to domestic violence: Assessment and treatment protocols. In A. R. Roberts & G. J. Greene (Eds.), *Social workers' desk reference* (pp. 673–679). New York: Oxford University Press.

Saunders, D. G. (1995). Domestic violence: Legal issues. In R. L. Edwards (Ed.), *Encyclopedia of social work* (19th ed., Vol. 1, pp. 789–795). Washington, DC: NASW Press.

2002), *Handbook of Domestic Violence Intervention Strategies: Policies, Programs, and Legal Remedies* (Roberts, 2002), or perhaps *Alternatives to Domestic Violence: A Homework Manual for Battering Intervention Groups* (Fall, Howard, & Ford, 1999).

If you then used the computer to access the Library of Congress (LOC) on-line library catalog at http://catalog.loc.gov,[1] you might notice that the LOC uses the subject heading "family violence" instead of "domestic violence." Clicking on that subject heading would produce several pertinent subheadings and other links to resource materials about family and domestic violence. If you repeated the search that you conducted at the university library, you might find some reference works housed in the Library of Congress that your own library does not possess (see Box 3.12 for a selected list).

## BOX 3.12 • *Selected Family Violence Reference Works from the Library of Congress*

Bolton, F. G., & Bolton, S. R. (1987). *Working with violent families: A guide for clinical and legal practitioners.* Newbury Park, CA: Sage.

Center on Crime Communities and Culture. (1997). *Pathfinder on domestic violence in the United States.* New York: Center on Crime Communities and Culture.

Centre for Social Development and Humanitarian Affairs (United Nations). (1993). *Strategies for confronting domestic violence: A resource manual.* New York: United Nations.

Deaton, W., & Hertica, M. (2001a). *Growing Free: A manual for survivors of domestic violence.* New York: Haworth Press.

Deaton, W., & Hertica, M. (2001b). *A therapist's guide to Growing Free: A manual for survivors of domestic violence.* New York: Haworth Press.

Fall, K. A., Howard, S., & Ford, J. E. (1999). *Alternatives to domestic violence: A homework manual for battering intervention groups.* Philadelphia, PA: Accelerated Development.

Feindler, E. L., Rathus, J. H., & Silver, L. B. (2003). *Assessment of family violence: A handbook for researchers and practitioners.* Washington, DC: American Psychological Association.

Gondolf, E. W. (1988). *Research on men who batter: An overview, bibliography and resource guide* (1st ed.). Bradenton, FL: Human Services Institute.

Henderson, H. (2000). *Domestic violence and child abuse sourcebook: Basic consumer health information about spousal/partner, child, sibling, parent, and elder abuse.* Detroit, MI: Omnigraphics.

Jaising, I. (2001). *Law of domestic violence: A user's manual for women.* Holmes Beach, FL: William W. Gaunt & Sons.

Lukawiecki, T., Ross, N., Canada. Health Canada., & Canada. Family Violence Prevention Unit. (1999). *Annotated inventory of research reports completed through the five research centres on family violence and violence against women and children.* Ottawa: Health Canada.

**BOX 3.12** • *Continued*

---

Mariani, C., & Sokolich, P. (1996). *Domestic violence survival guide.* Flushing, NY: Looseleaf Law Publications.

McCue, M. L. (1995). *Domestic violence: A reference handbook.* Santa Barbara, CA: ABC-CLIO.

Roberts, A. R. (2002). *Handbook of domestic violence intervention strategies: Policies, programs, and legal remedies.* Oxford and New York: Oxford University Press.

United States Congress, House Committee on Education and Labor, Subcommittee on Select Education. (1988). *Reauthorization of the Child Abuse Prevention and Treatment Act and the Family Violence Prevention and Services Act: Hearing before the Subcommittee on Select Education of the Committee on Education and Labor, House of Representatives, One Hundredth Congress, first session, hearing held in Washington, DC, April 29, 1987.* Washington DC: U.S. Government Printing Office.

Van Hasselt, V. B. (1988). *Handbook of family violence.* New York: Plenum Press.

Virginia Commission on Family Violence Prevention. (1997). *Family violence reference manual.* Richmond, VA: Virginia Commission on Family Violence Prevention.

Virginia Commission on Family Violence Prevention. (1999). *Annotated bibliography of research related to family violence.* Richmond, VA: Virginia Commission on Family Violence Prevention.

Watts, T. J. (1988). *Public policy toward family and domestic violence: A bibliography.* Monticello, IL: Vance Bibliographies.

---

### Books

Reference works such as encyclopedias and dictionaries are, of course, books. Other scholarly books may provide general or specific information as well. Textbooks and edited books may include chapters or sections that pertain to your topic. You may be fortunate enough to find a scholarly book that directly addresses your practice-effectiveness query. Handbooks, manuals, and practice guides often contain especially pertinent information about practice or service models and approaches. Box 3.13 includes an abbreviated list of selected handbooks and manuals. Some, but not all, are based on empirical evidence of practice effectiveness.

The search for books is similar to the search for reference works. Unlike major reference works, however, other books are usually shelved in open stacks. Unless placed on reserve, they may be checked out for off-site use. Fortunately, you may use the on-line library catalog to search for relevant books in the same way that you seek reference works. As you discover relevant books, including reference works, make note of the International Standard Book Number (ISBN) or the call number. These numbers represent an efficient way to locate books in libraries and bookstores.

Use your keywords and synonyms to search catalogs from university libraries or the Library of Congress On-line, or services such as Bowker's Global Books-in-Print to identify relevant books.[2] Some library catalogs contain information about tables of contents, including the authors and titles of chapters in edited books. As you proceed with your search, you will undoubtedly identify experts who have written significant works in the field. Add their names to your table of keywords and synonyms.

## BOX 3.13 • *Selected List of Practice Handbooks and Manuals*

Achieving Evidence-Based Practice: A Handbook for Practitioners

Child Sexual Abuse: An Interdisciplinary Manual for Diagnosis, Case Management, and Treatment

Clinical Handbook of Psychological Disorders: A Step-By-Step Treatment Manual

Cognitive Processing Therapy for Rape Victims: A Treatment Manual

Cognitive-Behavioral Coping Skills Therapy Manual: A Clinical Research Guide for Therapists Treating Individuals with Alcohol Abuse and Dependence

Comparative Psychology: A Handbook

Eating Disorders and Obesity: A Comprehensive Handbook

Handbook for Action Research in Health and Social Care

Handbook of Aging and the Social Sciences

Handbook of Asian American Psychology

Handbook of Assessment and Treatment Planning for Psychological Disorders

Handbook of Child Psychology

Handbook of Community Psychology

Handbook of Comparative Interventions for Adult Disorders

Handbook of Culture and Psychology

Handbook of Effective Psychotherapy

Handbook of Empirical Social Work Practice

Handbook of Forensic Sexology: Biomedical and Criminological Perspectives

Handbook of Group Psychotherapy: An Empirical and Clinical Synthesis

Handbook of Health Psychology

Handbook of Humanistic Psychology: Leading Edges in Theory, Research, and Practice

Handbook of Personality Psychology

Handbook of Psychotherapy and Behavior Change

Handbook of Qualitative Research

Handbook of Research Methods: A Guide for Practitioners and Students in the Social Sciences

Handbook of School Psychology

Handbook of Social Cognition

Handbook of Social Psychology

Handbook of Social Studies in Health and Medicine

Handbook of Social Support and the Family

Handbook of Social Work Direct Practice

Handbook of Social Work Practice

Handbook of Social Work Practice with Vulnerable and Resilient Populations

Handbook of Social Work Practice with Vulnerable Populations

Handbook of Treatment for Eating Disorders

Incest: A Treatment Manual for Therapy with Victims, Spouses, and Offenders

International Handbook on Social Work Theory and Practice

Motivational Enhancement Therapy Manual: A Clinical Research Guide for Therapists Treating Individuals with Alcohol Abuse and Dependence

Multicultural Clients: A Professional Handbook for Healthcare Providers and Social Workers

Psychology of Sexual Orientation, Behavior, and Identity: A Handbook

Psychology of Women: A Handbook of Issues and Theories.

Social Psychology: Handbook of Basic Principles

Social Work in Health Care: A Handbook for Practice

Treatment Alternatives to Street Crime: Training Manual

Searches of library catalogs using the terms *program manual, practice manual, treatment manual, best practice, guidelines, standards, practice guidelines, expert consensus statements,* and *clinical practice guidelines (CPGs)* often yield helpful resources—although they may vary in terms of their empirical base. Some are clearly supported by credible evidence that includes research-based knowledge, while others reflect the expert opinions of a group of authorities. Works such as those listed in Box 3.14 are representative of the kinds of practice guidelines likely to become more prevalent and prominent within the next several years.

If you decided to search the Library of Congress on-line catalog for books about domestic violence between adult partners (husbands and wives, spouses, intimates, lovers), you could go the Basic Search page at http://catalog.loc.gov, enter the term *violence*, and select the subject browse type of search. You might use the broad term *violence* to begin in order to determine if it is a subject heading that has subdivisions, such as domestic or family violence, or intimate partner violence. If you did, you would find that *violence* is both a Library of Congress Subject Heading (LCSH) and a Medical Subject Heading (MeSH) term. You might also discover that the subject

## BOX 3.14 • *Selected List of Practice Guidelines and Standards*

AHNA Standards of Holistic Nursing Practice: Guidelines for Caring and Healing

American Psychiatric Association Practice Guideline for the Treatment of Patients with Eating Disorders

American Psychiatric Association Practice Guideline for the Treatment of Patients with Substance Use Disorders: Alcohol, Cocaine, Opiods

American Psychiatric Association Practice Guidelines for the Treatment of Patients with Borderline Personality Disorder

American Psychiatric Association Practice Guidelines for the Treatment of Patients with HIV/AIDS

American Psychiatric Association Practice Guidelines for the Treatment of Patients with Major Depression

American Psychiatric Association Practice Guidelines for the Treatment of Patients with Panic Disorder

Early Identification of Alzheimer's Disease and Related Dementias

Narcotic Treatment Programs: Best Practice Guidelines

NASW Standards for Continuing Professional Education

NASW Standards for Cultural Competence in Social Work Practice

NASW Standards for School Social Work Services

NASW Standards for Social Work Case Management

NASW Standards for Social Work Personnel Practices

NASW Standards for Social Work Practice in Child Protection

NASW Standards for Social Work Services in Long-Term Care Facilities

NASW Standards for the Practice of Clinical Social Work

NASW Standards for the Practice of Social Work with Adolescents

NASW Standards of Practice for Social Work Mediators

*violence* includes several subcategories, including family violence, fighting (psychology), prison violence, school violence, violent crimes, violent deaths, dating violence, children and violence, political violence, road rage, and youth and violence.

If you clicked on the hyperlinked subject heading **Family Violence,** you could quickly view a list of the titles and authors of nearly a hundred books on the topic. Furthermore, you could select those that you thought might pertain to your topic and save the list to your computer or send it to your e-mail account.

To conduct a more focused search, you could go back to the Library of Congress search page (http://catalog.loc.gov) and select guided rather than basic search. The LOC guided search allows you to use advanced features in your search, including Boolean operators.

University libraries, the Library of Congress on-line catalogs, and Web sites such as Bowker's Global Books-in-Print are efficient ways to identify the titles, authors, and publishers of relevant books. Once identified, however, you must obtain them through your own library, interlibrary loan, or, if you have sufficient resources, by purchasing them from a bookseller.

You may also be able to read some books electronically—through the Internet or as downloads to your personal computer. For example, *The Merck Manual of Diagnosis and Therapy* (Beers & Berkow, 1999) is available on line free of charge at http://www.merck.com/pubs/mmanual, as is *The Merck Manual of Medical Information Home Edition* (Berkow, 2000) at http://www.merck.com/pubs/mmanual_home. Your university library may permit access to some e-books, and some publishers give Internet users access to a few of their books as well. For example, current members of the Council on Social Work Education (CSWE) may access on-line copies of *Practice-Sensitive Social Work Education* (Teare & Sheafor, 1995) and *Expanding Partnerships for Vulnerable Children, Youth, and Families* (Hooper-Briar & Lawson, 1996). In addition, the Gutenberg Project (http://promo.net/pg/) provides access to many books, including classics, and the University of Pennsylvania Library sponsors the Online Books Page at http://onlinebooks.library.upenn.edu. Under the Books Online section of that site, you may click on **Subjects** to access the Library of Congress classifications. If you scrolled down the page and clicked on the *HV: Social Service, Welfare, Criminology* hyperlink, you would soon retrieve a long list of free on-line books. A single click loads each book so that you could read it cover to cover, or examine selected portions.

## Dissertations

University and research libraries often have copies of doctoral dissertations, especially those of their own graduates. You may locate them through a basic search of the on-line catalog. There are also other means to locate dissertations.

If you were to search a major university library on-line catalog using the term *dissertation abstracts*, you would probably find a reference to abstracts published by University Microfilms International. These include *Dissertation Abstracts International: Humanities and Social Sciences* and *Dissertation Abstracts International: Science and*

*Engineering.* You may also see a reference to *Dissertation Abstracts International: Cumulated Author Index. Social Work Abstracts* might also be identified, since that bibliographic database includes information about doctoral dissertations in social work and related disciplines.

The library may have printed copies of the dissertation abstracts or may provide access via CD-ROM or on-line connection. Many university libraries subscribe to the ProQuest® Digital Dissertations service (http://www.lib.umi.com/dissertations). The search feature enables users to search for relevant dissertations in about the same way that scholars look for books and periodicals through their library on-line catalog. You may select the basic or advanced search methods and use the usual Boolean operators AND, OR, or NOT as you search for author, keyword, title, school, subject, abstracts, sponsoring university, degree, and other database fields.

You may also use the browse feature to review dissertations cataloged by subject. If you do, you will notice how subjects are organized into the humanities and social sciences, and the sciences and engineering. Most social workers would browse subdivisions within each of these two major categories. For example, social work appears within the social sciences subdivision of the humanities and social sciences category along with other related subjects (anthropology, business administration, economics, gerontology, recreation, urban and regional planning, women's studies). The sociology subdivision contains related subject areas as well (general, criminology and penology, demography, ethnic and racial studies, individual and family studies, industrial and labor relations, public and social welfare, social structure and development, theory and methods).

Education is another subdivision within the humanities and social sciences category and contains many subject areas of potential relevance for social workers (adult and continuing, bilinqual and multicultural, curriculum and instruction, early childhood, educational psychology, guidance and counseling, health, special education, technology, tests and measurements).

Health sciences and psychology are subdivisions within the sciences and engineering category. Psychology contains the following interesting subject areas (general, behavioral, clinical, cognitive, developmental, experimental, industrial, personality, physiological, psychobiology, psychometrics, and social). Health sciences includes several relevant subjects (education, health care management, human development, mental health, oncology, pharmacology, public health, recreation, rehabilitation and therapy, speech pathology).

If you were to conduct a basic search of the UMI ProQuest Digital Dissertations database for keywords using *domestic violence OR family violence OR partner violence*, you would generate a list of more than 1,250 dissertation citations—if you limited the search to those published in 1998 or later. Obviously, this topic is attractive to doctoral students. If you narrowed the search by searching only the **Titles** field, you would still produce more almost 550 dissertations titles. If you then used the **Refine Search** feature to search the **Abstracts** field within that set of results, using the terms *treatment AND research*, you would generate almost 70 citations. A review of the titles and brief abstracts might lead you to become interested in a dissertation entitled *Effectiveness of a Court-Ordered Domestic Violence Treatment Program: A Clinical Utility*

*Study* by David J. Ley, Jr. (2001). If so, you might ask your own reference librarian for help in obtaining a copy of the dissertation through interlibrary loan. If that proves unsuccessful, you could use your Web browser to download a copy in Adobe Reader (PDF) format from the ProQuest® Digital Dissertations at http://www.lib.umi.com/dissertations. Unfortunately, that would require a credit card payment of about $25.

Recently completed dissertations that closely address your subject area are often extremely useful. They almost always include a thorough review of the research literature and an extensive list of references.

## Professional and Scientific Journals

In the search for evidence of effectiveness upon which to base your service to clients in need, you must locate and read articles from scholarly journals. As professionals, you should be especially interested in research papers that pertain to the nature and outcomes of various strategies of prevention or intervention. In most circumstances, articles from scholarly journals represent the major source of information about practice effectiveness. Popular magazine and newspaper articles may provide leads and ideas for your search by identifying contemporary scholars or research studies. However, they cannot be considered credible scholarly sources.

The information and technology revolution has resulted in increased production of periodicals. There are literally thousands of scholarly journals. Although most are still published in print format, many now appear in both print and electronic (online) form, and several are presented exclusively on the World Wide Web.

A definitive list of journals of relevance to social workers is impossible to produce because the profession addresses such a wide range of diverse issues and because several new publications emerge each year. In addition, social workers must be familiar with journals from other disciplines that relate to their practices, settings, and clientele. For example, social workers in the fields of medical and mental health must be familiar with medical, psychiatric, and psychological journals as well as social work journals. Those involved in policy and planning must be cognizant of journals in the areas of law, politics, economics, business administration, and management, among others. Those in school social work must be familiar with periodicals in the fields of education, child and adolescent development, child and family welfare, and a host of other areas. All social workers must conscientiously identify and review journals that provide credible and relevant information, regardless of the discipline with which the periodicals are affiliated.

The selected list of journal titles in Box 3.15 may be of some value to you. However, it is far from complete. Many scholarly publications that pertain to your topical interests are almost certainly not included here.

In seeking information, you may be tempted to immediately search for the articles themselves rather than looking for the titles of potentially relevant journals. Try to identify the journals first. Sometimes knowledge of specialized publications helps you locate the best and most applicable articles. This is especially important for advanced scholars who realize that electronic searches of bibliographic databases in-

## BOX 3.15 • *Selected List of Social Work-Relevant Journals*

Accent on Living
Acta Psychiatrica Scandinavica
Addiction
Addiction & Recovery
Addiction Biology
Addiction Letter
Administration in Social Work
Adolescence
Adoptive Families
Advances in Social Work: Linking Research, Education & Practice
Affilia: Journal of Women & Social Work
Age & Ageing
Alcoholism Treatment Quarterly
American Journal of Art Therapy
American Journal of Family Therapy
American Journal of Nursing
American Journal of Orthopsychiatry
American Journal of Psychiatry
American Journal of Psychoanalysis
American Journal of Psychotherapy
American Psychologist
Annual Review of Psychology
Archives of General Psychiatry
Archives of Pediatrics & Adolescent Medicine
Australian and New Zealand Journal of Psychiatry
Australian Journal of Psychology
Australian Journal of Social Issues
Bandolier
Behavior Therapy
Behavioral & Brain Sciences
Behavioral Health Management
Behavioral Medicine
Behavioral Science
Behaviour Research & Therapy

British Journal of Clinical Psychology
British Journal of Guidance & Counselling
British Journal of Psychiatry
British Journal of Psychology
British Medical Journal
Brown University Child & Adolescent Behavior Letter
Brown University Long-Term Care Letter
Bulletin of the Menninger Clinical
Canadian Journal of Experimental Psychology
Canadian Journal of Psychiatry
Canadian Journal of Psychology
Canadian Social Trends
Career Development Quarterly
Child & Adolescent Social Work Journal
Child Abuse & Neglect
Child Development
Child Health Alert
Child Maltreatment
Child Study Journal
Child Welfare
Clinical Evidence
Clinical Nursing Research
Clinical Pediatrics
Clinical Social Work Journal
Cognitive Psychology
Cognitive Science
Cognitive Therapy and Research
Community Mental Health Journal
Counseling & Values
Counselor Education & Supervision
Countdown
Criminal Justice & Behavior
Crisis
Current Psychology

*(continued)*

## BOX 3.15   Continued

DATA: The Brown University Digest of Addiction Theory & Application

Death Studies

Ecological Monographs

Educational & Psychological Measurement

Educational Gerontology

Educational Measurement: Issues & Practice

Educational Psychology

Educational Psychology Review

Effective Healthcare Bulletins

Elementary School Guidance & Counseling

Evidence Based Healthcare

Evidence Based Medicine

Evidence Based Mental Health

Evidence Based Nursing

Families in Society

Family & Conciliation Courts Review

Family & Consumer Sciences Research Journal

Family Economics & Nutrition Review

Family Journal

Family Planning Perspectives

Family Relations

Family Safety & Health

Federal Probation

Focus on Autism & Other Developmental Disabilities

Focus on Autistic Behavior

General Hospital Psychiatry

Genetic, Social & General Psychology Monographs

Geriatrics

Gerontologist

Gifted Child Quarterly

Harvard Mental Health Letter

Health & Social Work

Health Psychology

Innovation: The European Journal of Social Sciences

International Journal of Aging & Human Development

International Journal of Comparative Psychology

International Journal of Geriatric Psychiatry

International Journal of Offender Therapy & Comparative Criminology

International Journal of Psychotherapy

International Journal of Social Psychiatry

International Review of Psychiatry

International Social Work

Intervention in School & Clinic

Issues in Law & Medicine

Journal for Specialists in Group Work

Journal of Abnormal Child Psychology

Journal of Abnormal Psychology

Journal of Addictions & Offender Counseling

Journal of Adolescence

Journal of Adolescent & Adult Literacy

Journal of Adolescent Research

Journal of Affective Disorders

Journal of Aging Studies

Journal of Applied Gerontology

Journal of Behavioral Health Services & Research

Journal of Black Psychology

Journal of Business & Psychology

Journal of Child Psychology & Psychiatry & Allied Disciplines

Journal of Child Sexual Abuse

Journal of Clinical and Experimental Neuropsychology

Journal of Clinical Psychiatry

Journal of Clinical Psychology

Journal of Cognitive Neuroscience

Journal of Comparative Psychology

Journal of Consulting and Clinical Psychology

Journal of Counseling & Development

Journal of Counseling Psychology

Journal of Cross-Cultural Psychology

Journal of Early Adolescence

Journal of Economic & Social Measurement

Journal of Educational Measurement

Journal of Employment Counseling

Journal of Experimental Psychology/Animal Behavior Processes

Journal of Experimental Psychology/Human Perception & Performance

Journal of Family Issues

Journal of Family Nursing

Journal of Gay & Lesbian Psychotherapy

Journal of General Psychology

Journal of Genetic Psychology

Journal of Gerontological Social Work

Journal of Group Psychotherapy, Psychodrama & Sociometry

Journal of Holistic Nursing

Journal of Home Economics

Journal of Humanistic Counseling Education & Development

Journal of Humanistic Psychology

Journal of Intellectual & Developmental Disability

Journal of Learning Disabilities

Journal of Marital & Family Therapy

Journal of Marriage & the Family

Journal of Mental Health

Journal of Mental Health Administration

Journal of Mental Health Counseling

Journal of Multicultural Counseling & Development

Journal of Multicultural Social Work

Journal of Neuropsychiatry and Clinical Neurosciences

Journal of Personality

Journal of Personality & Social Psychology

Journal of Rehabilitation Research & Development

Journal of Reproductive & Infant Psychology

Journal of Social Issues

Journal of Social Political & Economic Studies

Journal of Social Work Education

Journal of Social Work Research and Evaluation: An International Publication

Journal of Substance Abuse Treatment

Journal of the American Academy of Child & Adolescent Psychiatry

Journal of the American Geriatric Society

Journal of the American Medical Association

Journal of Youth & Adolescence

Journals of Gerontology

Lancet

Mainstream

Marriage & Family Review

Measurement & Evaluation in Counseling & Development

Mental Health Weekly

Mental Retardation

Monographs of the Society for Research in Child Development

New England Journal of Medicine

Omega: Journal of Death & Dying

Palaestra

Personnel Psychology

Philosophical Psychology

Practising Evidence Based Mental Health

PriMHE journal

Professional School Counseling

Psychiatric Rehabilitation Journal

Psychiatric Services

Psychiatry

Psychiatry—Interpersonal and Biological Processes

*(continued)*

**BOX 3.15    Continued**

| | |
|---|---|
| Psychoanalytic Study of the Child | Social Cognition |
| Psychological Assessment | Social Education |
| Psychological Bulletin | Social Indicators Research |
| Psychological Medicine | Social Policy |
| Psychology and Aging | Social Research |
| Psychology of Women Quarterly | Social Security Bulletin |
| Psychopharmacology Update | Social Service Review |
| Psychosocial Rehabilitation Journal | Social Work |
| Psychotherapy Letter | Social Work in Education |
| Rehabilitation Counseling Bulletin | Social Work in Health Care |
| Research on Aging | Social Work Research |
| Research on Social Work Practice | Social Work with Groups |
| RN | Teaching Exceptional Children |
| Rural Special Education Quarterly | Tikkun |
| Schizophrenia Bulletin | Topics in Early Childhood Special Education |
| School Counselor | |
| School Psychology Review | Western Journal of Nursing Research |
| Small Group Research | Women & Therapy |
| Social Alternatives | Youth & Society |

variably fail to identify at least some important articles. Doctoral students and professors frequently conduct hand searches of the most critical journals in order to ensure that they have located all key articles. Try to identify the titles of those journals that are most pertinent before you begin to search for articles within those and other periodicals. As you find journals that relate to your topic, make note of their titles and library call numbers, and perhaps their International Standard Serial Numbers (ISSN) as well. This information will help you easily locate them again in the future.

In your search for relevant journals, you may again use your university library or the Library of Congress on-line catalogs. Many on-line catalogs permit users to search for periodical titles. For example, a quick search of the Indiana University on-line catalog (http://iucat.edu) for periodical titles containing the term *violence* produces a list of more than forty journals, including *Journal of Interpersonal Violence, Violence against Women, Family Violence and Sexual Assault Bulletin, Violence Update, Journal of Family Violence, Violence and Victims, Response to Violence in the Family, Aggressive Behavior,* and *Violent Relationships.* Of course, journals with titles that do not contain the term *violence* also contain articles about the topic.

You might also search for journal titles through the Library of Congress on-line catalog. For example, you could go to http://catalog.loc.gov and chose **Guided Search**. You might then click on the **Set Search Limits** button. Once there, you could move your cursor to the **Type** window, and use the scroll feature to highlight **Serial (Newspaper, Periodical, etc.)**. If you wished, you could limit the search to English-language publications and then click the **Set Search Limits** button. That would return you to the **Guided Search** page with the limits in place. You might then enter a term such as *violence* in the **Search** window, and highlight **Keywords Anywhere (GKEY)** in the **Search As** window. If you click on the **Begin Search** button, you would obtain a list of about two hundred titles.

If you searched the LOC on-line catalog for periodicals about violence in this manner, you might discover journals you had not previously identified through the search of your university library. Among others you might identify are *Accidents and Violence; Aggression and Violent Behavior; Criminal Justice Journal; Current Research on Peace and Violence; Domestic Abuse Incident Report; Domestic Violence Law Bulletin; Domestic Violence Monograph Series; Journal of Aggression, Maltreatment, and Trauma; National Bulletin on Domestic Violence Prevention; National Campaign to Stop Violence; Response to the Victimization of Women and Children; Trauma, Violence, and Abuse;* and *Violence and Abuse Abstracts*. You might also be interested in some of the periodicals produced by various state-sponsored domestic violence commissions or boards. They would also appear on your list.

One of the more comprehensive sources of information about periodicals is Ulrich's Periodical Directory (available at http://www.ulrichsweb.com/ulrichsweb). A similar service is available at http://www.publist.com. A quick search of Ulrich's for titles containing the keyword phrase *social work* would produce the names of about 160 periodicals from around the world. A similar search of PubList would yield more than 100 journals or magazines with *social work* in their title. A search for periodicals containing *violence* in the title would generate 34 publications through Ulrich's and 23 through PubList.

Identification of pertinent journal titles is a necessary, but insufficient, step in the search process. Journal titles alone do not provide substantive information. Obviously, you must locate and retrieve pertinent articles contained within the scholarly journals, and then review and analyze them to assess their value for your search. At times, you may choose to visit libraries that house the most relevant journals, then carefully hand search the table of contents of each issue—just as doctoral students and professors often do. Indeed, some journals may focus so specifically on your topic that you should decide to do just that!

## *Searching Library Resources: Exercises*

The following exercises are intended to help you develop skill in searching library resources for books and journals that may contain information about practice effectiveness. Please word process your responses, and label the computer file *EBSW Ch3 Library Search Exercises*.

**1.** Go to the Library of Congress Web site at http://www.loc.gov. Click **Search The Catalog** near the top of the page. You should be taken to the on-line search page at http://catalog.loc.gov. Click **Help On Searching**. You should be directed to http://catalog.loc.gov/help/contents.htm. Read the general information about the Library of Congress on-line catalog. Locate and make note of the approximate number of records contained in LOC on-line catalog database. Note the date of your electronic visit to the LOC Web site.

Following that, move your cursor over to the left side of the page. Click on **FAQs.** You should be directed to the Frequently Asked Questions page at http://catalog.loc.gov/help/faq.htm. Review the information presented there. Make note of the days and times when it might be most difficult to access the LOC on-line catalog.

Once again, move your cursor over to the left side of the page. Click on **Basic Searching**. You should be directed to the basic search overview page at http://catalog.loc.gov/help/combinedsearch.htm. The basic search process enables scholars to search the LOC on-line catalog from multiple perspectives. Review the material and make note of several methods by which you might search for information via the basic search approach.

Move your cursor over to the left side of the page. Click on **Titles** under **Basic Searching.** You should be directed to the Basic Search—Title help page at http://catalog.loc.gov/help/title.htm. The basic title search process enables scholars to search titles of single works, periodicals, or series contained in the LOC on-line catalog. In a few sentences, word process what you might do to increase the number of hits if a search for titles generated fewer than you anticipated.

Move your cursor over to the left side of the page. Click on **Author/Creator Browse** under **Basic Searching.** You should be directed to the basic search—author/creator help page at http://catalog.loc.gov/help/name.htm. The basic author/creator search process enables scholars to search for personal or group authors or creators contained in the LOC on-line catalog. In your word-processed file, discuss whether it would be better to search for authors using last name followed by first name or first name followed by last name.

Move your cursor over to the left side of the page. Click on **Subject Browse** under **Basic Searching.** You should be directed to the Basic Search—Subject Browse help page at http://catalog.loc.gov/help/subject.htm. The basic subject search process enables scholars to search for materials contained in the LOC on-line catalog that match entries in a controlled vocabulary such as the Library of Congress Subject Headings (LCSH). In a few sentences, discuss what you think might be the advantages and disadvantages of searches using subject headings.

Move your cursor over to the left side of the page. Click on **Keyword** under **Basic Searching.** You should be directed to the Basic Search—Keyword help page at http://catalog.loc.gov/help/keyword.htm. The keyword search process enables scholars to search for materials contained in the LOC on-line catalog that include terms contained in the other fields (for example, title, author/creator, subject) and to use certain symbols (+, !, ?, *) to manage the keyword search. Briefly discuss the pros and cons associated with keyword searches.

Now move your cursor over to the left side of the page. Click on **Command Keyword** under **Basic Searching.** You should be directed to the Basic search—command keyword help page at http://catalog.loc.gov/help/command.htm. The command keyword process is the most powerful and sophisticated of the basic search processes. It enables scholars to set search limits and use the question mark symbol for truncation, quotation marks for exact phrases, parentheses to nest operations, and Boolean operators such as AND, OR, or NOT. Review the materials in the help page and briefly discuss what makes the command keyword search so powerful.

Following that, move your cursor over to the left side of the page. Click on **Guided Searching** under **Searching.** You should be directed to the Guided Search help page at http://catalog.loc.gov/help/buildersearch.htm. The guided search process enables scholars to use some of the features of command keyword searches through drop-down menus. In a short paragraph, discuss how guided searches differ from command keyword searches.

2. Now that you have a general sense of how to use the LOC search features, go to the Library of Congress on-line catalog at http://catalog.loc.gov. Click on **Basic Search.** If you attempt to access the catalog during a busy time, you will receive a message that "All available connections to the LC On-line Catalog are in use. Please try again in a few minutes." You may indeed wait several seconds and then click on basic search once again. Or you may try during hours likely to have less traffic (such as late evening). The Library of Congress on-line catalog is an incredible resource that is freely accessible. However, it has a finite capacity. We cannot always access the catalog exactly when we wish to.

Once you have gained access to the basic search screen, review the basic search tips to again familiarize yourself with the features. Then scroll back up to the top of the screen. Type *reference books* in the **Search Text** window. Highlight **Title** in the **Search Type** window, and click the **Begin Search** button. Record the results of that search by describing the number of hits and kinds of materials identified.

Return to the basic search page and again enter *reference books* in the **Search Text** window. This time, highlight **Subject Browse** in the **Search Type** window, and click the **Begin Search** button. Briefly describe the kinds of materials identified by each of these two searches.

The term *reference books* is a Library of Congress Subject Heading (LCSH). When a scholar conducts a subject search using a LCSH, materials classified within that heading emerge. In many instances, the LCSH term may be linked to a broader or narrower term. This is indicated by the **MORE INFO** icon. By clicking on the **MORE INFO** button adjacent to the first reference books subject heading hit, several narrower subject heading terms emerge, including Encyclopedias and Dictionaries, which includes approximately a thousand works.

Return to the basic search page and again enter *reference books* in the search text window. This time, highlight **Keyword** in the **Search Type** window, and click the **Begin Search** button. Briefly describe the results of that search (for example, the kinds of materials identified), and discuss whether that approach is useful or not.

Return to the basic search page. This time type *encyclopedia AND social AND work* in the **Search Text** window. Highlight **Title** in the **Search Type** window, and click the **Begin Search** button. Briefly describe the results of that search (number and kinds of materials identified).

If you were redirected to another page, return to the basic search page and use the same search phrase—*encyclopedia AND social AND work*—in the **Search Text** window. This time, highlight **Keyword** in the **Search Type** window, and click the **Begin Search** button. Describe the results of that search, and discuss the difference in outcomes for the title search and the keyword search.

Return to the basic search page and enter the same search phrase—*encyclopedia AND social AND work*. What happens when you highlight **Command Keyword** in the **Search Type** window and conduct a search? Which process seems more useful in this instance—**Keyword** or **Command Keyword**? What happens when you conduct a search using the same search phrase but highlight **Subject Browse** in the **Search Type** window? Which process seems more useful in this instance—subject, keyword, or command keyword?

Return to the home page of the Library of Congress on-line catalog. This time click on **Guided Search** rather than **Basic Search**. Move your cursor to the middle-right side of the page. Click the **Set Search Limits** button. Note that you may set limits for your search according to five dimensions: **Date, Language, Type (of publication), Location,** and **Place of Publication.** Select **English** as the language and reference collections as the location. Click **Set Search Limits** to return to the **Guided Search** page. What happens when you conduct a **Keyword Anywhere (GHEY)** search using the phrase *social work*? We may omit the term *encyclopedia* because we have limited the search to reference sections of the Library of Congress on-line catalog. Remember to clear the limits you set before conducting additional searches.

3. Go to The Online Books Page at http://onlinebooks.library.upenn.edu. Click on the **Titles** hyperlink to reveal a **Search Titles** window. Enter the words *Violence in Families: Assessing Prevention and Treatment Programs* to locate a book by that title. Click on the hyperlinked title to go to the National Academies Press Web page that contains the book. Move your cursor over to the upper left quadrant of the screen and click on **Read Online for Free** to reveal a hyperlinked table of contents. Click on **Executive Summary** and then go to page 3 (tools to move around the book are located at both the top and bottom of the screen). Read the section entitled "The Role od Science in the Assessment of Interventions." In particular, read the "Conclusions" and "Recommendations" subsections. Briefly summarize the fifth and sixth recommendations.

4. Turn now to your own topic of interest. Review your practice-effectiveness question (the one you created in the Chapter 2 exercises) and the table of keywords and synonyms that you created earlier. Identify four to six words from your table of keywords and synonyms that capture the major elements of your practice-effectiveness questions. Go to your university library on-line catalog and conduct a basic, general keyword search for each of those terms. After that, go to the Library of Congress on-line catalog and complete the same searches. Briefly describe the results of each search.

   Use Boolean operators to add the terms *reference, dictionary, handbook, manual, directory,* and *guideline* to your earlier searches in your university library and the Library of Congress. Identify the most relevant reference works and other books that you generated through these new searches.

   Now use Boolean operators to create three search strings that capture the central elements of your practice-effectiveness question and the major keywords and synonyms associated with those aspects. Use those strings to search your own university library on-line catalog and that of the Library of Congress. Describe the results.

5. Conduct a search for dissertations that might contain information pertinent to your practice-effectiveness question. If you can access the UMI ProQuest Digital Dissertations Web site through your university account, conduct an on-line search. If not, use the dissertation abstracts or social work abstracts resources within the reference section of your university library. Make note of two or three dissertations that might help you address your practice-effectiveness question.

6. Conduct a search for the titles of professional journals that might contain articles, especially research articles, about your practice-effectiveness question. Start with your university library on-line catalog to identify journal titles available to campus scholars. If you can use your university account to access the Ulrich's Periodical Directory on line, also search that database for relevant journals. If you cannot, go to the PubList Web site at http://www.publist.com. If necessary, complete the free registration process, and then use your keywords to conduct a search for potentially relevant journals. Identify five to ten professional journals that might help you address your practice-effectiveness question.

## Searching Bibliographic Databases

Most university libraries provide students and faculty free access to one or more commercial electronic bibliographic database services. Libraries subscribe to those most relevant to the research and professional interests of their scholars. As a member of a university community, you may underestimate the real market value of the bibliographic databases because you do not directly pay the costs. Libraries pay substantial subscription fees for use of these commercial products. Large universities often invest hundreds of thousands of dollars per year in these services. You would be shocked at the actual cost of individual subscriptions!

Accompanying this book is information about Pearson Education's Research Navigator On-line Databases. Among the materials is a student access code to enable you to register for a subscription to the service at http://www.researchnavigator.com. The subscription enables you to search the Research Navigator bibliographic databases free of charge. Research Navigator is provided to you courtesy of the publisher. It is an invaluable resource for evidence-based social work.

The Research Navigator home Web page has special features for scholars. Within **Understanding the Research Process,** the **Start Writing** section contains guidelines and resources for preparing research papers. **Internet Research** contains resources about search services as well as tips for searching and evaluating resources. **Citing Sources** contains information about proper citation and reference formats in major editorial styles. **Links Library** contains hyperlinks to resources in several academic disciplines.

Articles from hundreds of professional journals are available through more than a dozen Research Navigator databases. Indeed, you may seek and access reference information and full-text articles from journals in social work, sociology, psychology, education, criminal justice, political science, anthropology, communications, the medical sciences, and other disciplines.

Research Navigator allows scholars to conduct basic or advanced searches. The Boolean operators AND, OR, and NOT may be used, and completed searches may be refined to improve results. The following codes may be incorporated into search strings: AU (Author), TI (Article Title), SU (Subject), AB (Abstract), AN (Accession Number), IS (International Standard Serial Number—ISSN), SO (Source—Journal Title), and AS (Author Supplied Abstract).

To conduct a search for journal articles through Research Navigator, you must first log in, and then select the databases you wish to search. If, for example, you are interested in the topic of domestic violence between adult partners or spouses, you could select databases in criminal justice; education; helping professions; nursing, health, and medicine; political science; psychology; and sociology to search for professional journal articles about the topic. You could limit your search to the helping professions database to reduce the number of results. However, you might miss significant articles from journals not included in that particular database.

After selecting one or more databases, enter a keyword or phrase and click **Go** to initiate a basic search process. You might select the **Advanced Search Feature** to enter a search string such as the following: *"domestic violence" OR "partner violence" OR "conjugal violence" OR "family violence" OR "spouse abuse."* If you then clicked on the search button, you would return a list of more than eight hundred references to articles about the topic. More than five hundred of the articles are available as full-text documents. This enables you to read them in their entirety.

If you wanted to focus on articles that describe research about the effectiveness of practices or services to persons involved in or affected by domestic violence, you could then add a new search string such as *research OR evaluation OR outcome OR effectiveness OR study OR review OR meta-analysis.* The revised search produces a more manageable number of returns. Several contain hyperlinks to full-text versions of the articles in either HTML or Adobe portable document (PDF) format. PDF-formatted versions are especially useful because they contain full-page images of the published articles. You can see the page numbers and graphics as actually published in the print version of the journal. In effect, you access a photocopied image of the original article. This makes citing quoted or paraphrased material easier because you can refer accurately to the actual page numbers.

If you scanned the article titles, you might become interested in an article by Eileen Abel (2000), who reviewed empirical research studies related to the effectiveness of psychosocial treatments for battered women. In that article, Abel describes several important studies of outcome effectiveness and makes reference to numerous relevant papers.

Bibliographic systems such as Research Navigator are difficult to overvalue. Imagine being able to find Abel's work and read the entire article online within a few minutes! Despite their obvious merits, there are certain dangers to bibliographic services. Scholars may be unaware that some key journals are excluded from particular databases. They may conclude they have conducted comprehensive searches of the literature when they have actually failed to search the contents of several highly relevant journals. Ensure that you know what journals are included within each database searched. Most databases include a means to identify the journal titles or publications included among their collections. When you realize that important journals are excluded from a bibliographic database, find them in some other way. You should also check to see whether excluded journals are published electronically. If your library subscribes to print versions, you may be able to access them free of charge through the World Wide Web. Check with your reference librarian to determine which journals are available electronically as well as in print form.

Scholars may be tempted to use full-text services exclusively—because it is so easy to review entire articles online. Limiting a search for evidence in such a way represents a major scholarship flaw. Sometime in the future, you may be able to access full-text versions of all scholarly materials online. However, many extremely valuable materials are still unavailable in electronic form today. Sometimes you must obtain the printed version of some documents, perhaps by actually visiting a library building. Failure to do so raises questions of scholarly integrity and places the value of findings and conclusions in doubt. How could you support a claim that a practice reflects evidence of effectiveness if you have not examined some of the most pertinent information?

Universities that offer accredited programs in social work often purchase the rights to the CD-ROM or on-line versions of Social Work Abstracts (SWABS), published by SilverPlatter. WebSPIRS is SilverPlatter's interface for World Wide Web access to the more than 250 bibliographic and full-text databases included within their collections. University libraries may also subscribe to the Gale Group (InfoTrac) Expanded Academic ASAP™ service, which provides subscribers access to bibliographic and full-text materials from both scholarly and popular periodicals from a wide range of academic subjects and disciplines. Expanded Academic ASAP™ includes materials from more than a thousand periodicals. EBSCO Publishing Services also provides a wide range of bibliographic and full-text services, including those contained in your Research Navigator database. OVID Technologies sponsors databases widely used in medical schools and hospitals. Some OVID subscriptions allow access to a rich array of resources, including citations, abstracts, and full-text articles from dozens of databases.

Several on-line bibliographic databases do not require paid subscription, although they usually do not provide full-text access. For example, the United States National Library of Medicine (NLM) (http:www.nlm.nih.gov) provides open access to several extraordinary bibliographic databases and other valuable resources.[3]

The National Library of Medicine offers numerous resources and databases, including Bioethics, Cancer Information, Chemical Information, Clinical Alerts, Clinical Trials, Consumer Information, Environmental Health Information, Directory of Health Organizations (DIRLINE®), DOCLINE®, Drug Information, Health Service Research and Health Care Technology, NLM Gateway, HIV/AIDS Resources, Interlibrary Loan, Locatorplus, Medical Subject Headings (MeSH®), MEDLINE® (professionals), MEDLINEplus (consumers), NLM On-line Exhibitions, Population Information, Profiles in Science, PubMed®, TOXNET®, and Visible Human Project®. The NLM gateway (http://gateway.nlm.nih.gov/gw/Cmd) allows users to conduct a simultaneous search of multiple services. For example, if you were interested in searching for treatment manuals or practice guidelines that might help you serve persons affected by violence, you might use the gateway and enter a search string such as *("treatment manual" OR "practice guideline") AND violence*. If you then hit the enter key, that string would lead to a search of the MEDLINE/PubMed bibliographic database (1966–present) and OLDMEDLINE (1957–1965), LOCATORplus (catalog of books, serials, and audiovisual materials), MEDLINEplus Health Topics (health information from the National Institutes of Health), MEDLINEplus Drug Information, MEDLINE Plus Medical Encyclopedia, DIRLINE (directory of health organizations), AIDS Meetings (abstracts of presentations), Health Services Research Meetings (presentation abstracts), Space Life Sciences Meetings (abstracts), and HSRProj (current health services research projects). The search would produce reference information about more than a hundred journal articles, ten books, and references to current health services research projects.

The MEDLINE® database is available through the PubMed® interface at http:www.ncbi.nlm.nih.gov/entrez. MEDLINE®/PubMed® is an extraordinarily valuable resource for social workers, especially those in the health and mental health fields. The National Library of Medicine provides users free access to more than 12 million bibliographic references from health-and life-science related journals. More than 4,300 journals are abstracted and indexed within the MEDLINE®/PubMed® bibliographic database. A great many would interest social workers. For example, about 250 of their journals contain the term *social* in their titles, more than 50 contain *sociology*, about 150 have *psychology*, more than 130 *education*, more than 80 *psychiatry*, more than 30 *political*, more than 110 *policy*, more than 100 *child*, more than 10 *abuse*, more than 50 *behavior*, and more than 700 contain the term *research*. Several also include *evidence* in their titles (for example, *Clinical Evidence, Evidence-Based Mental Health, Evidence-Based Nursing*). The sheer amount of potentially relevant bibliographic information is incredible.

Research Navigator and most other bibliographic database services offer features similar to those provided via MEDLINE®/PubMed®. The interfaces operate much like library on-line catalogs and other electronic databases, although there are variations from service to service. Each bibliographic database service is likely to yield a unique set of results. This is understandable because each database contains its own selection of journals and operates through its own algorithms. Whenever possible, use multiple services to capture a comprehensive set of results. You may obtain dramatically different outcomes when using alternate features or processes within a single bibliographic database, even when the search terms are identical. An advanced search and a basic search might not yield identical results, and a keyword search produces different returns than a title search. Obviously, a search for the term *Smith* within the **Author** field obtains quite different results from a search for *Smith* within the **Title** field. Similarly, searches using the strings *child abuse*; *child AND abuse*; and *child OR abuse* would produce distinct lists of citations.

If you visited the National Library of Medicine Web site at http://www.nlm.nih.gov and clicked on **Health Information,** you would be transferred to a Web page containing a list of services. You might briefly review those and then click on the MEDLINE®/PubMed® hyperlink to access the MEDLINE® bibliographic database at http://www.ncbi.nlm.nih.gov/entrez. The PubMed® interface allows users to search all fields by simply inserting one or more search terms in the empty **Search for** window. Unless your keyword is rare, the basic search process tends to yield a large number of returns. For example, a basic search of PubMed® using the term *violence* produces more than 30,000 hits.

A search may be narrowed or focused by clicking on the **Limits** button, which permits more advanced operations. Other bibliographic database interfaces may use the terms *basic, guided,* and *advanced* to distinguish various search modes. The limits feature in PubMed® allows scholars to limit a search to fields such as **Title, Title/Abstract, Journal, Language, Publication Date, Publication Type, MeSH Subject Heading,** and **Text Word.**

You may also limit the search to certain kinds of publication types (clinical trial, editorial, letter, meta-analysis, practice guideline, randomized controlled trial, review). This is an extremely useful feature when searching for evidence of practice effectiveness. You are much more likely to locate pertinent research-based information about practice outcomes in articles that contain meta-analyses, reports of clinical and randomized controlled trials, reviews, and descriptions of practice guidelines. You are less likely to find relevant evidence of practice effectiveness in editorials or letters.

PubMed® searches may include the Boolean operators AND, OR, or NOT, which permits further refinement. For example, an unlimited search of all fields using the string *domestic AND violence* would produce a return of nearly 20,000 citations. If you placed quotation marks around the words so that the phrase *"domestic violence"* was sought, the number of citations would decrease to about 2,000. If you changed the search string to *"domestic violence" AND research*, you would generate a list of about 350 article citations. If you added *AND outcome* to that string, you would locate about 25 articles. If you conducted a search using the string *"domestic violence" OR "family violence" OR "partner violence"* and restricted the search to practice guidelines through the limits feature and the limited to pull-down menu, you would obtain about 40 titles. By scanning the titles, you would find that about 10 articles contain information about practice guidelines for persons affected by some form of domestic violence.

You could easily select those particular references by clicking on the select box adjacent to each title and then use the **Send To** button to e-mail or save them to a computer file (Box 3.16 shows citations presented in PubMed® format). You can not directly access the full-text versions of the articles through PubMed®. However, you may use bibliographic information to search library holdings, print or electronic journals, and those database services that contain full-text material.

If you were interested in articles that contained reports of studies that adopted rigorous research designs, you could use the same search string—*"domestic violence" OR family violence OR partner violence*—but limit the search to **Randomized**

**BOX 3.16** • *PubMed-Formatted Bibliographic References*

Ferris LE, Norton PG, Dunn EV, Gort EH, Degani N. Guidelines for managing domestic abuse when male and female partners are patients of the same physician. The Delphi Panel and the Consulting Group. JAMA. 1997 Sep 10;278(10):851–7. Review. PMID: 9293995 [PubMed—indexed for MEDLINE]

[No authors listed] Ambulatory care criteria set: intervention for domestic violence. Number 20, November 1996. Committee on Quality Assessment. American College of Obstetricians and Gynecologists. Int J Gynaecol Obstet. 1997 Apr;57(1):93–4. No abstract available. PMID: 9175679 [PubMed—indexed for MEDLINE]

[No authors listed] ACOG technical bulletin. Domestic violence. Number 209—August 1995 (replaces no. 124, January 1989). American College of Obstetricians and Gynecologists. Int J Gynaecol Obstet. 1995 Nov;51(2):161–70. PMID: 8635639 [PubMed—indexed for MEDLINE]

[No authors listed] Mississippi State Medical Association & Alliance Physician Resource Directory. Diagnostic & treatment guidelines on domestic violence. J Miss State Med Assoc. 1995 Oct-Nov;36(10):331–46. No abstract available. PMID: 8537963 [PubMed—indexed for MEDLINE]

Jordan CE, Walker R. Guidelines for handling domestic violence cases in community mental health centers. Kentucky Department for Mental Health and Mental Retardation Services. Hosp Community Psychiatry. 1994 Feb;45(2):147–51. PMID: 8168794 [PubMed—indexed for MEDLINE]

Braham R, Furniss KK, Holtz H. Nursing protocol on domestic violence. Nurse Pract. 1992 Nov;17(11):24, 27, 31. No abstract available. PMID: 1436772 [PubMed—indexed for MEDLINE]

Bishop J, Patterson PG. [Guidelines for the evaluation and management of family violence.] Can J Psychiatry. 1992 Sep;37(7):458–81. Review. No abstract available. PMID: 1423145 [PubMed—indexed for MEDLINE]

[No authors listed] Violence against women. Relevance for medical practitioners. Council on Scientific Affairs, American Medical Association. JAMA. 1992 Jun 17;267(23):3184–9. PMID: 1593741 [PubMed—indexed for MEDLINE]

Jezierski M. Guidelines for intervention by ED nurses in cases of domestic abuse. J Emerg Nurs. 1992 Feb;18(1):28A–30A. No abstract available. PMID: 1740871 [PubMed—indexed for MEDLINE]

**Controlled Trials.** If you did so, you would obtain a list of more than a hundred citations. By scanning the titles, you would notice that many involve research about child abuse services. However, you would find several that address aspects of partner violence (see Box 3.17).

If you conducted another search with the same string but limited it to **Clinical Trials,** you would identify more than two hundred articles. You would find that most of them also address child abuse issues. However, about twenty-five describe and discuss clinical trials research related to some form of partner violence.

The National Library of Medicine (NLM) offers a related service called MEDLINEplus (http://www.nlm.nih.gov/medlineplus) that contains health information. Geared more to consumers than to professionals, the materials and resources published through MEDLINEplus are nonetheless highly credible. Users may access medical information about numerous health topics, a medical encyclopedia, a medical dictionary, physician and hospital directories, and links to related resources. Basic and advanced searches are available, and users may browse the site.

Domestic violence is one of many health-related topics addressed on the site. A click on that hyperlinked topic heading would take you to a domestic violence Web page (http://www.nlm.nih.gov/medlineplus/domesticviolence.html) that contains a wealth of relevant resources. In addition to news and general information, the domestic violence page includes specific material about diagnosis, prevention, coping, law and policy, and statistics. Information about both men and women is available. Directories and links to relevant organizations are identified. For example, a click on one hyperlinked heading would reveal a reference list of about fifty recently published research articles about spouse abuse. Another click would display information about male batterers (http://www.cdc.gov/ncipc/factsheets/malebat.htm) published by the National Center for Injury Prevention and Control. This is an especially scholarly fact sheet. Unlike many such documents, it contains citations within the publication and a complete reference list. As you might imagine, thousands of fact sheets are available in electronic or print versions. A surprisingly large proportion of them report statistics and other information as facts without citations and references.

Other on-line bibliographic database services function in ways that are essentially similar to those of MEDLINE®/PubMed®. Social Work Abstracts (SWABS), for example, has a WebSPIRS interface that affords users basic and advanced search features. **Words Anywhere**, **Subject**, **Title**, or **Author** searches can be conducted. There is a **Suggest** feature that produces alternate terms that increase the number or improve the quality of returns. An index of keywords in the database can be searched and articles associated with them retrieved. For instance, a **General Index** search of articles abstracted in SWABS between 1977 and June 2002 using the string *violence OR violent* would generated a list of citations for more than two thousand articles or dissertations. One of the valuable aspects of SWABS is that it contains abstracts about dissertations as well as journal articles.

As do many bibliographic database services, SWABS allows users to combine previous searches or to use them in conjunction with new terms. This may be called the **Search History** feature. For example, if you conducted a search using the string *domestic violence OR family violence OR partner violence* (SWABS does not require quotation marks or parentheses), you would obtain a set of more than four hundred cita-

## BOX 3.17 • *PubMed-Formatted Bibliographic References*

Campbell JC, Coben JH, McLoughlin E, Dearwater S, Nah G, Glass N, Lee D, Durborow N. An evaluation of a system-change training model to improve emergency department response to battered women. Acad Emerg Med. 2001 Feb;8(2):131–8. PMID: 11157288 [PubMed—indexed for MEDLINE]

Thompson RS, Rivara FP, Thompson DC, Barlow WE, Sugg NK, Maiuro RD, Rubanowice DM. Identification and management of domestic violence: a randomized trial. Am J Prev Med. 2000 Nov;19(4):253–63. PMID: 11064229 [PubMed—indexed for MEDLINE]

Dunford FW. The San Diego Navy experiment: an assessment of interventions for men who assault their wives. J Consult Clin Psychol. 2000 Jun;68(3):468–76. PMID: 10883563 [PubMed—indexed for MEDLINE]

Easton C, Swan S, Sinha R. Motivation to change substance use among offenders of domestic violence. J Subst Abuse Treat. 2000 Jul;19(1):1–5. PMID: 10867294 [PubMed—indexed for MEDLINE]

Coonrod DV, Bay RC, Rowley BD, Del Mar NB, Gabriele L, Tessman TD, Chambliss LR. A randomized controlled study of brief interventions to teach residents about domestic violence. Acad Med. 2000 Jan;75(1):55–7. PMID: 10667876 [PubMed—indexed for MEDLINE]

Stalker CA, Fry R. A comparison of short-term group and individual therapy for sexually abused women. Can J Psychiatry. 1999 Mar;44(2):168–74. PMID: 10097838 [PubMed—indexed for MEDLINE]

Sullivan CM, Bybee DI. Reducing violence using community-based advocacy for women with abusive partners. J Consult Clin Psychol. 1999 Feb;67(1):43–53. PMID: 10028208 [PubMed—indexed for MEDLINE]

Foshee VA, Bauman KE, Arriaga XB, Helms RW, Koch GG, Linder GF. An evaluation of Safe Dates, an adolescent dating violence prevention program. Am J Public Health. 1998 Jan;88(1):45–50. PMID: 9584032 [PubMed—indexed for MEDLINE]

Sutherland C, Bybee D, Sullivan C. The long-term effects of battering on women's health. Womens Health. 1998 Spring;4(1):41–70. PMID: 9520606 [PubMed—indexed for MEDLINE]

Foshee VA, Linder GF, Bauman KE, Langwick SA, Arriaga XB, Heath JL, McMahon PM, Bangdiwala S. The Safe Dates Project: theoretical basis, evaluation design, and selected baseline findings. Am J Prev Med. 1996 Sep–Oct;12(5 Suppl):39–47. PMID: 8909623 [PubMed—indexed for MEDLINE]

Saunders DG. Feminist-cognitive-behavioral and process-psychodynamic treatments for men who batter: interaction of abuser traits and treatment models. Violence Vict. 1996 Winter;11(4):393–414. PMID: 9210279 [PubMed—indexed for MEDLINE]

Mullin CR, Linz D. Desensitization and resensitization to violence against women: effects of exposure to sexually violent films on judgments of domestic violence victims. J Pers Soc Psychol. 1995 Sep;69(3):449–59. PMID: 7562390 [PubMed—indexed for MEDLINE]

Stosny S. "Shadows of the heart": a dramatic video for the treatment resistance of spouse abusers. Soc Work. 1994 Nov;39(6):686–94. PMID: 7992138 [PubMed—indexed for MEDLINE]

Sullivan CM, Campbell R, Angelique H, Eby KK, Davidson WS 2nd. An advocacy intervention program for women with abusive partners: six-month follow-up. Am J Community Psychol. 1994 Feb;22(1):101–22. PMID: 7942642 [PubMed—indexed for MEDLINE]

Sullivan CM, Tan C, Basta J, Rumptz M, Davidson WS 2nd. An advocacy intervention program for women with abusive partners: initial evaluation. Am J Community Psychol. 1992 Jun;20(3):309–32. PMID: 1415030 [PubMed—indexed for MEDLINE]

tions. This set is called S1 or Search Number 1. If you conduct another search using a string such as *study OR research OR outcome OR evaluation*, you would obtain a set of several thousand citations. This new set is called S2 or Search Number 2. If you wished, you could combine the two searches by clicking on the **Search History** button to reveal a list of your prior searches, selecting Search Number 1 and Search Number 2, and clicking on the **And** button to combine and search the two sets. The combined search would generate articles containing references to some form of research about some aspect of domestic violence. You could, of course, further refine the results by conducting additional searches and combining them through the **Search History** feature. For instance, you might search for articles about treatment, program, practice, service, or therapy and then combine those results with your first and second searches. If you did, you might identify articles such as those displayed in Box 3.18 and formatted according to the American Psychological Association publication manual. You could then try to locate the articles through electronic full-text sources or by locating the respective journals in your own or in other libraries.

You could also use the advanced search feature to locate articles by important researchers in the field of domestic violence. You could use their names connected by the Boolean operator OR to locate relevant works. You could also then use the search history feature to combine those results with early searches.

The Educational Resources Information Center (ERIC) at http://www .eric.ed.gov and its companion service AskERIC at http://www.askeric.org permit users free access to the ERIC bibliographic database. Although targeted for educators, the database includes bibliographic information from several social work journals (such as *Social Work, Social Work Research, Journal of Social Work Education, Health and Social Work, and Journal of Ethnic* and *Cultural Diversity in Social Work*) excluded from some other databases.

Cambridge Scientific Abstracts at http://www.csa.com offers scholars fee-based access to several bibliographic databases, including Social Services Abstracts. Like SWABS, Social Service Abstracts provides basic and advanced search features. In addition, the user may browse the indexes, search the database thesaurus, or review search histories.

Although most bibliographic database services offer similar features, a few are atypical. Social Services Citations Index, sponsored by Thomson/ISI Web of Knowledge® (http://www.isinet.com/isi), is an example. In addition to searches by

**BOX 3.18 • *APA-Formatted Bibliographic References***

Abel, E. M. (2000). Psychosocial treatments for battered women: A review of empirical research. *Research on Social Work Practice, 10*(1), 55–77.

Aldarondo, E. (1996). Cessation and persistence of wife assault: A longitudinal analysis. *American Journal of Orthopsychiatry, 66*(1), 141–152.

Attala, J. M., and Hudson, W. W., & McSweeney, M. (1994). A partial validation of two short-form partner abuse scales. *Women and Health, 21*(2/3), 125–139.

Barnett, O. W. (2001). Why battered women do not leave, part 2: External inhibiting factors-social support and internal inhibiting factors. *Trauma, Violence, & Abuse,* 2(1), 3–35.

Bennett, L. W. (1995). Substance abuse and the domestic assault of women. *Social Work, 40*(6), 760–771.

Berns, S. B., Jacobson, N. S., & Gottman, J. M. (1999). Demand/withdraw interaction patterns between different types of batterers and their spouses. *Journal of Marital and Family Therapy, 25*(3), 337–348.

Brannen, S. J., & Rubin, A. (1996).Comparing the effectiveness of gender-specific and couples groups in a court-mandated spouse abuse treatment program. *Research on Social Work Practice, 6*(4), 405–424.

Buttell, F. (1998). Issues and ethics in social work with batterers. *The New Social Worker, 5*(2), 7–9.

Davis, L. V., & Srinivasan, M. (1995). Listening to the voices of battered women: What helps them escape violence. *AFFILIA: Journal of Women and Social Work, 10*(1), 49–69.

Dwyer, D. C., Smokowski, P. R., Bricout, J. C., & Wodarski, J. S. (1995). Domestic violence research: Theoretical and practice implications for social work. *Clinical Social Work Journal, 23*(2), 185–198.

Gondolf, E. W. (1997). Batterer programs: What we know and need to know. *Journal of Interpersonal Violence, 12*(1), 83–98.

Hamberger, L. K. (1997). Research concerning wife abuse: Implications for physician training. *Journal of Aggression, Maltreatment & Trauma, 1*(1), 81–96.

Harway, M., Hansen, M., & Cervantes, N. N. (1997). Therapist awareness of appropriate intervention in treatment of domestic violence: A review. *Journal of Aggression, Maltreatment & Trauma,* 1(1), 27–40.

Horton, A. L., & Johnson, B. L. (1993). Profile and strategies of women who have ended abuse. *Families in Society: The Journal of Contemporary Human Services, 74*(8), 481–492.

Jones, L., Hughes, M., & Unterstaller, U. (2001). Post-traumatic stress disorder (PTSD) in victims of domestic violence: A review of the research. *Trauma, Violence, & Abuse, 2*(2), 99–119.

Lundy, M., & Grossman, S. (2001). Clinical research and practice with battered women: What we know, what we need to know. *Trauma, Violence, & Abuse, 2*(2), 120–141.

McNamara, J., & Brooker, D. J. (2000). The Abuse Disability Questionnaire: A new scale for assessing the consequences of partner abuse. *Journal of Interpersonal Violence,* 15(2), 170–183.

Mullender, A. (1996). Groupwork with male "domestic" abusers: Models and dilemmas. *Groupwork, 9*(1), 27–47.

Rondeau, G., Brodeur, N., Brochu, S., & Lemire, G. (2001). Dropout and completion of treatment among spouse abusers. *Violence and Victims, 16*(2), 127–143.

Shamai, M. (2000). Rebirth of the self: How battered women experience treatment. *Clinical Social Work Journal, 28*(1), 85–103.

Whitman, C. (1995). Residential care and treatment for abused women and their children. *Adult Residential Care Journal, 9*(1), 22–34.

subject term, author name, journal title, or author affiliation, users may conduct a cited reference search. This process identifies articles that contain the names of selected authors among the references. When you know the name of an acknowledged expert, you can identify related articles—often ones that have only recently been published. For example, a search for articles in which one or more of E. Gondolf's works are cited produces more than sixty hits. Box 3.19 includes several such articles.

OVID bibliographic database services (http://www.ovid.com) tend to address the needs of health and medical professionals. Universities with medical schools are likely to subscribe to several OVID services. For example, Journals@OVID Full-Text abstracts scholarly journals in the fields of clinical medicine, behavioral and social science, the life sciences, nursing, the physical sciences and engineering, and psychology. Although few social work-specific journals are included, many topics of interest to social workers are addressed. Books@OVID provides full-text access to several medical textbooks, handbooks, and guides.

OVID offers a rich array of services that allow users to search for information about medical symptoms, illnesses, and diseases. Even more relevant to social workers, however, are several services related to evidence-based medicine. Depending on the nature and level of subscription, users may be able to access the full text of the journal *Clinical Evidence* and several other evidence-based resources.

Fee-based bibliographic services such as Research Navigator and EBSCOHost, InfoTrac, Social Work Abstracts, Social Service Abstracts, Social Service Citation Index, and OVID are invaluable for social workers interested in searching for evidence of practice effectiveness. However, some social workers do not have university access or cannot afford to purchase access. As noted earlier, the United States National Library of Medicine (http://www.nlm.nih.gov) sponsors free and open access to the MEDLINE®/PubMed® bibliographic database. In addition, the commercial service INGENTA (http://www.ingenta.com) allows users to search an enormous bibliographic database without charge. Dozens of journals of relevance to social workers are included. However, you may have to pay a fee to retrieve copies of articles. Nonetheless, it represents an excellent way to identify reference information about pertinent articles. Then you may go to your university library to review the journal or request a copy through interlibrary loan.

A search of the INGENTA database using the search string *partner AND violence* within the title, keyword, and abstract fields, limited to publications from 1997

**BOX 3.19** • *APA-Formatted Bibliographic References (E. Gondolf)*

Coben, J. H., & Friedman, D. I. (2002). Health care use by perpetrators of domestic violence. *Journal of Emergency Medicine*, 22(3), 313–317.

Fleck-Henderson, A. (2000). Domestic violence in the child protection system: Seeing double. *Children and Youth Services Review*, 22(5), 333–354.

Gondolf, E. W. (1999). A comparison of four batterer intervention systems—Do court referral, program length, and services matter? *Journal of Interpersonal Violence*, 14(1), 41–61.

Gondolf, E. W. (1999). MCMI-III results for batterer program participants in four cities: Less "pathological" than expected. *Journal of Family Violence*, 14(1), 1–17.

Gondolf, E. W. (2000). A 30-month follow-up of court-referred batterers in four cities. *International Journal of Offender Therapy and Comparative Criminology*, 44(1), 111–128.

Gondolf, E. W. (2000). Mandatory court review and batterer program compliance. *Journal of Interpersonal Violence*, 15(4), 428–437.

Gondolf, E. W. (2002). Service barriers for battered women with male partners in batterer programs. *Journal of Interpersonal Violence*, 17(2), 217–227.

Gondolf, E. W., & White, R. J. (2001). Batterer program participants who repeatedly reassault—Psychopathic tendencies and other disorders. *Journal of Interpersonal Violence*, 16(4), 361–380.

Goodrum, S., Umberson, D., & Anderson, K. L. (2001). The batterer's view of the self and others in domestic violence. *Sociological Inquiry*, 71(2), 221–240.

Heckert, D. A., & Gondolf, E. W. (2000). Assessing assault self-reports by batterer program participants and their partners. *Journal of Family Violence*, 15(2), 181–197.

Heckert, D. A., & Gondolf, E. W. (2000). The effect of perceptions of sanctions on batterer program outcomes. *Journal of Research in Crime and Delinquency*, 37(4), 369–391.

Jones, A. S., & Gondolf, E. W. (2002). Assessing the effect of batterer program completion on reassault: An instrumental variables analysis. *Journal of Quantitative Criminology*, 18(1), 71–98.

Morgan, M., & O'Neill, D. (2001). Pragmatic post-structuralism (II): An outcomes evaluation of a stopping violence programme. *Journal of Community & Applied Social Psychology*, 11(4), 277–289.

Nosko, A., & Wallace, B. (1988). Group work with abusive men—A multidimensional model. *Social Work with Groups*, 11(3), 33–52.

Peterman, L. M., & Dixon, C. G. (2001). Assessment and evaluation of men who batter women. *Journal of Rehabilitation*, 67(4), 38–42.

Rouse, L. P. (1990). The dominance motive in abusive partners—Identifying couples at risk. *Journal of College Student Development*, 31(4), 330–335.

Scher, M., & Stevens, M. (1987). Men and violence. *Journal of Counseling and Development*, 65(7), 351–355.

Silverman, J. G., & Bancroft, R. L. (1998). When men batter women: New insights into ending abusive relationships. *Contemporary Psychology*, 43(10), 704–706.

White, R. J., & Gondolf, E. W. (2000). Implications of personality profiles for batterer treatment. *Journal of Interpersonal Violence*, 15(5), 467–488.

Wood, G. G., & Roche, S. E. (2001). Situations and representations: Feminist practice with survivors of male violence. *Families in Society—The Journal of Contemporary Human Services*, 82(6), 583–590.

through 2002, produces approximately 160 article references. To review an article abstract, select the **Summary** button adjacent to the publication of interest.

INFOTRIEVE at http://www.infotrieve.com also offers a free bibliographic database service called ArticleFinder. It operates in about the same manner as INGENTA.

FINDARTICLES at http://www.findarticles.com is another Web site that allows users free access to bibliographic information and full-text versions of many publications. The range of publications and their applicability to social work is not as great as some other sources. Nonetheless, you may be able to access some useful materials.

NORTHERNLIGHT (http://www.northernlight.com) is a search service that accesses articles and reports from a variety of publications (journals, books, magazines, reference works, news reports). Geared primarily to the needs of the business sector, some resources of interest to social workers are incorporated in their collections. Users may search for references at no cost. However, payment of a fee is required to access the articles themselves. Social workers might find it helpful to use the **Power Search** feature to limit their search to magazines and journals. Otherwise, the search includes newspapers, press releases, broadcast news transcripts, and numerous business-related publications.

YAHOO at http://www.yahoo.com also has a search feature that limits returns to research documents. This approach restricts results primarily to articles from journals rather than newspapers and popular magazines.

In addition to the general bibliographic services, it may be necessary to search the tables of contents of journals either by hand in a library or electronically through the periodical's Web site (for example, *Social Service Review* at http://www.journals.uchicago.edu/SSR/home.html). In addition, there are numerous specialized electronic databases that may be searched without charge. Box 3.20 contains a few examples.

**BOX 3.20 •** *Selected List of Specialized Bibliographic Databases*

Center for Sex Offender Management (U.S.) documents database: http://www.csom.org/asp

Educational Resources Information Center (ERIC) database: http://www.eric.ed.gov/searchdb/searchdb.html

Harvard Family Research Project database of afterschool-program evaluations: http://www.gse.harvard.edu/hfrp/projects/afterschool/evaldatabase.html

National Clearinghouse on Child Abuse and Neglect (NCCAN) database: http://basis1.calib.com/BASIS/chdocs/canweb/SF/

National Criminal Justice Reference Service (NCJRS) database: http://abstractsdb.ncjrs.org/content/AbstractsDB_Search.asp

PAVNET database on U.S. federally funded violence-related research: http://www.pavnet.org

PsiTri database of randomized and controlled trials in mental health: http://www.terkko.helsinki.fi/eu-psi/psitri.htm

UK National Health Service NRR (National Research Register): http://www.update-software.com/nrr/CLIBNET.EXE?A=1&U=1001

**BOX 3.20    Continued**

U.S. Housing and Urban Development (HUD) Bibliographic Database: http://www.huduser.org/bibliodb/pdrbibdb.html

World Bank Group Documents: http://www=wds.worldbank.org

## *Searching Bibliographic Databases: Exercises*

The following exercises are intended to help you learn to search bibliographic databases to locate journal articles related to evidence of practice effectiveness. Please word process your responses, and label the computer file *EBSW Ch3 Search Bib Databases Exercises.*

1.  Go to your university library to identify the on-line or CD-ROM bibliographic databases accessible with your university account and password. You may be able to access some from a computer workstation in the library. Others may be accessible via the Internet with your account information, and some may not require any special permission or subscription. List the array of bibliographic databases that you may use to search for practice-effectiveness information from professional journals. Also identify those journals that may be accessed electronically. Describe how you might access these sources (such as Web site addresses or other guidelines and instructions). Make special note of those that permit access to full-text versions of articles. Show your completed list to a reference librarian to identify any that you may have missed. Add those to your list as well.

2.  Proceed to the National Library of Medicine PubMed tutorial Web site at http://www.nlm.nih.gov/bsd/pubmed_tutorial/m1001.html. The PubMed tutorial provides a rich learning experience for users. The knowledge gained will transfer to many other bibliographic databases. The linked words or phrases on the left side of the introductory screen allow users to move from one section of the tutorial to another. However, the best way to proceed through the tutorial is simply to click on the **Next** arrow after you have carefully read each page. As you go through the lessons, take advantage of the various **Show Me** links. They provide illustrations and examples.

Based on your study of the PubMed tutorial, prepare brief responses to the following questions:

a.  What are MeSH hierarchies and automatic explosions?
b.  What happens when you use a MeSH heading as a search term?
c.  What is the MeSH browser? The journal browser? The single citation matcher?
d.  What are clinical queries and link outs?

e. What is a cubby? How might you use one?

f. What is a journal translation table?

g. What are stopwords and what effect do they have on searches?

h. What is truncation? What is the wildcard symbol used for truncation in the PubMed system?

i. What functions do quotation marks and parentheses serve in PubMed searches?

j. In PubMed, how would you search for articles authored by James Gordon Jones?

k. How would you search for articles authored by a Dr. Foa when you do not know her or his first name?

l. What are three Boolean operators used in the PubMed searches? How should they be entered as part of a search string: lowercase, uppercase, either?

m. What PubMed format would you use if you wanted to download reference records into a bibliographic management software program?

n. In PubMed, how could you increase the number of citations displayed on the screen?

o. In PubMed, how could you sort the list of reference records alphabetically by author name, alphabetically by journal name, and by date of publication?

p. What is a clipboard? In PubMed, how might you select and add records to your clipboard?

q. In PubMed, how might you select and save records to your own computer?

r. In PubMed, how could you change the displayed records into regular text to facilitate copying or printing?

s. In PubMed, what purposes does the **Limit** feature serve? How might you restrict searches to a particular year of publication (such as 2000), a specific journal (such as *Social Work Research*), or a single language (such as English)?

 3. PubMed allows users to limit searches to a particular kind of article through its **Publication Types** drop-down menu. Identify the different types of journal publications, available through PubMed and make note of those types that you would commonly hope to find in searches for evidence of practice effectiveness?

 4. Now shift from the PubMed bibliographic databases. Go to the Pearson Education Research Navigator Web site at http://www.researchnavigator.com. On the left side of the home page, you should find a box entitled **Additional Resources**. Within that box are several hyperlinks. Click first on the one labeled **About**. Familiarize yourself with the general contents of Research Navigator, and then click on the **Take a Tour** hyperlink to develop a more specific understanding of the features. If you review the information carefully, you will notice an opportunity to review the journals contained in each of the EBSCOHost ContentSelect databases within Research Navigator. Click on **Helping Professions** to identify several social work journals. Make note of those social work journals of most relevance to your search for practice-effectiveness

evidence. Also identify major social work journals that are not included in that database. Do the same for the criminal justice, education, health, nursing, and medicine, political science, psychology, and sociology databases. Make note of journals that may contain information of use to you in your search for evidence.

5. In the upper-right portion of the Research Navigator home page at http://www.researchnavigator.com, you should see a box entitled **Understanding the Research Process.** Within that box is a window that contains a drop-down menu. The menu items include **Start Writing, Searching the Internet,** and **Citing Sources.** Click on the each item in sequence, and review the materials. Summarize two or three things from each section that may help you in your search for evidence of practice effectiveness.

6. If you have not yet done so, use the access code included with this book to register your account at the Research Navigator Web site. Once you have logged into the site, go to the box entitled Search for Source Material to locate EBSCO's ContentSelect Academic Journal Database. Select those databases that may contain journals that pertain to your practice-effectiveness question. Refer to the table of keywords and synonyms you previously prepared to guide your search. Using the general-to-specific or broad-to-narrow search principles, begin your search of the Research Navigator bibliographic databases with one or two key words before incorporating additional terms through the use of Boolean operators. Use a word-processor program or the **Save As** feature of your Web browser to maintain a record of the search strings and the processes used. Also save the citations of the most relevant records in word-processed, text, or bibliographic software format. Finally, print or save an electronic copy of the full-text versions of those articles that appear most pertinent to your search.

7. Go to the PubMed interface to search MEDLINE/PubMed for bibliographic references. Use the search strings and processes you used in your search of the Research Navigator databases. Add pertinent references to those you previously identified through your search of Research Navigator.

8. Now visit the INGENTA Web site at http://www.ingenta.com. Reproduce the search processes you conducted through the Research Navigator and the MEDLINE/PubMed databases. Add any additional journal article references to your growing list of potentially useful materials. Complete the same search of the ERIC database at http://www.askeric.org and then repeat it through the INFOTRIEVE ArticleFinder service at http://www.infotrieve.com. Supplement your bibliography with new references.

9. Determine which bibliographic databases you may access through your university library (InfoTrac, Expanded Academic ASAP, Social Work Abstracts, Social Service Abstracts, Social Services Citations Index, PsychINFO, or Sociological Abstracts). Then repeat the search process as needed until you are sure you have located all relevant articles.

## *Searching Evidence-Based Collaborations and Government Resources*

As discussed earlier, organized efforts to complete systematic reviews of evidence of practice effectiveness have emerged during the last ten to fifteen years. Some are sponsored by the federal government, others by various professional associations. The Cochrane Collaboration (http://www.cochrane.org) is an international initiative geared toward the promotion of evidence-based practice within the health services.

If your university library subscribes to OVID services (http://www.ovid.com), you may be able to gain on-line access to the full resources of the Cochrane Collaboration Library EBM Reviews. The following are especially relevant for professionals interested in evidence of practice effectiveness: *Clinical Evidence* (an evidence-based medicine journal), *Database of Abstracts of Reviews of Effectiveness (DARE), EBM (Evidence Based Medicine) Reviews—Best Evidence, EBM Reviews—Cochrane Database of Systematic Reviews, EBM Reviews—Database of Abstracts of Reviews of Effectiveness (DARE)*

If your university does not subscribe to OVID, you may still search or browse titles and abstracts of the Cochrane Reviews free of charge at http://www.update-software.com/Cochrane/default.HTM and the DARE abstracts at http://nhscrd.york.ac.uk/darehp.htm. Tables of contents of *Clinical Evidence* may be searched and viewed at http://www.clinicalevidence.com. However, only scholars at subscribing institutions may access the complete, full-text versions of the Cochrane Library resources.

Although the Cochrane Collaboration emphasizes medical research, several reviews pertain to topics of interest to social workers. For example, if you browsed abstracts of systematic reviews published by the Cochrane Developmental, Psychosocial and Learning Problems Group, you might notice a reference to a Cochrane Review entitled "'Scared Straight' and Other Juvenile Awareness Programs for Preventing Juvenile Delinquency." The systematic analysis of the evidence suggests that the use of juvenile awareness programs such as "Scared Straight"

> are likely to have a harmful effect and increase delinquency relative to doing nothing at all to the same youths. Given these results, agencies that permit such programmes must rigorously evaluate them not only to ensure that they are doing what they purport to do (prevent crime)—but at the very least they do not cause more harm than good. (Petrosino, Turpin-Petrosino, & Buehler, 2002a, para 8)

If you had not previously reviewed the professional literature, you might think that such programs were generally helpful. How many well-intentioned professionals remain unaware of findings such as these?

Full access to the Cochrane Library databases permits users to examine complete reviews to assess their nature and quality. Scholars may consider the objectives for the review, criteria adopted for including or excluding studies, description of the search strategy, review methodology, qualities of the reviewed studies, results, discussion, and conclusions with implications for practice and research. For example, the reviewers of "Scared Straight" used these terms in their search strings:

'scared straight'

('prison or jail or reformatory or institution') and ('orientation or visit or tour')

'prisoner run' or 'offender run' or 'inmate run'

'prison awareness' or 'prison aversion' or 'juvenile awareness'

('rap session' or 'speak out' or 'confrontation') and ('prisoner' or 'lifer' or 'inmate' or 'offender'). (Petrosino, Turpin-Petrosino, & Buehler, 2002b, Search strategy for identification of studies section, para. 5)

These terms were used to search the following bibliographic databases and publication years for relevant research studies.

Criminal Justice Abstracts, 1968–September 2001

Current Contents, 1993–2001

Dissertation Abstracts, 1981–August 2001

Education Full Text, June 1983–October 2001

ERIC (Education Resource Information Clearinghouse), 1966–2001

GPO Monthly (Government Printing Office Monthly), 1976–2001

MEDLINE 1966–2001

National Clearinghouse on Child Abuse and Neglect (through 2001)

NCJRS (National Criminal Justice Reference Service)–2001

PAIS International (Public Affairs Information Service), 1972–October 2001

Political Sciences Abstracts, 1975–March 2001

PsycINFO (Psychological Abstracts) 1987–November 2001

Social Sciences Citation Index, February 1983–October 2001

Sociofile (Sociological Abstracts and Social Planning and Development Abstracts) January 1963–September 2001. (Petrosino et al., 2002b, Search strategy for identification of studies section, para. 4)

The reviewers obtained nearly five hundred citations from their searches. They carefully examined these articles to determine whether they met the inclusion criteria. Importantly, they limited their review to randomized controlled studies (RCT) and based their conclusion on their analysis of research that met the rigorous RCT criteria. It appears that their findings and conclusions are based on strong evidence and scholarly analysis.

The Cochrane Collaboration and its growing library of systematic reviews are valuable resources, especially for physicians but also for social workers and other helping professionals. The Campbell Collaboration (C2) at http://www .campbellcollaboration.org is a Cochrane-like initiative that currently provides free access to more than 10,000 studies in the fields of criminal justice, education, and social welfare through its Sociological, Psychological, Educational, and Criminological Trials Register (C2-SPECTR) database.

C2-SPECTR users may conduct basic or advanced searches to locate pertinent bibliographic references—many of which include brief annotated summary reviews of the study. In the United Kingdom, the Electronic Library for Social Care (eLSC) provides the CareData bibliographic database (http://www.elsc.org.uk) to users interested in locating research-based information to guide their social service practice. Social workers from North America may access Caredata via the Internet at no cost.

Scotland has established a similar initiative, reSearchWeb, to enable social workers to access relevant research-based knowledge. The Web site (http://www.researchweb.org.uk) has a number of useful features, including links to Caredata. These sites are enormously helpful to social workers in the United Kingdom and throughout the world. North American social workers could benefit from specialized knowledge information services similar to those provided by CareData and reSearchWeb.

Turning Research into Practice (TRIP) at http://www.tripdatabase is yet another extraordinary site originating from the United Kingdom. More than a bibliographic database, TRIP contains various resources of direct use to health professionals interested in turning research into practice.

Although few are social work-specific, numerous resources are available to North American professionals. The federal government provides an enormous volume of valuable information to U.S. citizens and indeed to the citizens of the world. You have already learned about the Library of Congress and the National Library of Medicine. There are hundreds more. For example, the United States Agency for Healthcare Research and Quality (AHRQ) promotes practice-relevant research, especially through its twelve Evidence-based Practice Centers. You may visit the AHRQ Web site at http://www.ahrq.gov. A review of the evidence reports available through AHRQ (http://www.ahrq.gov/clinic/epcix.htm) would enlighten many social workers.

Many of the studies and reports are primarily for consumption by medical professionals. However, several apply to social workers. There are evidence-based reports, for example, that address topics of sleep apnea, brain injuries among children, alcohol dependence, depression, attention deficit and hyperactivity disorder, diet and cancer, chronic fatigue, pain management for spinal cord-injured patients, and speech-language disorders.

The Agency for Healthcare Research and Quality has also established the National Guideline Clearinghouse™ (NGC). The NGC Web site (http://www.guidelines.gov) provides free access to a substantial array of resources.[4] In addition to the evidence reports mentioned above, scholars may review annotated bibliographies about guidelines (development methodologies, evaluation, implementation, structure), browse an index and conduct searches for guidelines. The NGC Web site allows for basic and detailed searches.

A basic search of the NGC using the term *domestic violence* generates a list of about twelve guidelines that pertain to some aspect of the topic. You may review brief and complete summaries as well as full-text versions of the guidelines on-line using your Internet browser.

By selecting the guideline entitled "Domestic Violence," you would see a brief summary from which you could quickly identify the source, publication date, major recommendations, and clinical highlights for providers. If that material appeared to be of interest, you could readily retrieve and read the complete document.

The National Library of Medicine sponsors the Health Services/Technology Assessment Text (HSTAT) databases at http://hstat.nlm.nih.gov, which provide full-text access to health information, technology assessment, and guideline information. In conducting a search, scholars may choose to incorporate the databases of the National Guideline Clearinghouse, the Center for Disease Control, or PubMed to supplement those directly included within HSTAT.

The United States National Institutes of Health along with the National Library of Medicine publishes the ClinicalTrials database (http://clinicaltrials.gov) that contains information about current clinical research studies. The listed studies often address current or pressing issues conducted by prestigious researchers. A review of current studies in an area may help you gain a sense of what is cutting-edge.

For example, a basic search of the ClinicalTrials database using the term *violence* yields information about a study sponsored by the National Institute on Alcohol Abuse and Alcoholism (NIAAA). Entitled "Effect of Fluoxetine (Prozac) on Domestic Violence," the study plans to determine whether the antidepressant medication Prozac, when provided along with psychotherapy, reduces aggressive behavior among people who engaged in intimate partner violence.

A similar Web site, sponsored by the National Institutes of Health Clinical Center (http://www.cc.nih.gov), also provides a means to locate information about clinical research studies. The Search the Studies page at http://clinicalstudies.info.nih.gov enables users to search a database that contains descriptions of clinical investigations or browse studies by the principal investigator's institute.

The Combined Health Information Database (CHID) is another resource of value to social workers (http://chid.nih.gov). CHID is updated four times yearly, and several different federal agencies contribute to its collections. Users may conduct basic or detailed searches, or browse by topical area. The detailed search feature allows use of Boolean operators and other advanced search features.

A search of CHID for information about domestic violence yields numerous references to articles, books, videos, and organizations. You might notice, among the citations, a reference to the "Domestic Violence Community Education Manual for Healthy Start" published by the Birmingham, Alabama, Family Violence Center. That manual describes a domestic violence protocol for hospital emergency rooms.

Several other U.S. federal agencies and departments conduct research and present information of use to social workers and their clients. Much information is available through their Web sites. The selected list of federal agencies and departments shown in Box 3.21 may pertain to social workers.

You may find it useful to explore some of the agency or department Web sites that pertain to your topic. A few specific governmental databases are central to the work of most social workers and should be highlighted. For example, the U.S. Department of Health and Human Services sponsors the National Clearinghouse on Child Abuse and Neglect Information (http://www.calib.com/nccanch). The clearinghouse provides interested users with access to databases of both documents and organizations.

**BOX 3.21** • *Selected List of U.S. Federal Agencies and Departments*

Administration on Aging: (AoA) http://www.aoa.gov/
Administration for Children and Families (ACF): http://www.acf.dhhs.gov/
Agency for Healthcare Research and Quality (AHRQ): http://www.ahrq.gov/
Agency for International Development: http://www.usaid.gov/
Best Practices Initiative, Department of Health and Human Services: http://www.osophs.dhhs.gov/ophs/BestPractice/default.htm
Bureau of the Census: http://www.census.gov/
Centers for Disease Control and Prevention (CDC): http://www.cdc.gov/
Center for Information Technology (CIT formerly DCRT, OIRM, TCB): http://www.cit.nih.gov/home.asp
Centers for Medicare & Medicaid Services (formerly the Health Care Financing Administration): http://cms.hhs.gov/default.asp
Center for Scientific Review (CSR): http://www.csr.nih.gov/
Civil Rights Division, Department of Justice: http://www.usdoj.gov/crt/crt-home.html
Congressional Budget Office (CBO): http://www.cbo.gov/
Corporation for National and Community Service: http://www.cns.gov/
Department of Agriculture (USDA): http://www.usda.gov/
Department of Commerce: http://home.doc.gov/
Department of Defense (DoD): http://www.defenselink.mil/
Department of Education: http://www.ed.gov/
Department of Energy: http://www.energy.gov/
Department of Health and Human Services (HHS): http://www.hhs.gov/
Department of Housing and Urban Development (HUD): http://www.hud.gov
Department of the Interior: http://www.doi.gov/
Department of Justice: http://www.usdoj.gov/
Department of Labor (DoL): http://www.dol.gov/
Department of State: http://www.state.gov/
Department of Transportation (DOT): http://www.dot.gov/
Department of the Treasury: http://www.ustreas.gov/
Department of Veterans Affairs (VA): http://www.va.gov/
Disability Employment Policy Office: http://www.dol.gov/odep/welcome.html
Domestic Policy Council: http://www.whitehouse.gov/dpc/index.html
Drug Enforcement Administration (DEA): http://www.usdoj.gov/dea/
Educational Research and Improvement: http://www.ed.gov/offices/OERI/
Elementary and Secondary Education: http://www.ed.gov/offices/OESE/
Equal Employment Opportunity Commission: (EEOC): http://www.eeoc.gov/
Executive Office for Immigration Review: http://www.usdoj.gov/eoir/
Fair Housing and Equal Opportunity: http://www.hud.gov/offices/fheo/index.cfm
Faith-Based and Community Initiatives Office: http://www.whitehouse.gov/infocus/faith-based/
Food and Drug Administration (FDA): http://www.fda.gov/
General Accounting Office (GAO): http://www.gao.gov/
General Services Administration (GSA): http://www.gsa.gov/Portal/home.jsp
Government Printing Office (GPO): http://www.access.gpo.gov/
Health Resources and Services Administration: http://www.hrsa.gov/
House of Representatives http://www.house.gov/

*(continued)*

## BOX 3.21 Continued

Immigration and Naturalization Service (INS): http://www.ins.usdoj.gov/graphics/index.htm

Indian Health Service: http://www.ihs.gov/

Institute of Peace: http://www.usip.org/

Justice Programs Office (Juvenile Justice, Victims of Crime, Violence Against Women, Family Violence, and more): http://www.ojp.usdoj.gov/

Legal Services Corporation: http://www.lsc.gov/index2.htm

Medicare Payment Advisory Commission (formerly the Physician Payment Review Commission and the Prospective Payment Assessment Commission): http://www.medpac.gov/

Minority Business Development Agency: http://www.mbda.gov/

National AIDS Policy Office: http://www.whitehouse.gov/onap/aids.html

National Cancer Institute (NCI): http://www.nci.nih.gov/

National Center for Complementary and Alternative Medicine (NCCAM): http://nccam.nih.gov/

National Center on Minority Health and Health Disparities (NCMHD): http://ncmhd.nih.gov/

National Center for Research Resources (NCRR): http://www.ncrr.nih.gov/

National Clearinghouse on Child Abuse and Neglect Information: http://www.calib.com/nccanch/

National Council on Disability: http://www.ncd.gov/

National Criminal Justice Reference Service (NCJRS): http://www.ncjrs.org

National Eye Institute (NEI): http://www.nei.nih.gov/

National Health Information Center: http://www.health.gov/NHIC/

National Heart, Lung, and Blood Institute (NHLBI): http://www.nhlbi.nih.gov/index.htm

National Human Genome Research Institute (NHGRI): http://www.genome.gov/

National Institute on Aging (NIA): http://www.nia.nih.gov/

National Institute on Alcohol Abuse and Alcoholism (NIAAA): http://www.niaaa.nih.gov/

National Institute of Allergy and Infectious Diseases (NIAID): http://www.niaid.nih.gov/default.htm

National Institute of Arthritis and Musculoskeletal and Skin Diseases (NIAMS): http://www.niams.nih.gov/

National Institute of Child Health and Human Development (NICHD): http://www.nichd.nih.gov/

National Institute on Deafness and Other Communication Disorders (NIDCD): http://www.nidcd.nih.gov/

National Institute of Dental and Craniofacial Research (NIDCR): http://www.nidr.nih.gov/

National Institute of Diabetes and Digestive and Kidney Diseases (NIDDK): http://www.niddk.nih.gov/

National Institute on Drug Abuse (NIDA): http://www.nida.nih.gov/

National Institute of Environmental Health Sciences (NIEHS): http://www.niehs.nih.gov/

National Institute of General Medical Sciences (NIGMS): http://www.nigms.nih.gov/

National Institutes of Health (NIH): http://www.nih.gov/

National Institute of Justice: http://www.ojp.usdoj.gov/nij/
National Institute of Mental Health (NIMH): http://www.nimh.nih.gov/
National Institute of Neurological Disorders and Stroke (NINDS): http://www.ninds
.nih.gov/
National Institute of Nursing Research (NINR): http://www.nih.gov/ninr/
National Library of Medicine (NLM): http://www.nlm.nih.gov/
National Science Foundation: http://www.nsf.gov/
Office of Management and Budget (OMB): http://www.whitehouse.gov/omb/index.html
Office of Public Health and Science: http://www.surgeongeneral.gov/ophs/
Office of Scientific and Technical Information: http://www.osti.gov/ostipg.html
Peace Corps: http://www.peacecorps.gov/indexf.cfm
Policy Development and Research, Department of Housing and Urban Development:
http://www.hud.gov/bdfy2000/summary/pdandr/pdrindex.cfm
Postsecondary Education: http://www.ed.gov/offices/OPE/
Presidential Task Force on Employment of Adults with Disabilities: http://www
.dol.gov/_sec/programs/ptfead/
Public and Indian Housing: http://www.hud.gov/offices/pih/index.cfm
Rural Development: http://www.rurdev.usda.gov/
Senate: http://www.senate.gov/
Social Security Administration (SSA): http://www.ssa.gov/
Special Education and Rehabilitative Services: http://www.ed.gov/offices/OSERS/
Stennis Center for Public Service: http://www.stennis.gov/
Student Financial Assistance Programs: http://www.ed.gov/offices/OSFAP/
Substance Abuse and Mental Health Services Administration: http://www.samhsa.gov/
Supreme Court of the United States: http://www.supremecourtus.gov/
Thomas Legislative Information: http://thomas.loc.gov/
Vocational and Adult Education: http://www.ed.gov/offices/OVAE/
Warren Grant Magnuson Clinical Center: http://www.cc.nih.gov/index.cgi
White House: http://www.whitehouse.gov/
Women's Bureau (Labor Department): http://www.dol.gov/wb/

A review of the National Clearinghouse's documents database keyword list reveals numerous topics of immediate interest to social workers. It contains references and links to resources, books, and journal articles published inside and outside the federal government.

The organization's database is equally valuable. For example, a search of all states by keyword terms related to topics of domestic, family, and partner violence, results in a list of organizations displayed in Box 3.22.

Among many other U.S. government databases, social workers may find the National Clearinghouse for Alcohol and Drug Information at http://www.health.org and the National Clearinghouse on Families and Youth (NCFY) at http://www.ncfy.com especially helpful. In addition, certain government-wide gateways enable users to search for information from most federal agencies. In line with the general principle of proceeding from the general to the specific, you may begin to search via general gateways before moving to more specialized Web sites.

**BOX 3.22** • *Selected List of Family Violence Organizations*

Center for the Prevention of Sexual and Domestic Violence: http://www.cpsdv.org/
Domestic Violence Institute: http://www.tutt.com/walker/
Family Violence and Sexual Assault Institute: http://roseillus.com/clients/FVSAI/
Family Violence Prevention Fund: http://endabuse.org/
Institute on Domestic Violence in the African American Community: http://www
.dvinstitute.org/
National Council on Child Abuse and Family Violence: http://nccafv.org/
National Coalition Against Domestic Violence: http://www.ncadv.org/
National Latino Alliance for the Elimination of Domestic Violence: http://www
.dvalianza.org/
National Resource Center on Domestic Violence, Child Protection and Custody:
http://www.nationalcouncilfvd.org/

Perhaps the biggest and best is FirstGov (http://www.firstgov.gov). The
FirstGov Web site allows users to search federal, state, local, tribal, and international
governmental organizations. Users may conduct basic or advanced searches. You do
not need to include AND or + (plus) in your basic search string because FirstGov automatically searches for all entered keywords. Use mixed lowercase and uppercase letters when you seek a specific match (Washington Monument). All uppercase or all
lowercase entries will result in a broad search for all occurrences (monument or
MONUMENT) of the term. All searches begin as basic searches. However, once you
obtain your first results you may access the **Advanced Search** button.

Another major gateway of the federal government helps users locate and retrieve
statistical information. The FedStats Web site (http://www.fedstats.gov) provides free
access to statistical information from more than a hundred governmental agencies.
Users may browse topics and agencies, or may conduct a search across all agencies.

Suppose, for instance, you wished to conduct a search for statistics about inti-
mate partner violence. A search using relevant keywords would identify at least four
agencies that produced statistics related to the topic: the Bureau of Justice Statistics
(BJS), the Federal Bureau of Investigation, the Center for Disease Control, and the
Forum on Child and Family Statistics. If you clicked on the hyperlinked title from the
Bureau of Justice Statistics Web site, you would be directed to a document entitled
"BJS Special Report on Intimate Partner Violence." That report contains the follow-
ing information.

> As defined in this report, intimate relationships involve current or former spouses,
> boyfriends, or girlfriends. These individuals may be of the same gender. Violent acts
> examined include murder, rape, sexual assault, robbery, aggravated assault, and sim-
> ple assault. . . . In 1998 women were victims in about 876,340 violent crimes and
> men were victims in about 157,330 violent crimes committed by an intimate part-
> ner (table 1). Women were victims of intimate partner violence at a rate about 5
> times that of males (767 versus 146 per 100,000 persons, respectively). (Rennison &
> Welchans, 2002, p. 2)

Knowledge of such statistical information could help social workers in numerous ways. You might understand client populations more completely or serve as a better advocate. Statistical information about populations and problems may help in program development, grant writing, and service delivery.

The HealthFinder Web site permits users to search for health-related information available through the federal government (http://www.healthfinder.gov). Although directed more toward consumers than professionals, it provides access to information resources of considerable value to many social workers and especially their clients.

The United States Government Printing Office (GPO) at http://www.access.gpo.gov provides access to the vast world of government publications. You may search its on-line catalog to locate GPO on-line materials or those published in print, microfiche, or audiovisual format. You probably already know that many government publications are available in selected libraries throughout the country.

A search of the GPO on-line catalog using the string *"domestic violence" OR "family violence" OR "partner violence"* returns citations for more than a hundred relevant government documents, many available online. Some social workers might be interested in publications such as "The Effects of Arrest on Intimate Partner Violence: New Evidence from the Spouse Assault Replication Program" (Maxwell, Garner, & Fagan, 2001), a bibliography of nearly seven hundred citations related to the topic of "Domestic Violence Assessment by Health Care Practitioners" published during the 1990–1997 time period (Glazer, Glock, & Page, 1997), and a report entitled "Documenting Domestic Violence: How Health Care Providers Can Help Victims" (Isaac & Enos, 2001).

## Searching Evidence-Based Collaborations and Government Resources: Exercises

The following exercises should help you gain some experience searching evidence-based collaborations and government resources for information about practice effectiveness. Word process your responses, and save them to a computer file as *EBSW Ch3 Search EB and Gov Exercises.*

1. Go to the Cochrane Collaboration Library Web site at http://www.update-software.com/Cochrane/default.HTM. Move your cursor to the left side of the screen, and click on the **What's in** button to familiarize yourself with the different elements of the Cochrane Library. In a paragraph or so, briefly describe the features of the Cochrane Database of Systematic Reviews (CDSR), the Database of Abstracts of Reviews of Effectiveness (DARE), the Cochrane Controlled Trials Register (CCTR), the Cochrane Methodology Register (CMT), and the Cochrane Database of Methodology Reviews (CDMR).

2. Go to your university library. Identify which electronic bibliographic databases are accessible to students and faculty. In particular, determine whether your library subscribes to the evidence-based medical (EBM) services of the

Cochrane Library that are offered through OVID. If your university has a medical school, there is a good chance that you will be able to use the EBM services. Consult with a reference librarian to make sure.

If you have full access, go to the OVID databases and search the Cochrane Database of Systematic Reviews with the terms *psychological debriefing preventing PTSD* to locate the full-text version of the review entitled, "Psychological Debriefing for Preventing Post Traumatic Stress Disorder (PTSD)." Read the Discussion and the Conclusions: Implications for Practice sections. Summarize the material.

If you do not have access to the full-text versions of the Cochrane reviews, return to the Cochrane Collaboration Library Web site at http://www.update-software.com/Cochrane/default.HTM. Move your cursor to the left side of the screen, and click on **Abstracts of Cochrane Reviews.** If a Web page that contains a search window does not appear, go to http://www.update-software .com/cochrane/abstract.htm. Once there, enter the string *psychological debriefing preventing PTSD* in the window, and then click on the **Search** button. An abstract of the "Psychological Debriefing" review should appear. Read the abstract, and briefly summarize the findings.

3. Return to the Cochrane Collaboration Library Web site at http://www.update-software.com/Cochrane/default.HTM. Move your cursor to the left side of the screen, and click on **Abstracts of Cochrane Reviews.** If a Web page that contains a search window does not appear, go to http://www.update-software .com/cochrane/abstract.htm. Once there, enter one or more of the major keywords for your own practice-effectiveness question and begin the search. If you use more than one keyword, use the Boolean operator OR to connect them. Describe the results of your search. Record the citations of abstracts of systematic reviews that pertain to your topic. Read the most pertinent abstracts and summarize the findings in your computer file.

4. Go to the Campbell Collaboration (C2) SPECTR on-line abstracts database at http://www.campbellcollaboration.org. Once there, enter one or more of the major keywords for your practice-effectiveness question and begin the search. If you use more than one term, use the Boolean operator OR to connect them. Record the results of your search in your computer file. Record the citation of any abstracts of systematic reviews that pertain to your topic. Read the most pertinent abstract, and word process a short summary of the findings.

5. Go to the CareData on-line abstracts database at http://www.elsc.org.uk. Once there, enter one or more of the major keywords for your own practice-effectiveness question and begin the search. If you use more than one term, use the Boolean operator OR to connect them. Word process the results of your search. Record the citation of any abstracts of systematic reviews that pertain to your topic. Read the most pertinent abstracts, and summarize the findings in your computer file.

6. Go to the Turning Research into Practice Web site at http://www. tripdatabase.com. Enter one or more of the keywords from your practice-effectiveness question and begin to search. Record the results of your search, and save copies of those documents that relate to your topic.

7. Go to the Agency for Healthcare Research and Quality Web site at http://www.ahrq.gov. Once there, enter one or more of the major keywords for your practice-effectiveness question and begin the search. If you use more than one keyword, use the Boolean operator OR to connect them. Word-process the results of your search. Record the citations of materials that pertain to your topic. Read the most pertinent documents and summarize the findings.

8. Go to the National Guidelines Clearinghouse at http://www.guidelines.gov. Once there, enter one or more of the major keywords for your practice-effectiveness question and begin the search. If you use more than one keyword, use the Boolean operator OR to connect them. Word-process the results of your search and record the citations of materials that pertain to your topic. Read the most pertinent documents and summarize the findings.

9. Go to the HSTAT database at http://hstat.nlm.nih.gov. Use the keywords, synonyms, and subject headings associated with your practice-effectiveness question to conduct a search. Word process the results and record the citations of those documents that pertain to your topic. Read the most pertinent materials and summarize the contents.

10. Go to the National Institutes of Health Clinical Trials site at http:// clinicaltrials.gov. Once there, enter one or more of the major keywords for your practice-effectiveness question and begin the search. If you use more than one keyword, use the Boolean operator OR to connect them. Word process the results of your search and identify those research studies that pertain to your topic. Read the most pertinent documents and summarize the findings.

11. Go to the Search the Studies site at http://clinicalstudies.info.nih.gov. Once there, enter one or more of the major keywords for your practice-effectiveness question and begin the search. If you use more than one keyword, use the Boolean operator OR to connect them. Word process the results of your search and identify those research studies that pertain to your topic. Read the most pertinent documents and summarize the findings.

12. Go to the Combined Health Information Database at http://chid.nih .gov/index.html. Once there, enter one or more of the major keywords for your practice-effectiveness question and begin the search. If you use more than one keyword, use the Boolean operator OR to connect them. Word process the results of your search and record the citations of those materials that pertain to your topic. Read the most pertinent documents and summarize the findings.

13. Go to the FirstGov site at http://www.firstgov.gov. Once there, enter one or more of the major keywords for your practice-effectiveness question and begin the search. If you use more than one keyword, use the Boolean operator OR to connect them. Word process the results of your search and record the citations of materials that pertain to your topic. Read the most pertinent documents and summarize the findings.

14. Go to the FedStats site at http://www.fedstats.gov. Once there, enter one or more of the major keywords for your own practice-effectiveness question and begin the search. If you use more than one keyword, use the Boolean operator OR to connect them. Word process the results of your search and record the citations of materials that pertain to your topic. Read the most pertinent documents and summarize the findings.

15. Go to the HealthFinder site at http://www.healthfinder.gov. Once there, enter one or more of the major keywords for your own practice-effectiveness question and begin the search. If you use more than one keyword, use the Boolean operator OR to connect them. Word process the results of your search and record the citations of materials that pertain to your topic. Read the most pertinent documents and summarize the findings.

16. Go to the Government Printing Office Access site at http://www.access.gpo.gov. Once there, enter one or more of the major keywords for your own practice-effectiveness question and begin the search. If you use more than one keyword, use the Boolean operator OR to connect them. Word process the results of your search and record the citations of materials that pertain to your topic. Read the most pertinent documents and summarize the findings.

## Searching the World Wide Web

A search of the World Wide Web for evidence of practice effectiveness has distinct advantages and serious disadvantages. Thus far, you have learned about sources that have a reasonably high degree of credibility (reference works and books from university and research library catalogs including the U.S. Library of Congress; journal articles discovered through electronic bibliographic databases and evidence-based collaborations; and materials sponsored by agencies of the U.S. and other governments). The World Wide Web, however, contains all sorts of information. Some is credible, much is suspect, and a great deal is simply false. The World Wide Web is full of marketing and advertising material as well as outright propaganda and other forms of biased information. Therefore, social workers must be especially careful to assess materials for credibility and legitimacy.

Open or unlimited searches of the Web must be approached with caution. However, a great deal of useful information can be obtained. In seeking such material, social workers may use various search engines or services. Each search service has its own Web site that contains a description of the operational principles and procedures of the service. Several use meta-search processes (multiple search engines or services) to generate their results. Several popular search engines are displayed in Box 3.23. As you visit these sites, take a moment to review their Help guidelines, which are typically hyperlinked to the home page. Do so before you begin to search. Some knowledge about how a particular search engine operates contributes to more productive results and may save a good deal of time.

General search and meta-search services are a great means by which to identify and locate the names, addresses, and Web site addresses of professional organizations, consumer and advocacy groups, research centers and institutes, hospitals and clinics, universities and colleges, social service agencies, and sometimes expert practitioners and researchers. However, the World Wide Web is massive. The number of returns from any search is often unmanageably large.

For example, a search using the term *violence* through AllTheWeb returns a list of about 13 million Web pages. The same keyword produces 8 million hits through AltaVista, 8 million through Google, and 12 million through ixquick. These returns are too numerous to be useful. Some services classify content, which makes the process somewhat more coherent. For example, both Yahoo and WebCrawler have specific categories related to the topic of domestic violence. A click on a hyperlinked domestic violence category would return numerous Web sites, many of which are relevant. The Yahoo domestic violence category contains more than 250 Web sites,

**BOX 3.23 • *Selected List of Popular Web Search Engines***

AllTheWeb: http://www.alltheweb.com
AltaVista: http://www.altavista.com
CNET Search: http://www.search.com
Dogpile: http://www.dogpile.com
Excite: http://www.excite.com
Google: http://www.google.com
Infomine Scholarly Internet Resources: http://infomine.ucr.edu
Ixquick: http://ixquick.com
Librarians' Index to the Internet (LII): http://lii.org/search/file/searchtools
LookSmart: http://www.looksmart.com
Mamma: http:www.mamma.com
Metacrawler: http://www.metacrawler.com
NorthernLight: http://www.northernlight.com
SurfWax.com: http://www.surfwax.com
WebCrawler: http://www.webcrawler.com
Yahoo: http://www.yahoo.com

including the National Coalition against Domestic Violence at http://www.ncadv.org, the National Domestic Violence Hotline at http://www.ndvh.org, the Domestic Violence Shelter Tour at http://www.dvsheltertour.org, and the American Institute on Domestic Violence at http://www.aidv-usa.com.

A few services may be especially valuable for social workers interested in searching for scholarly rather than popular resources. Even with these services, however, you must carefully assess the quality of each identified Web site and the materials published on it. For example, the Librarians' Index to the Internet (Best Search Tools) at http://lii.org/search/file/searchtools is a subject-oriented database containing several thousand Web sites that have been assessed and selected by librarians. As a result, searches are likely to produce fewer results than some other services. However, the quality of the identified sites is often superior. For instance, a search of the Librarians' Index for sites about *family violence* produces about fifteen results, including Stop Abuse for Everyone (SAFE) at http://www.safe4all.org, the Family Violence Prevention Fund at http://endabuse.org, the Violence against Women Office at http://www.ojp.usdoj.gov/vawo, and MenWeb at http:www.batteredmen.com.

The INFOMINE Scholarly Internet Resources collection at http://infomine.ucr.edu is another librarian-created and -operated search service.

> INFOMINE is a virtual library of Internet resources relevant to faculty, students, and research staff at the university level. It contains useful Internet resources like databases, electronic journals, electronic books, bulletin boards, mailing lists, on-line library card catalogs, articles, directories of researchers, and many other types of information. (INFOMINE Scholarly Internet Resources Collections, 1994, para. 1)

A search of INFOMINE using the search string *domestic violence* generates a list of about fifty Web sites. Among others, social workers might be interested in Pathfinder on Domestic Violence in the United States at http://www.soros.org/crime/pfdv, the California Crime and Violence Prevention Center at http://caag.state.ca.us/cvpc, the Reports of the Surgeon General of the United States at http://sgreports.nlm.nih.gov/nn, the Violence Policy Center at http://www.vpc.org, and the Institute for Women's Policy Research at http://www.iwpr.org.

General or meta-search services are also useful for locating experts in the field. Many experts, especially if they are university professors, actually value hearing from students and other scholars interested in their research and expertise. Some may respond generously and graciously to your requests for information, especially if the inquiry is focused. Global questions (such as "Please tell me everything I should know about this topic") are likely to be dismissed or ignored.

Searching for the organizational affiliation of individual experts may be quite straightforward. At other times, it may require considerable ingenuity. Recent journal articles by experts often contain contact information about the author. For example, in a search for information about domestic or intimate partner violence, you might review an article coauthored by Edward W. Gondolf (Gondolf & White, 2001), one of the experts in the field. At the end of the article, following the list of references, you might notice that Dr. Gondolf is a professor of sociology at Indiana University of Pennsylvania and associate director of research at the Mid-Atlantic Addiction Training Institute. If a specific address is not provided, you could use a search engine such as Google to search for *"Indiana University Pennsylvania"*—rather than the Indiana University in the state of Indiana. You would find that the university has a Web site (http://www.iup.edu) that contains a directory database through which you could search for Dr. Gondolf. You could readily adopt the same process in attempting to locate Dr. Jeffrey L. Edleson, a professor in the School of Social Work at the University of Minnesota and director of the Minnesota Center against Violence and Abuse, and Dr. Richard J. Gelles, social work professor at the University of Pennsylvania and co-director of two organizations: the Center for the Study of Youth Policy and the Center for Children's Policy, Practice, and Research.

Often, when attempting to locate an expert's affiliation and address, you may learn about a research center or institute. If you then use a service such as Teoma (http://www.teoma.com) or AllTheWeb (http://www.alltheweb.com) to conduct a search, you might locate information about them or perhaps even identify their Web sites. For example, the Mid-Atlantic Addiction Training Institute (MAATI) has a Web site at http://www.iup.edu/maati; the Minnesota Center against Violence and Abuse Services (MINCAVA) has one at http://www.mincava.umn.edu; the Center for Children's Policy, Practice, and Research sponsors a site at http://www .ssw.upenn.edu/CCPPR; and the Web site for the Center for the Study of Youth Policy is located at http://www.ssw.upenn.edu/CSYP.

The Web sites of most professional associations are easily located by conducting searches through any of the major search engines. Among dozens of others, Web sites of the following associations provide access to many resources of value to helping professionals: National Association of Social Workers at http://www.socialworkers.org, the Clinical Social Work Federation at http://www.cswf.org, the Council on Social Work Education at http://www.cswe.org, the American Psychiatric Association at http://www.psych.org, the American Psychological Association at http://www.apa.org, the American Nursing Association at http://www.nursing-world.org, the American Sociological Association at http://www.asanet.org, the American Counseling Association at http://www.counseling.org, and the American Association for Marriage and Family Therapy at http://www.aamft.org. For example, the American Psychiatric Association publishes electronic copies (http://www.psych .org/clin_res/prac_guide.cfm) of their practice guidelines for the treatment of several conditions including major depression, eating disorders, bipolar disorder, substance use disorders, nicotine dependence, schizophrenia, Alzheimer's disease, panic disorder, HIV/AIDS, and borderline personality disorder (American Psychiatric Association, 1993a, 1993b, 1995a, 1995b, 1996a, 1996b, 1997a, 1997b, 2000a, 2000b, 2000c, 2001). Many of these guidelines may be of value to social workers and clients as they address mental health and addictions issues.

## *Searching the World Wide Web: Exercises*

The following exercises are intended to acquaint you with ways to search the World Wide Web for information related to evidence of practice effectiveness. Word process your responses and label the computer file *EBSW Ch3 Search WWW Exercises.*

1. Go to the AllTheWeb Web site at http://www.alltheweb.com and click on the hyperlinked **Help** button. Review the help and FAQs information regarding the basic search feature. Then scan the help guidelines regarding advanced and FTP searches, and information about the results page. After gaining some familiarity with the search procedures go back to the basic search page at http://www.alltheweb.com and enter the words *social work*. Select the **Exact Phrase** box and click the **Search** button. Use your word processor to record the number of hits. Scan the first page of returns and make note of a few social work-related Web sites that might be of interest to you or perhaps of some use in your search for evidence of practice effectiveness.

2. Shift your focus to the keywords, synonyms, and search strings associated with your evidence-based practice-effectiveness question. Use the terms and strings that you used to search for reference works, books, and journal titles through library catalogs; articles through various bibliographic databases; and evidence-based collaborations and governmental resources to conduct your search of the World Wide Web. Choose two or three of the major search engines to conduct identical searches. Also search the Web sites of relevant professional organizations. Use the same terms and strings in each search. Use your word processor to record those Web sites and materials that relate to your practice-effectiveness question. Make note of the advantages and disadvantages of the various search engines. Identify which of them produced the most pertinent returns. Note those that you would be likely to use again in searches for credible evidence of practice effectiveness.

3. In completing the exercises for this chapter, you conducted searches of library resources for reference works, books, dissertations, and journals; bibliographic databases and other sources for journal articles; the databases and Web sites of evidence-based collaborations and government resources for guidelines, reports, and documents; and the World Wide Web for information published by professional associations and other interested organizations. You undoubtedly have an extensive reference list along with many other materials. You have kept logs related to your search activities, written or word processed summary notes or quoted passages, and probably saved copies of most pertinent documents. Briefly review the materials and organize them into labeled folders in preparation for analysis and synthesis.

# Notes

1. Scholars may also use the On-line Computer Library Center (OCLC) First Search World Cat service (http://www.oclc.org) to search electronic library catalogs from throughout the world. Many public and university libraries subscribe to the service so that students and faculty may have free access. To locate a participating library in your area, go to http:www.oclc.org/contacts/libraries.

Bowker's Global Books-in-Print (http://www.globalbooksinprint.com) is another place to identify books in print. It is a commercial service that may be available through your university or local library.

2. You may sometimes find it helpful to search the on-line catalogs of commercial bookstores to identify pertinent books. In addition to major booksellers such as http://www.amazon.com, http:www.bn.com, http://www.borders.com, http:www.half.com, you may also use services that search multiple bookstores (http://www.bestwebbuys.com/books and http://www.isbn.nu).

3. You can find a Guide to Finding Health Information via the NLM at http://www.nlm.nih.gov/services/guide.html.

4. In July 2002 there were nearly one thousand guidelines available for review via the http://www.guidelines.gov Web site.

# 4

## *Analyzing*

The analyzing phase of evidence-based social work involves the evaluation and synthesis of information collected and compiled during the search process (Rothman, Damron-Rodriguez, & Shenassa, 1994; Slavin, 1986). In this chapter, you will learn to assess the credibility and quality of sources and their contents, synthesize the evidence in the form of conclusions and recommendations, and prepare a practice-effectiveness evidence report (PEER) to share with professional colleagues and consumers.

### *Evaluating Evidence*

Social work involves consideration of complex issues and multidimensional factors within and surrounding people and communities. The nature of the populations served and the problems addressed varies widely according to agency mission, program goals, and social work roles. Social workers serve diverse client groups and deal with challenging social problems. Some groups and certain social problems have been extensively studied. Others have received little scholarly attention. Consequently, the nature and amount of practice-effectiveness knowledge varies considerably from topic to topic. In order to analyze and evaluate the quality of different forms and levels of evidence, social workers require organized conceptual schemes and processes. Indeed, a fundamental step in the process of analysis and evaluation is to determine and specify what you will accept as legitimate evidence, the dimensions you will consider for analysis, and how you will conduct your evaluation.

In effect, you need to define evidence. Of course, the definition should flow naturally from the practice-effectiveness question and match the current state of knowledge in the field. Typically, the definition involves identification of selection criteria for the inclusion and exclusion of information products. The selection criteria commonly include references to types of sources and the nature and quality of their contents.

Cochrane Collaboration reviewers, for example, select only those products that meet "all of the inclusion criteria and none of the exclusion criteria" (Khan, Popay, & Kleijnen, 2001, Section 1.2.4, p. 8). Your definition of evidence should be clear and precise so that others could apply the same selection criteria and obtain similar results.

In their systematic review of assertive community treatment (ACT) for people with severe mental disorders, Marshall and Lockwood (2002) adopted definitional criteria that included findings only from randomized controlled trial (RCT) research studies that compared ACT to case management, traditional community care, or hospital-based rehabilitation. The reviewers excluded authority-based information, less rigorous research studies, and RCT studies that compared ACT with other programs (such as hospital diversion programs or crisis intervention activities).

A clear conception or definition of evidence and associated criteria are needed to determine what information to include and what to exclude from analysis. The specific definition depends upon several considerations. The most important is your evidence-based question. The query reflects your purpose for seeking practice-effectiveness evidence. Another factor involves the current state of knowledge in the subject area. Most professionals prefer information based on well-designed research studies that involve randomized assignment and control groups. However, sometimes the depth and breadth of knowledge development in particular subject areas is limited. To accommodate such realities, a more inclusive definition of evidence may be needed. Recognize, however, that as the breadth of the definition increases, the confidence level of the findings decreases. Furthermore, definitions may be expanded prematurely based on ignorance or incomplete scholarship. Some social workers may fail to review the literature adequately and decide that there are few research studies about the topic when a substantial research base actually exists. Based on an uninformed or incomplete estimate of the current state of knowledge, you could unnecessarily broaden your definition of evidence and diminish the credibility of your conclusions.

Scholarly understanding of the contemporary practice-effectiveness research literature is essential to develop a definition of evidence that appropriately matches the state of knowledge. In medicine, there is a wealth of research-based information about health practices. Physicians can usually adopt precise conceptions of evidence to include only findings derived from research studies that reflect adequate controls (such as randomly controlled trials and clinical trials).

As a social worker, you may choose to adopt a similarly precise and rigorous definition of evidence to minimize the danger of reaching invalid and unreliable conclusions. You may decide to wait until someone conducts the controlled research studies. In so doing, however, you may exclude information that could be of some benefit to clients. This issue may be conceptualized as a tension between potential risks and potential benefits. For example, when medical doctors and their patients consider a surgical procedure or the prescription of powerful medicines, they weigh the risks to life or disability. They also consider the likely consequences of no action. Social workers and their clients engage in similar appraisals. Sometimes, the risks to life may be just as immediate for social workers' clients as they are for doctors' patients. When social workers estimate the risk of child abuse, intervene with a suicidal or homicidal person, or attempt to secure shelter for an intoxicated homeless person during subzero weather conditions, the threats to life are real and profound. Certain actions may increase risk, while others reduce it. Doing nothing may have serious consequences as well. Such circumstances require balancing risks and benefits.

Of course, all social workers should be familiar with research regarding lethality assessment and crisis intervention in life-threatening situations. However, risk-benefit considerations occur in other contexts as well—even where danger to life is not an immediate issue. This is where professional social workers may differ in some respects from their medical colleagues. Unless the risk of doing nothing is extreme, physicians must be essentially conservative in their treatment of patients. The risks of doing harm are so severe that extreme caution is required. Social workers, on the other hand, must often be innovative, radical, or even revolutionary in efforts to serve underserved peoples or address social injustice and oppression. In such cases, the risks of doing little or nothing are so morally extreme that some action is required—even if the effectiveness of the intervention has not been confirmed through controlled studies. Rather, the action is based on professional values and principles.

Formulating a definition of evidence and its associated inclusion and exclusion criteria often involves balancing the potential for true or false positives and negatives (see Table 4.1). Social workers hope to adopt practices and undertake actions based on an accurate appraisal of the validity of the information. If your appraisal is accurate and the evidence valid, you can maximize use of effective practices and minimize the application of ineffective services. When information is invalid or your appraisal incorrect the consequences can be unfortunate.

A *true positive* exists when a social worker concludes that a particular action or inaction is an effective approach for service to a client and it actually is effective. A *true negative* occurs when a worker believes that an action is ineffective when it is indeed ineffective. Obviously, true positives and true negatives are preferred. When social workers know what works and what does not, they can perform their professional duties in accord with accurate understanding of valid information.

Conversely, a *false positive* occurs when a worker believes that something works when it actually does not. *False negatives* exist when social workers conclude that something does not work when it does. In the case of false positives and negatives, the information or a worker's appraisal may be inaccurate, leading to the adoption of ineffective or harmful practices and avoidance of those that could be effective and helpful.

In serving clients, social workers routinely reflect upon questions such as: Will this intervention do more harm than good? What is likely to happen if we do noth-

TABLE 4.1   *True and False Positives and Negatives*

|  | *Actually True* | *Actually False* |
|---|---|---|
| *Believed True* | True Positive (Accurate) | False Positive (Inaccurate) |
| *Believed False* | False Negative (Inaccurate) | True Negative (Accurate) |

ing? How do the potential benefits of an intervention compare with the potential risks? What happens if the intervention we've decided to implement doesn't work? Needless to say, these questions involve complex personal and philosophical considerations. Evidence of what works and what does not often helps social workers and clients consider these issues. However, not all evidence is equally valid, reliable, or relevant, and there are different kinds and levels of knowledge in various subject areas. An analysis and evaluation framework is needed to help determine quality and increase the likelihood of accurate appraisals of evidence.

Several authors have proposed classification and evaluation systems (Agency for Healthcare Research and Quality, 2002; Appraisal of Guidelines Research and Evaluation, 2001, 2002; Cluzeau et al., 2002; Greenhalgh, 1997; Guyatt, Sackett, & Sinclair, 1995; Powers, 1999). Most involve consideration of several dimensions or aspects of the quality of the information and its source.

In the context of evidence-based social work, *quality* refers to the nature or character of the information, including consideration of the relative credibility and legitimacy of the author or publisher and, more importantly, the accuracy, validity, relevance, reasonableness, and currency of the material. Evaluation of the quality of practice-effectiveness evidence involves consideration of *source* and *contents* in terms of probabilities, degrees, or levels such as "inferior," "marginal," "satisfactory," or "superior."

## Source

*Source* refers to the nature, form, kind, type, and origin of the information product. The concept includes consideration of the author, creator, researcher, presenter, producer, or publisher as well as the form in which the information is disseminated (book, journal article, Web site, conference presentation, personal communication). Tangible evidence that can be examined and reexamined is superior to undocumented expressions. Written or published products are preferred over verbal accounts.

*Classification* of source represents an initial step in the process of evaluating the quality of information products. In classifying, social workers ask questions such as: What kind of a source is this? Is the information product a general or specialized reference work (encyclopedia, dictionary), scholarly book or book chapter (textbook, handbook, manual), professional journal article, practice guideline, dissertation, government document, research center or institute report, clinic or agency publication, professional association newsletter, consumer organization or advocacy brochure, expert opinion paper, colleague or consumer feedback, personal communication, or popular material (book, magazine, newspaper)? Different kinds of sources generally reflect different levels of quality.

In assessing source quality, social workers may also ask questions such as: Who created and disseminated this information? Is the author a researcher, scholar, practitioner, advocate, consumer, stakeholder, or perhaps an interested observer? Who published and disseminated the information? Different authors, researchers, and publishers may reflect biases and perhaps conflicts of interest that threaten accuracy and credibility. Those who identify and attempt to control for threats to validity are valued more highly than those who do not.

In actual practice, social workers often weigh the quality and credibility of various sources and types of information. Consider, for example, a school social worker who seeks to address alleged violence between two students. In exploring what happened, the worker may hear one story from a teacher, another from one involved student, a third from the other student, and a fourth from a student who reportedly witnessed the event. She or he may hear other perspectives on the matter from the principal, other teachers, and perhaps one or more parents. The social worker may never know the precise truth of the matter. However, she or he would probably assign greater value to the words of people closest to the event, those previously found to be reliable, those who describe events logically and consistently in considerable detail, and those who support their conclusions with substantiating evidence.

Similarly, sources of practice-effectiveness evidence reflect a relative credibility value. Identifiable sources are more credible than anonymous ones; credentialed more than noncredentialed authorities; experts more than amateurs; experienced more than inexperienced professionals; and actual consumers more than external observers. The words of people who acknowledge their biases or conflicts of interests and describe how they attempt to control them are valued more than those who fail to do so.

Sources may be primary or secondary in nature. *Primary* sources are those closest to the events described or investigated and are presented or published by the researchers or authors themselves. *Secondary* sources are more distant from the experience. They represent a secondhand report of primary materials. In a sense, secondary sources are similar to hearsay information in legal proceedings. The secondary author presents information originally expressed by someone else. A journal article about a study written by the researchers who actually conducted the scientific work is a primary source. A newspaper article in which that study is described and summarized is a secondary source. For example, three researchers (Pomeroy, Rubin, & Walker, 1995) conducted a study of the effectiveness of a psychoeducational and task-centered group practice approach with family members of people with AIDS. They describe the study and discuss the findings of their original research in an article published in the journal *Social Work Research*. The research article is a primary source. Abstracts may be included in bibliographic databases and published at the beginning of journal articles. However, they are secondary sources even when written by the authors of the original research.

A textbook description and summary of findings from several research studies—perhaps including that of Pomeroy, Rubin, and Walker—is a secondary source. A book review is a secondary source for information about the book itself. Doctoral dissertations typically contain a chapter or section in which the relevant literature is extensively reviewed. These comprehensive reviews serve as a foundation for the development of doctoral research questions or hypotheses. The literature review chapter or section of the dissertation is a secondary source, while those portions that include description and discussion of the original doctoral research itself are primary.

Secondary sources are often extremely useful—especially for the purposes of identifying primary materials—but they are not typically as credible or reliable as the primary sources. Summaries may omit details needed to assess the quality of the evidence, and may occasionally be inaccurate or distorted. Indeed, certain secondary sources are highly suspect. Some fail to cite or reference the primary sources. Quite a few fact sheets published on popular Web sites contain an array of statistics without citing the primary researchers or the studies from which the facts were taken. Others discuss selected materials that support a preferred position. Indeed, a surprisingly large number of publications include only references to those research studies that confirm the author's point of view, while neglecting those that constitute a challenge.

In general, information products are either *authority based* or *research based*. Authority-based products are derived from the ideas and conclusions of persons or organizations that have a stake in the subject. Professors, practitioners, directors of agencies, advocacy organizations, professional associations, clients, and consumer groups are authorities that frequently share information in the form of opinions, assertions, claims, or arguments. Many theoretical books, book chapters, essays, conceptual articles, position papers, letters, advocacy statements, and letters are authority-based products, as are the opinions and suggestions of professional colleagues. Consumers also possess authority. Indeed, as users of services, consumers often have valuable and relevant perspectives based on direct and personal experience. Other stakeholders (family members, representatives of funding sources, lay people interested in a topic) may contribute their knowledge and ideas in one form or another. Derived from their observations, perspectives, and experience, such information is authority based.

Conversely, research-based information products result from qualitative and quantitative studies. They tend to be valued on the basis of the quality of the research design and implementation, and the logical bases on which findings and conclusions are reached. Less dependent on the status or prestige of the author, findings of research studies published in refereed, professional journals such as *Social Service Review*, *Research on Social Work Practice*, *Social Work Research*, or the *New England Journal of Medicine* reflect greater credibility than authority-based materials.

Although these categories of primary versus secondary and research-based versus authoritative findings are dichotomized, they are probably more accurately viewed as continua. Primary sources may be placed at one pole of a horizontal axis and secondary sources at the other. Research-based materials may be positioned at one end of a vertical axis and authority-based on the other. Integration of the two axes might yield a matrix as reflected in Figure 4.1.

Social workers interested in evidence of practice effectiveness search for and analyze relevant authority-based and especially research-based information that may be available. In addition to discrete articles and research papers, literature reviews, systematic reviews, and meta-analyses are often rich sources of both primary and secondary source material. Indeed, your own effort to seek, discover, and analyze pertinent information is, in effect, a systematic review. In trying to serve clients with effective practices, you rely on knowledge discovered through your examination of the nomothetic evidence. As you apply and evaluate the outcomes of your evidence-based services with clients, you generate ideographic data. If you do so in a systematic manner, you may produce research-based, primary source material that may prove valuable to other professional helpers and consumers facing similar issues and circumstances.

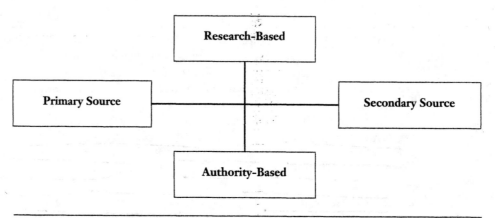

**FIGURE 4.1**   *Primary and Secondary Research-Based and Authority-Based Information*

As you learned through your search efforts, information appears in a large and expanding variety of forms and media. Audiovisual, electronic, and digital formats now complement the vast and growing array of print materials. Like printed products, they too vary in quality and credibility. Table 4.2 reflects a selected array of source types commonly considered in evidence-based social work.

There are numerous other kinds of materials that could be included. Add them to the table if you like. However, the primary function of the table is to consider source type as an indication of probable quality. When combined with the primary versus secondary, and research-based versus authority-based classifications, you have a basic template for evaluation to add to your source cards or bibliographic database (see Chapter 3). You might take a source card (see Box 4.1) and record classifications to the citation information. It would be even more efficient to use an electronic bibliographic database to add classification dimensions and ratings.

Such classification yields a preliminary estimate of relative quality. Suppose, for example, you find a relevant article in a professional journal. Cursory examination reveals whether it is better described as research based or authority based, and whether it is primary or secondary source material. Research-based papers selected for publication through peer review processes represent a preferred form of evidence. Editors of professional journals usually, but not always, ask two to five reviewers to read and evaluate submitted manuscripts. For example, manuscripts submitted to the journal *Social Work* are reviewed by three reviewers and the editor-in-chief through procedures that maintain the anonymity of the authors throughout the process. Fewer than two of every ten submitted manuscripts are accepted for publication. Even the most prestigious journals, however, include editorials, occasional invited articles, letters to the editor, and book reviews. In general, products selected through peer-review processes reflect greater credibility than those published without them. Similarly, a self-published work typically reflects less quality than one produced by a well-known publishing company. However, just as you may sometimes rely on authority-based information to supplement or complement research findings, self-published or unpublished works occasionally contain useful information.

**TABLE 4.2** *Product: Source Types*

Professional Journal: Refereed Article
Professional Journal: Invited Article
Professional Journal: Editorial
Professional Journal: Letter to Editor
Professional Journal: Abstract
Professional Journal: Book Review
Published Scholarly Book: Authored
Published Scholarly Book: Edited
Published Scholarly Book Chapter
Published Scholarly Monograph
Professional Conference Paper/Presentation: Refereed
Professional Conference Paper/Presentation: Invited
Dissertation/Thesis
General Reference Section (Encyclopedia, Dictionary)
Specialized Reference Section (Encyclopedia, Dictionary)
Practice Guideline
Practice Standard
Policy Recommendation
Government Report or Document
Professional Association Report or Document
Research Center Report or Document
Advocacy Group Report or Document
Consumer Organization Report or Document
Service Organization/Agency Report or Document
Client Case Record or Report
Committee Meeting Minutes
Legislative Hearing Minutes
Testimony Transcript
Unpublished Manuscript (Book, Chapter, Article, Monograph)
Self-Published Manuscript (Book, Chapter, Article, Monograph)
Internet Source (Web site)
Audiovisual Material (Audio or Videotape, Slideshow, CD-ROM)
Computer Program
Bill
Law, Statute, or Legal Regulation
Personal Communication or Correspondence
Popular Book
Popular Magazine or News Source: Reported Article
Popular Magazine or News Source: Commentary
Popular Magazine or News Source: Editorial
Popular Magazine or News Source: Letter
Popular Magazine or News Source: Book Review
Bibliography: Annotated
Bibliography: Not Annotated
Research/Grant Proposal
Other Source

## Box 4.1 • *Expanded Source Card*

24. Edleson, J. L. (1999). The overlap between child maltreatment and woman battering. *Violence against Women, 5*(2), 134–155.

    a. Research-based
    b. Primary source
    c. Professional journal: Referred article

In attempting to evaluate the quality of sources, refer to the source rating rubric presented in Table 4.3. In addition to the research-based and authority-based primary and secondary dimensions discussed earlier, several additional aspects are presented to facilitate analysis and evaluation. Evaluate the product in terms of the authors and their authority, expertise, and affiliations. Also consider the reputation of the publisher and publication as well as the currency of the product.

The source rating rubric is a qualitative tool intended to facilitate analysis and evaluation of sources. The dimensions are not equally weighted, and the ratings do not reflect equal intervals. Therefore, summed or averaged dimension ratings would be inappropriate. Nonetheless, the rubric may help you evaluate the general quality of the sources you consider.

In assessing the authors of a source, determine their identity, credentials, or qualifications and how they may be contacted. Unidentified authorship raises serious questions of quality and credibility. Once identified, consider the authors' authority and expertise as well as their affiliations as indications of their competence to prepare a high-quality product. Ask questions such as: What other products have the authors published? What roles and positions have they fulfilled, and what professional and research experiences have they had that contribute to their expertise in this area? With what organizations are they or have they been affiliated? How well do these characteristics, experiences, and affiliations support the authors' readiness to contribute valid and useful evidence? Might any of these things constitute a conflict of interest or suggest a potential for bias?

Also consider the *publisher* and the *publication* as indicators of quality. For example, books produced by the presses of major professional associations such as the National Association of Social Workers, the American Psychiatric Association, the American Psychological Association, the American Sociological Association, and the American Medical Association tend to have the explicit or implicit endorsement of the organizations. Many universities also have nonprofit academic presses that publish books of importance to specialized audiences (see http://aaupnet.org/membership/directory.html). For example, Indiana University Press (http://www.indiana.edu/~iupress) specializes in the publication of works in the humanities and social sciences, and both Columbia University Press (http://www.columbia.edu/cu/cup) and the University of Chicago Press (http://www.press.uchicago.edu) publish a large number of social work books.

**TABLE 4.3**   *Source Rating Rubric*

| Assessment Dimensions | Source Rating | | | |
| --- | --- | --- | --- | --- |
| | *Inferior* −2 | *Marginal* −1 | *Satisfactory* +1 | *Superior* +2 |

Use the numerical rating associated with the statement that best reflects your evaluation of the source of the product in terms of the assessment dimensions presented in the first column. Use a 4-point rating scale where Inferior = −2; Marginal = −1; Satisfactory = +1; and Superior = +2.

| Assessment Dimensions | *Inferior* −2 | *Marginal* −1 | *Satisfactory* +1 | *Superior* +2 |
| --- | --- | --- | --- | --- |
| **AUTHOR**<br><br>Rating: _____ | Authors are unidentified and their credentials or qualifications are not presented. | Authors are identified but their credentials or qualifications are not presented. | Authors are identified and their credentials or qualifications are presented in general terms. | Authors are identified and their credentials or qualifications are presented in specific detail. |
| **AUTHORITY AND EXPERTISE**<br><br>Rating: _____ | Information about the authors' competence and experience is not available or, if available, reveals incompetence and inexperience indicative of an unsatisfactory level of expertise. | Information about the authors' competence and experience is available but does not relate to the topics or does not indicate a satisfactory level of expertise. | Information about the authors' competence and experience is available, relevant, and suggests at least a general level of expertise. | Information about the authors' competence and experience is available, relevant, and suggests a superior level of expertise. |
| **AFFILIATIONS**<br><br>Rating: _____ | The agencies, institutes, universities, hospitals, or associations with which the authors are affiliated are unidentified. | The agencies, institutes, universities, hospitals, or associations with which the authors are affiliated are identified but do not directly bear upon the topics addressed or the authors' expertise. | The agencies, institutes, universities, hospitals, or associations with which the authors are affiliated are identified and directly relate to the topics addressed or the authors' expertise. | The agencies, institutes, universities, hospitals, or associations with which the authors are affiliated are identified and clearly and directly relate to the topics addressed and clearly support the authors' expertise. |

**TABLE 4.3**  *Continued*

| Assessment Dimensions | Source Rating | | | |
|---|---|---|---|---|
| | *Inferior* −2 | *Marginal* −1 | *Satisfactory* +1 | *Superior* +2 |

Use the numerical rating associated with the statement that best reflects your evaluation of the source of the product in terms of the assessment dimensions presented in the first column. Use a 4-point rating scale where Inferior = −2; Marginal = −1; Satisfactory = +1; and Superior = +2.

| Assessment Dimensions | *Inferior* −2 | *Marginal* −1 | *Satisfactory* +1 | *Superior* +2 |
|---|---|---|---|---|
| PUBLISHER AND PUBLICATION<br><br>Rating: _____ | Unpublished, self-published, vanity publication, promotional materials, or the publisher and publication are poorly regarded, unidentified or, if identified, reflect an unmanaged bias or conflict of interest. | The publisher and publication are identified but reflect an uncertain reputation, where the potential for bias or conflict of interest is apparent and procedures for their management are not presented. | The publisher and publication are identified and reflect a satisfactory reputation, where the potential for bias or conflict of interest is stated and managed. | The publisher and publication are identified and reflect an outstanding reputation, where the potential for bias or conflict of interest is explicitly stated and scrupulously managed. |
| CURRENCY<br><br>Rating: _____ | The product was published or updated more 20 years ago. | The product was published or updated 10 to 20 years ago. | The product was published or updated 5 to 10 years ago. | The product was published or updated within the past 5 years. |
| SUMMARY RATING | −2 | −1 | +1 | +2 |

Most major commercial publishing companies reflect strength in certain but not all topical areas. Partly motivated by profit, most are also concerned with quality and accuracy. Indeed, many are highly regarded for their product lines. Most have Web sites and on-line catalogs. For a categorical list, visit the Yahoo publishers page at http://dir.yahoo.com/Business_and_Economy/Shopping_and_Services/Publishers.

The editors and publishers of journals, like those that produce books, often focus on specialized topics, perspectives, or themes (see http://www.publist.com). Several are associated with or sponsored by professional associations or academic institutions. For instance, *Social Work* and *Social Work Research* are published by the National Association of Social Workers. The *Journal of Social Service Research* is affiliated with the George Warren Brown School of Social Work at Washington University, *Advances in Social Work* with the Indiana University School of Social Work, *Areté* with the University of South Carolina College of Social Work, *Child Welfare* with the Child Welfare League of America, and *Research on Social Work Practice* with the Society for Social Work Research and Practice.

Others are not directly affiliated with particular institutions, organizations, or associations. Examination of the names and credentials of the editors and the editorial board members often reveals a great deal about quality, as do the criteria for submission and selection of article manuscripts. The criteria are often described on a Guide for Authors page in each issue. Information about the percentage of submitted articles that are accepted and published may be presented in the journal itself or in books that compile information for authors. For example, NASW Press publishes *An Author's Guide to Social Work Journals* (Beebe, 1997) that provides detailed information about each journal's requirements for manuscript preparation, selection criteria and processes, time between acceptance and publication, and acceptance ratios.

In general, the age of the journal, its affiliation, the credentials and qualifications of the editors, the rigor of the selection criteria, and the proportion of submissions published are indicators of publication quality. For instance, the journal *Social Service Review*, affiliated with the University of Chicago School of Social Service Administration and published by the University of Chicago Press, has been published since 1927 and is issued quarterly. Editors give preference to research-based articles related to human behavior and social services. A peer review process takes four-to-six months, and the time between acceptance and publication is approximately six months. About 20 percent of submitted manuscripts are accepted for publication.

The journal *Research on Social Work Practice* specializes in the publication of quantitative, empirical research concerning social practice methods and outcomes. The selection process includes a blind peer review of manuscripts by at least three reviewers. Fewer than half of submitted articles are published.

Works that are unpublished, self-published, or published by vanity presses are valued less than those produced by academic or professional association presses and major commercial publishing houses. Unidentified publishers and publications should be viewed with great caution, as must promotional, advertising, or marketing brochures and materials. Sponsorship is a factor as well. For example, a document published by a tobacco company extolling the safety of modern cigarettes would be viewed as less credible than a publication by the National Institutes of Health cautioning people about the risks associated with smoking. Although not directly motivated by profit, professional associations and unions do promote themselves and their members. As a result, some of their publications, especially newsletters and Web-based documents that support their missions and agendas, may be more market-oriented than scholarly in nature.

Scholars generally consider papers accepted by journals and conference organizations through multiple peer reviews to be superior to those that do not require a review or involve a single reviewer. Even when both have been selected through rigorous review processes, research papers published in journals are usually considered more credible than those delivered during conferences. Journal articles may easily be read and reread many times, and other scholars may offer their own analyses or research findings to challenge or support those of original authors. The public dissemination of research and the ongoing process of peer review and criticism contribute to the publication of better-quality research studies.

Obviously, some journals are more prestigious than others; and some are more likely to contain articles pertinent to your search for evidence of practice effectiveness. Some journals emphasize the publication of high-quality research papers, while others publish theoretical or conceptual works, or perhaps opinion papers. Several factors enter into an appraisal of the quality of a professional journal. The credibility and credentials of the editor and editorial board members are key factors. The acceptance-to-submission ratio is another. For instance, a journal that receives one thousand manuscripts each year and publishes one hundred of them would reflect a 1-to-10 ratio. One manuscript is accepted for every ten submitted. Since nine of ten submissions are rejected, you may conclude that the quality of the accepted and published papers is generally superior to those in a journal that publishes seven of every ten submissions. In other words, a journal with a 10 percent acceptance rate would typically be considered of higher quality than one with a 70 percent acceptance rate.

Currency or timeliness also deserves consideration. In most instances, recent high-quality studies are more credible than equally well-designed research studies completed decades earlier. Competent scholars and researchers carefully and comprehensively explore previous research studies in order to confirm, advance, or extend knowledge and build upon earlier discoveries in building-block or perhaps spiral fashion. Obviously, people, problems, and practices change over time. Current studies are more likely to be relevant to contemporary target client groups and services. Older studies may refer to people and problems that are quite dissimilar to contemporary persons and issues. Suppose you have just read a research article about services to troubled adolescents the 1950s. Imagine the differences between the youth of 1950 and those of the early twenty-first century! Consider the social circumstances and problems faced by youth today and those fifty years ago! You would likely question the value and utility of information gained so long ago.

## Contents

*Contents* refer to the subjects, topics, and issues addressed within the product as well as to the nature and quality of the investigative methods and the reasonableness of the logic and argumentation. In evaluating contents, social workers consider whether and how the information relates to the practice-effectiveness question and the target client group.

*Source* and *contents* are not clearly distinct, mutually exclusive terms. They overlap. In attempting to evaluate the quality of relevant evidence of practice effectiveness, it is less important to distinguish what is source and what are contents than it is to think critically about dimensions that help you evaluate the quality and credibility of the information.

In assessing contents, consider the purpose and goals of the product, its organizational coherence, rationale, importance, depth, relevance, and utility. Assess the publication in terms of clarity and precision, honesty, integrity, and fairness, including breadth of understanding and coverage. Identify the intended audience, the methodology used to pursue the purpose and goals, and the degree to which they are achieved. Consider the value, ethical, and legal as well as the cultural implications of the contents as they might apply to or affect clients. Finally, and perhaps most importantly, evaluate the quality of the logic and reasoning reflected in the publication.

Table 4.4 may be used in conjunction with Tables 4.2 and 4.3 to help you to evaluate the contents of products that pertain to your search for evidence of practice effectiveness. The contents rating rubric is a qualitative guide for use in analyzing and evaluating the contents of information products.

Purpose and goals are fundamental to any scholarly consideration of the contents of a product. Some authors and publishers have different goals from those of social workers seeking to locate valid and reliable information to help clients. For instance, the author of a textbook may seek to provide a general introduction to and overview of a topic geared to students at an early stage of college education. A researcher may attempt to describe the results of an esoteric experiment that may be incredibly exciting to a handful of scientists but incomprehensible to the general public. An advocate for migrant workers may hope to change laws and policies to enhance the lives and well-being of constituents. A reporter for a daily newspaper seeks to publish current information that is interesting or newsworthy. A drug company may publish materials to advertise and market a new medicine.

These various purposes and goals may or may not match those reflected by your evidence-based practice-effectiveness question. For example, a newspaper report about a practice-relevant research study may highlight findings or implications that could lead you to seek the primary source but would not provide sufficient detail about the research design, the manner in which subjects were selected or assigned, the measurement instruments, or the intervention. Therefore, social workers would not be able to evaluate the quality of the study. The newspaper may be of excellent quality in terms of achieving its own purpose but of poor quality when it comes to helping professionals analyze a practice-related research study. Similarly, an advocacy group may do an excellent job preparing materials needed to promote its agenda. Those same materials, however, may be of limited value to social workers seeking high-quality evidence of what works to help clients.

In analyzing, ask whether the authors identify purposes and goals for their project. If they do not, try to infer them from the contents. Whether they are explicit or

**TABLE 4.4   Contents Rating Rubric**

Use the numerical rating associated with the statement that best reflects your evaluation of the contents of the product in terms of the assessment dimensions presented in the first column. Use a 4-point rating scale where Inferior = −2; Marginal = −1; Satisfactory = +1; and Superior = +2.

| Assessment Dimensions | Contents Rating | | | |
|---|---|---|---|---|
| | Inferior −2 | Marginal −1 | Satisfactory +1 | Superior +2 |
| PURPOSE AND GOALS  Rating: _____ | The purpose and goals for the project are unidentified and cannot be inferred from the contents of the product. | The purpose and goals for the project are unidentified, incomplete, or unclear and must be inferred from the contents of the product. | The purpose and goals for the project are identified and described in general terms. | The purpose and goals for the project are identified and clearly, precisely, and fully described in specific terms. |
| ORGANIZATION  Rating: _____ | The components that comprise the scholarly product are organized in a confusing or contradictory manner. | The logic underlying the organization of the scholarly product can only be inferred and may be subject to alternative interpretations. | Errors in interpretation are unlikely to occur as a result of the manner in which the components of the scholarly product are organized. | The components that comprise the scholarly product are organized in such a manner as to help facilitate an accurate interpretation of the product itself. |
| RATIONALE  Rating: _____ | The rationale for the project is unstated and cannot be inferred from the contents of the product. | The rationale for the project is unstated, incomplete, or unclear and must be inferred from the contents of the product. | The rationale for the project is clearly described in general terms and generally supported through logical argument or documentary evidence. | The rationale for the project is clearly, precisely, and fully described in specific terms, and consistently supported through explicit logical arguments and documentary evidence. |

**TABLE 4.4** *Continued*

| Assessment Dimensions | Contents Rating | | | |
|---|---|---|---|---|

Use the numerical rating associated with the statement that best reflects your evaluation of the contents of the product in terms of the assessment dimensions presented in the first column. Use a 4-point rating scale where Inferior = –2; Marginal = –1; Satisfactory = +1; and Superior = +2.

| Assessment Dimensions | Inferior –2 | Marginal –1 | Satisfactory +1 | Superior +2 |
|---|---|---|---|---|
| IMPORTANCE

Rating: _____ | The potential importance of the project is not established and the problems, topics, or issues addressed are meaningless, unsolvable, or trivial. | The potential importance of the project is not established although the problems, topics, or issues addressed might be important to some professional social workers or their clients. | The potential importance of the project is established and the problems, topics, or issues addressed are important to many professional social workers and their clients. | The potential importance of the project is clearly established and the problems, topics, or issues addressed are important to most or all professional social workers and their clients. |
| DEPTH

Rating: _____ | The contents reflect a shallow or superficial understanding of the central aspects of the topic or subject matter. | The contents reflect a marginal or modestly developed in-depth understanding of central aspects of the topic or subject matter. | The contents reflect a generally well-developed in-depth understanding of central aspects of the topic or subject matter. | The contents reflect an exceptionally well-developed in-depth understanding of central aspects of the topic or subject matter. |
| RELEVANCE AND UTILITY

Rating: _____ | The purpose and goals of the project, and the contents of the product do not pertain to your evidence-based practice-effectiveness question and have no apparent utility for service to identified clients. | The purpose and goals of the project, and the contents of the product indirectly or marginally pertain to your evidence-based practice-effectiveness question or have limited utility for service to identified clients. | The purpose and goals of the project, and the contents of the product directly pertain to your evidence-based practice-effectiveness question and are clearly useful for service to identified clients. | The purpose and goals of the project, and the contents of the product precisely pertain to your evidence-based practice-effectiveness question and are obviously and immediately useful for service to identified clients. |

**TABLE 4.4** *Continued*

| *Assessment Dimensions* | *Contents Rating* | | | |
|---|---|---|---|---|

Use the numerical rating associated with the statement that best reflects your evaluation of the contents of the product in terms of the assessment dimensions presented in the first column. Use a 4-point rating scale where Inferior = −2; Marginal = −1; Satisfactory = +1; and Superior = +2.

| *Assessment Dimensions* | *Inferior* −2 | *Marginal* −1 | *Satisfactory* +1 | *Superior* +2 |
|---|---|---|---|---|
| **CLARITY AND PRECISION**<br><br>Rating: _____ | Most or all of the contents are ambiguous, unclear, incomprehensible, imprecise, inconsistent, or inaccurate; definitions of key terms are not provided and cannot be inferred from the contents; errors of calculation, transcription, fact, or interpretation are evident; reference to and documentation of earlier scholarly work in the area are absent or incorrect. | Some or much of the contents are ambiguous, unclear, incomprehensible, imprecise, inconsistent, or inaccurate; definitions of key terms are unspecified, unclear, incomplete, or inconsistent, and must be inferred from the contents; some errors of calculation, transcription, fact, or interpretation are evident or likely; reference to and documentation of earlier scholarly work in the area are incomplete or contain errors of citation or interpretation. | Most of the contents are clear, understandable, precise, unambiguous, consistent, and accurate; definitions of key terms are provided and generally are used accurately throughout the product; errors of calculation, transcription, fact, or interpretation are not evident and are unlikely; reference to and documentation of earlier scholarly work in the area are generally complete and accurate. | All of the contents are clear, understandable, precise, unambiguous, consistent, and accurate; definitions of key terms are provided and consistently are used accurately throughout the product; errors of calculation, transcription, fact, or interpretation are not evident and are extremely unlikely; reference to and documentation of earlier scholarly work in the area are consistently complete and accurate. |

**TABLE 4.4** *Continued*

Use the numerical rating associated with the statement that best reflects your evaluation of the contents of the product in terms of the assessment dimensions presented in the first column. Use a 4-point rating scale where Inferior = −2; Marginal = −1; Satisfactory = +1; and Superior = +2.

| *Assessment Dimensions* | *Contents Rating* | | | |
| --- | --- | --- | --- | --- |
| | *Inferior* −2 | *Marginal* −1 | *Satisfactory* +1 | *Superior* +2 |
| HONESTY, INTEGRITY, AND FAIRNESS<br><br>Rating: _____ | The contents reflect a consistent lack of honesty, integrity, or fairness. | The contents reflect some lapses in honesty, integrity, or fairness. | The contents reflect honesty, integrity, and fairness. | The contents consistently reflect exceptional attention to honesty, integrity, and fairness. |
| BREADTH<br><br>Rating: _____ | The contents reflect an absence of understanding of the breadth of the topic or subject matter. | The contents reflect a marginal or modestly developed breadth of understanding of the topic or subject matter. | The contents generally reflect a well-developed breadth of understanding of the topic or subject matter. | The contents consistently reflect an exceptionally well-developed breadth of understanding of the topic or subject matter. |
| AUDIENCE<br><br>Rating: _____ | The audience for the product is unidentified and unclear from the contents. | The audience for the product is unidentified but may be inferred from the contents. | The audience for the product is clearly identified and generally reflected in the contents. | The audience for the product is explicitly identified and consistently reflected in the contents. |

**TABLE 4.4** *Continued*

| Assessment Dimensions | Contents Rating | | | | |
|---|---|---|---|---|---|

Use the numerical rating associated with the statement that best reflects your evaluation of the contents of the product in terms of the assessment dimensions presented in the first column. Use a 4-point rating scale where Inferior = −2; Marginal = −1; Satisfactory = +1; and Superior = +2.

| Assessment Dimensions | Inferior −2 | Marginal −1 | Satisfactory +1 | Superior +2 |
|---|---|---|---|---|
| METHODOLOGY<br><br>Rating: _____ | The approach selected to address the problem, topic, or issue is unidentified, incompletely described, or inappropriate for the purpose of the project. | The approach selected to address the problem, topic, or issue is identified and described but is inappropriate for the purpose of the project. | The approach selected to address the problem, topic, or issue is identified and described, and is appropriate for the purpose of the project. | The approach selected to address the problem, topic, or issue is clearly identified and explicitly described, and is especially appropriate for the purpose of the project. |
| ACHIEVEMENT<br><br>Rating: _____ | The stated purpose and goals of the product are neither pursued nor achieved. | The stated purpose and goals of the product are pursued and partially achieved. | The stated purpose and goals of the product are pursued and mostly achieved. | The stated purpose and goals of the product are pursued and fully achieved. |
| VALUES AND ETHICS<br><br>Rating: _____ | Adoption or application of contents of the product by professional social workers would be unethical, illegal, or immoral. | Adoption or application of the contents of the product by professional social workers would be of questionable or uncertain ethical, legal, or moral status. | Adoption or application of contents of the product by professional social workers would be clearly ethical, legal, and moral. | Adoption or application of contents of the product by professional social workers would be maximally ethical, legal, and moral. |

**TABLE 4.4** *Continued*

| Assessment Dimensions | Contents Rating | | | |
|---|---|---|---|---|
| | *Inferior* −2 | *Marginal* −1 | *Satisfactory* +1 | *Superior* +2 |

Use the numerical rating associated with the statement that best reflects your evaluation of the contents of the product in terms of the assessment dimensions presented in the first column. Use a 4-point rating scale where Inferior = −2; Marginal = −1; Satisfactory = +1; and Superior = +2.

| Assessment Dimensions | Inferior −2 | Marginal −1 | Satisfactory +1 | Superior +2 |
|---|---|---|---|---|
| CULTURE<br><br>Rating: ____ | Adoption or application of contents of the product by professional social workers would violate the personal, familial, or cultural values of clients. | Adoption or application of contents of the product by professional social workers could endanger the personal, familial, or cultural values of clients. | Adoption or application of contents of the product by professional social workers would be generally consistent with the personal, familial, and cultural values of clients. | Adoption or application of contents of the product by professional social workers would be uniformly consistent with the personal, familial, and cultural values of clients. |
| LOGIC AND REASONING<br><br>Rating: ____ | The contents reveal numerous logical fallacies, misinterpretations, and unsubstantiated assertions. | The contents reflect some logical fallacies, misinterpretations, and unsubstantiated assertions. | The contents generally reflect clear and logical thinking, reasonable interpretations, and support for assertions. | The contents consistently reflect clear and logical thinking, reasonable interpretations, and support for assertions. |
| SUMMARY RATING | −2 | −1 | +1 | +2 |

implicit, ask the question: Do the purposes and goals match those suggested by my practice-effectiveness question?

Organization refers to the logical consistency and coherence of the contents. Products may be presented in various ways and sequences. However, publications of higher quality generally reflect structure, direction, and flow. A plan, organizing framework, or logic model is apparent. Readers can easily recognize the beginning, middle, and end. Indeed, authors typically use an introductory section to introduce the topic, briefly summarize the contents, and outline how they will be presented. If there is a table of contents or if section headings appear throughout the publication, a logical framework should emerge.

In assessing organization ask: How have the authors organized this publication? Is there an introduction where the topic is identified and the format of the product outlined? Are the contents presented in a coherent fashion?

*Rationale, importance, depth, relevance*, and *utility* of products should also be considered in assessing quality. *Rationale* refers to the reasons why the topic should be explored. *Importance* involves the value or significance of the work. Authors may discuss the worth, relevance, and utility of the work explicitly within the rationale or introduction, or it may be implicit in the contents. The contents of some publications may powerfully affect human beings and their lives—for better or worse. Other information is essentially meaningless or trivial in nature. *Depth* refers to the level of intellectual sophistication and complexity involved in the topic. Some products reflect superficial coverage of a subject. Lacking depth, the contents may add little to the information needed to address your practice-effectiveness question.

*Relevance* and *utility* are also central to evaluating contents in evidence-based social work. You have heard television lawyers in courtroom scenes say, "I object! The question is irrelevant and immaterial." Evidence in legal proceedings should be relevant to the matter at hand. In the context of practice-effectiveness, you seek valid and reliable information that relates to your clients, the social problems affecting them, and the practices or services that may help. Contents that directly pertain to your clients are obviously more useful than those relevant to other groups and issues. Similarly, publications about interventions that social workers could conceivably adopt are more useful than those beyond their professional scope. For example, knowledge about biogenetics engineering is usually less relevant and useful to social workers than evidence about the validity and reliability of an alcoholism assessment instrument, the effectiveness of a family counseling approach for juvenile delinquency, or the outcomes of a prevention approach intended to reduce school violence. Unless there is an indirect or analogous relationship, you would typically not highly value knowledge that is unrelated or inapplicable to your clientele, their concerns or circumstances, or needed services.

Suppose, for example, you are interested in effective services for reducing violent behavior among low-income, youthful, inner-city gang members. Information about academic stresses experienced by college students at a small residential campus would usually not apply. Neither would research studies about programs designed to improve the diet, nutrition, and exercise of pregnant teenage mothers. Although interesting, such information does not directly relate to the service needs of young gang members and efforts to reduce violence.

In considering these aspects of quality, social workers ask questions such as: Is this serious work? How important, substantive, or meaningful is this material? Does this product contribute to the current knowledge base? What meaning does this material have for social workers and clients? Would the ideas and conclusions presented in this product be relevant to social workers and their clients? Are these contents related to my practice-effectiveness question? How useful are these contents?

*Clarity* and *precision* are additional dimensions for evaluation. Contents that contain clear and precise *definitions* of key terms tend to be especially valuable and useful to scholarly social workers seeking evidence. In the absence of explicit definitions or descriptions, readers may not be certain that their understanding of the meaning of key words or phrases matches the author's understanding. *Precision* in the presentation of facts, claims, and the ideas and conclusions of others contributes to accurate understanding. Careful scholarship and documentation of specific details add precision as well. For instance, suppose you are interested in the prevalence and incidence of child abuse and begin to read an article written by researchers who interviewed hundreds of college students about their childhood experiences. To understand and evaluate the quality of the study, you must know how the researchers define and determine *prevalence, incidence,* and *child abuse*; how they ask college students about the topic; and how they determine that a respondent had indeed been abused. Some researchers might adopt nonstandard conceptions of prevalence or incidence. Others could use a broad definition of *child abuse* and include the use of harsh words or mild spankings by adults. Some might define the term more narrowly to identify acts of physical violence that result in bodily harm or injury. Some researchers rely solely upon respondents' self-reports, while others attempt to corroborate respondents' statements with legal or medical records. Obviously, the definitions of *prevalence, incidence,* and *child abuse,* and the way they are measured affect the nature of the research findings.

Ask questions such as: Are core terms defined? How does the author define and use these terms? What does the author mean by this concept? Are terms used consistently through the product? How clear and understandable is the product? Would these contents be understood by the primary target audience? Are the contents accurate and valid? How is the presence or absence of a phenomenon determined, measured, or evaluated? How closely do the authors' definitions match those of other authors, my clients, and me? Are the assessment or evaluation tools and procedures used by the researchers consistent with their definitions? How accurate are the measurement processes? How reliable are the assessment instruments? Do the authors accurately report, quote, or summarize the words and ideas of others? Are citations and references precise and correct?

Clear definitions, an understandable presentation, and precise, consistent, and accurate use of important terms heighten the value and quality of publications. In their absence, readers may be left with inaccurate or distorted impressions, or perhaps a sense of uncertainty and confusion.

*Honesty* and *integrity* refer to the degree to which authors tell the truth, acknowledge mistakes, identify limitations, honor the work of others, and keep their promises and commitments. *Fairness* is a related concept that involves *breadth* of understanding, coverage, and openness to learning. Authors reflect fairness when they attempt to manage or control their own biases, preferences, and prejudices in their work. They manifest fairness when they purposefully examine literature and research from multiple perspectives rather than limiting their reviews to materials that support their own views. Authors reflect honesty and integrity when they discuss and reference opposing viewpoints or findings from research studies that challenge or differ from their own. Scholarship and documentation are important aspects of these processes. When authors accurately cite and reference original sources of facts and ideas and provide documentation in a full and accurate list of references, they reflect scholarly integrity.

In assessing honesty, integrity, and fairness, ask questions such as: How scholarly is this work? What is the quality of the documentation? How complete are the contents? Are there indications of distortion, bias, deceit, prejudice, or fraud in these materials? Do the assertions, claims, and conclusions reasonably and realistically match the evidence, or are they extreme and unrealistic? Do the authors acknowledge their own preferences, biases, expectations, and potential conflicts of interest? If so, do they take steps to minimize them? Are the authors fair and honest in summarizing others' work? Is there sufficient breadth of understanding, consideration, and coverage? Do the authors acknowledge the contributions of others' work through proper and complete citations and references? Are the sources mentioned and referenced reasonably representative of the literature, or are they limited to those that support the authors' own findings and views?

*Audience* refers to the targeted readership of the material and may be a consideration in evaluating contents. Materials geared toward scientists and researchers differ in sophistication, complexity, and quality from those disseminated to the general public. Similarly, textbooks for college students are often considerably more complicated than those for elementary school children. As professionals, social workers searching for and evaluating evidence of practice effectiveness generally prefer publications geared to highly educated, intellectually sophisticated, and critically thinking professional audiences.

Ask questions such as: To whom is this publication targeted? Who is likely to read this material? Is this publication intended for social workers or other professional helpers? Are these contents relevant for members of my selected target client group? Are the materials useful to the end-users?

*Method* or *methodology* refers to the processes, procedures, ways, and means by which the materials are produced. Although the term is often associated with formal research studies and may reference a particular research design (for example, experimental, pre-post, comparison group, focus group, ethnographic study, single-case), both authority-based and research-based publications reflect an investigative method. For example, some authors prepare products based on scholarly reviews of previous literature in the field. Others publish diaries or journals of their experiences; some write whatever comes to mind in stream of consciousness fashion; and still others report the results of their rational and logical analyses without much reference to research studies or the works of other authors. Almost all research-based products discuss the methods by which the studies were conducted. Authors of authority-based products may not explicate the method, but it can sometimes be inferred from the contents. Awareness of methodology helps readers evaluate the quality and credibility of the product.

Obviously, certain methods of investigation are likely to produce more valid or accurate, reliable, relevant, and useful information than others. For example, diaries or journals of consumers may be enormously helpful to social workers seeking to understand their clients' experiences, but less valuable for determining the likelihood that a particular intervention would help members of a specific population group.

Adoption of clearly described, systematically applied, and replicable scientific methods helps explain why research-based evidence is more highly valued than authority-based information. The claims, conclusions, and assertions of authorities are simply less subject to verification than are the results of research studies. Indeed, different authorities often make conflicting claims. For example, in court proceedings, plaintiffs and defendants often summon different experts to testify on their behalf. Judges and jurors frequently must weigh the relative credibility of the various authorities themselves rather than their testimony, because investigative methods remain unclear.

Social workers assessing the quality of evidence may consider questions such as: How did the authors reach their conclusions? What processes and procedures were used to generate the contents? What forms of inquiry or investigation are reflected? Are the methods identified and described? Do the methods logically match the needs and goals of the project? Could the processes and procedures be duplicated by someone else? What threats to validity and reliability are reflected in the methods used by the author?

Because well-designed research studies address many of these issues, and can be replicated, they are preferred over poorly designed research-based and authority-based information. When readers can determine the methods used by authors, they can consider the potential threats to internal and external validity as part of the process of assessing the contents of the publication.

*Achievement* refers to the degree to which the authors pursue and accomplish their purpose and goals. Achievement is not limited to success stories alone. Indeed, a scholar or researcher might discover something unexpected or unpredicted that constitutes an important achievement. For example, suppose a researcher evaluates the outcomes of individual counseling services when compared to group counseling services. The researcher fully anticipates that one-to-one counseling will be more helpful to clients than group experiences. Surprisingly, the researcher discovers that both counseling experiences seem about equally effective. Although the results of the study differ from what was expected, they constitute a substantial contribution. Based on the findings, future clients might be given a choice of individual or group services, and costs to consumers might become slightly lower as the number of group services increases.

In considering achievement, ask questions such as: Do the authors pursue the purposes and goals they establish or imply? How well do they accomplish them? How much did they achieve? What are the essential findings, results, or outcomes of this work?

Values and ethics are of central importance to social workers. Indeed, consideration of materials in terms of values and ethics as well as laws and regulations is part of what distinguishes professional from nonprofessional persons. As a social worker, you must consider the legal and ethical implications of perspectives, approaches, and actions you might take in your efforts to serve. Evidence from hundreds of studies and recommendations of world-renowned experts can not supercede your professional obligations and ethics. You may not let desirable goals or ends outweigh your respect for ethical means and processes. Even if they were shown to be 100 percent effective, you could not and should not adopt dishonest, deceitful, fraudulent, or oppressive practices. Even if you could guarantee a favorable outcome, you may not violate core social work values and ethics.

In evaluating the value and ethical aspects and implications of information products ask questions such as: Would actions suggested by the authors be legal and ethical? If I were to adopt the recommended practices with clients, what might be the ethical implications? If their ideas were implemented, what could be the risks or dangers to clients? How would I discuss the value and ethical implications of these issues with relevant clients?

Culture is another aspect that social workers routinely incorporate in their service to others. In assessing the quality of information, pay careful attention to product contents as they relate to the cultural traditions and beliefs of clients and consumers. This, of course, is fundamental to social work and consistent with a person-in-environment perspective. As professionals, you must consider each client's personal, familial, and cultural needs, orientation, and preferences in your efforts to help. For instance, you would respect clients' right to decline a proposed assessment process or intervention that violates their basic religious or cultural values—even when the evidence suggests that it could be helpful.

In assessing cultural dimensions, ask: How does this information relate to the cultural traditions of the target client group? Might the application of suggested practices lead consumers to feel culturally insulted, disrespected, or violated? Would the application of these ideas or suggestions reflect special respect for the cultural values and traditions of the clients for whom they are intended?

*Logic* and *reasoning* refer to the processes of rhetoric and argument evident in the publication's contents. There are many different forms and approaches to reasoning (such as symbolic logic, informal logic, non-Aristotelian logic, inductive and deductive reasoning). Professionals use logical analysis and reflective thought to identify and correct false arguments and thinking errors in their own and others' work. As you examine information of practice effectiveness, be alert for logical inconsistencies and reasoning flaws in both the contents and in your own review and analysis of them.

Involving critical thinking, reflection, and logical analysis, pertinent questions about the quality of contents include: Does this make sense? Do earlier passages logically lead to later sections? Are claims and assertions substantiated? What are the core elements of the argument? How are conclusions supported?

Also ask questions of your own reasoning: Am I being fair in evaluating these contents? In reviewing these materials, have I managed or compensated for my own biases, expectations, and preferences? Are my evaluative conclusions supported by evidence?

An important part of reasoning and critical thinking involves the identification of various forms of fallacious or faulty reasoning. The terms *pseudo-reasoning* (Moore & Parker, 1995), *pseudo-science* (Shermer, 1997), and *logical fallacies* have become popular in recent years. A logical fallacy may be described as a "bad argument, one in which the reasons advanced for a claim fail to warrant its acceptance" (Moore & Parker, 1995, p. 125). As you might imagine, a list of all the various forms of illogical or unreasonable arguments would be very long. Consider the following forms of pseudo-reasoning and logical fallacies that social workers may encounter as they assess the quality of evidence upon which to base their service activities (Engel, 1990; Gibbs & Gambrill, 1996; Moore & Parker, 1995; Paul, 1993; Toulmin, 2001):

*Ad Hominem:* A form of fallacious argument in which an author asserts that information should be rejected because of some perceived undesirable characteristic or circumstance of another author or source. For example, a psychoanalytically-oriented social worker might reject the findings of a research study because it was conducted by a behaviorist. Acceptance of such an argument could lead the social worker to exclude from consideration large amounts of potentially useful information.

*Anecdotal Evidence:* A form of fallacious argument in which an author asserts that a claim should be supported or rejected on the basis of one or two illustrative cases. For example, authors of an article might assert that "Students today are more troubled than those of twenty years ago." They might provide a case illustration of a boy who lies, steals, cheats, and behaves aggressively toward other children to "prove the point." If readers accepted this anecdotal report as representative of all students, they would have been swayed by the false anecdotal evidence argument.

*Apple Polishing:* A form of fallacious reasoning in which an author claims that something should be accepted as true because someone—often the reader—is a wonderful person. For example, an author might phrase a passage like this: "Intelligent readers and perceptive practitioners realize. . . ." The implication is that less intelligent and less perceptive readers would not be able to grasp the "truth."

*Begging the Question:* A form of fallacious argument in which an author supports a claim with another form of the same claim. For example, an author might assert that "experts endorse this model of practice." Later, in an effort to rebut anticipated criticisms, the author adds that "experts successfully refute the criticisms."

*Biased Sample:* A form of fallacious argument in which an unrepresentative sample is used to generalize to an entire population. For example, suppose a social worker wants to improve the quality and outcomes of the counseling services he or she provides to clients. The social worker decides to ask current long-term clients with whom he or she has worked for at least one year to identify those services that have been most helpful and those that have been least helpful. The plan is to use the information from the clients in services to all new clients from then on. Unfortunately, because the social worker does not plan to survey former clients, especially those who dropped out early, the sample is not representative. Finally, because clients who currently want or need services may be hesitant to identify negative aspects, the social worker may not obtain accurate information even from those he or she does ask.

*Burden of Proof:* A form of fallacious argument in which the responsibility for supporting a claim is placed upon the wrong person or thing. For example, an author claims that the nationally standardized social work licensing examinations are biased because "all multiple choice tests are biased." Anticipating challenges to this assertion, the author adds, "All aspects of society are racist, sexist, and classist. Why wouldn't the examinations be biased, too?" In effect, the author shifts the burden of proving the claim to readers—who did not make the claim in the first place.

*False Dilemma:* A form of fallacious argument in which an author asserts that there are only two options to consider. Other plausible options are ignored or rejected simply because they were not among the initial two. For example, an author might assert that there are only two intervention models or approaches that could be used to serve a certain clientele, then argue that since one is superior to the other, it is the best approach. Sometimes this "it's one or the other" formulation neglects other potential approaches that might be more effective that the two originally identified.

*Personal Experience, Subjectivism, or Relativism:* A form of fallacious reasoning in which an author claims that, since an issue is open to differences of opinion, all conclusions about it are equally valid. Therefore, everyone's personal choice is as good as anyone else's. For example, an author might assert that "all models of practice are equally effective, and every client is unique, so social workers and their clients may reasonably base their choice of intervention approach on the basis of subjective preference, personal experience, or intuition." This assertion may appeal to many social workers who value their personal experiences more than the results of research studies. Unfortunately, such decision-making processes contain numerous threats to validity.

*Pity:* A form of fallacious reasoning in which an author claims that something should be accepted as true because someone would be negatively affected if it were not. For example, authors might assert that readers must accept their proposition because "some people will lose their jobs."

*Popular Belief:* A form of fallacious reasoning in which an author claims that some or all others believe that something is true, so therefore it must be true. An author might cite findings from a survey that suggests that 75 percent of all social workers believe that programs such as Scared Straight are effective in reducing youth crime and delinquency. The author goes on to argue that "since so many social workers think these programs work, they should be implemented throughout the country."

*Popular Practice, Peer Pressure, Bandwagon:* A form of fallacious reasoning in which an author claims that some or all others are doing something, and therefore it is true or acceptable. For example, an author might argue that "since psychiatrists and psychologists often apply inaccurate diagnoses to secure reimbursement from managed care and insurance companies, social workers may do so as well."

*Red Herring, Smokescreen, or Diversion:* A form of fallacious reasoning in which unrelated and irrelevant information is introduced. If successful, the red herring diverts readers away from the original matter under consideration. For example, an author might propose to present information about the prevalence and incidence of domestic violence among lesbian couples but instead focuses on paternalism in society.

*Ridicule or Sarcasm:* A form of fallacious reasoning in which one claims that something is untrue because it would be ridiculous or stupid to accept the claim or to believe the person who made it. For example, an author might argue that social workers should never believe what psychiatrists say because "they all suffer from mental illness themselves."

*Same Cause:* A form of fallacious argument in which one asserts that two phenomena must have the same cause because they occurred at about the same time or in about the same place. For example, an author might claim that decreased academic achievement scores and increased rates of violence among youth are the result of the same cause—too much TV. This assertion also involves the error of confusing causation and association.

*Scare Tactics, Threats, or Intimidation:* A form of fallacious reasoning in which one claims that something should be accepted as true because some undesirable or unpleasant action might occur if it is not accepted. For example, authors might assert that if readers do not adhere to their recommendations, they will be sued for malpractice.

*Slippery Slope:* A form of fallacious argument in which a person claims that one event inexorably leads to another. For instance, an author might claim that implementation of government-sponsored health insurance for all would be the first step toward socialism.

*Spite or Indignation:* A form of fallacious argument in which one claims that something should be accepted as true because it would avenge a perceived wrong or injustice. For example, an author might argue that judges and jurors who convict innocent persons should be imprisoned for as long as those they mistakenly convicted.

*Straw Man:* A form of fallacious argument in which one substitutes an inaccurate, incomplete, or distorted characterization of another person's position and then proceeds to challenge the validity of the substitution (or straw man). For example, in advocating for continued application of the death penalty in capital crimes, an author might assert that "If we do away with the death penalty, murderers will be released to kill again." In this statement, the author argues against "releasing murderers from prison" instead of addressing the topic of the death penalty. Obviously, discontinuation of the death penalty does not mean that murderers will be released.

*Two Wrongs Make a Right:* A form of fallacious argument in which one claims that a wrong, unjust, or improper act is justified because the other party "would probably treat me unfairly, too." For example, someone might argue that it is acceptable to keep duplicate payments from an insurance company because "They would keep the money too."

*Wishful Thinking*: A form of fallacious reasoning in which one claims that something is true because it would be nice, good, convenient, or desirable for it to be true. For example, in discussing the case of a sexually abused eight-year-old, an author might argue that "The father could not have molested her. It's simply unthinkable that any father could do that to his own daughter."

*Unsubstantiated Assertion*: A form of incomplete reasoning in which supporting arguments or evidence for statements are absent. Support for the claim may or may not be available, but since it is not provided, the credibility of the assertion cannot be determined. For example, an author might state that adolescent clients are usually "resistant." In the absence of descriptions of behavior or documentation, examples, and illustrations, or findings of research studies, the assertion remains unverifiable.

## Assessing Authority-Based Evidence

Evidence-based social work reflects a clear preference for research-based knowledge. However, in seeking evidence of practice effectiveness, you may sometimes have to consider authority-based information. On occasion, the ideas, beliefs, opinions, judgments, and recommendations of experts, consumers, practicing professionals, and other stakeholders constitute the only available evidence. At other times, authoritative views supplement knowledge generated through scientific research processes. Indeed, the optimum condition occurs when evidence gained from studies coincides with that suggested by authorities. When both kinds of sources produce equivalent results and recommendations, a consensus best practice may emerge.

Authority-based information may appear in books and book chapters, essays, reports, journal articles, governmental or organizational publications, and a host of other contexts and media. You may correspond personally with experts in a field or subject area. Practicing professionals, agency executives, program funders, legislators, community representatives, or consumers and their family members may express their ideas. Much authoritative evidence involves opinion, anecdotes, claims, impressions, and reflections. Its validity and reliability are less subject to systematic evaluation than research-based evidence. Therefore, you must be cautious in your use of authoritative evidence.

Practice guidelines—sometimes called clinical or treatment guidelines, or perhaps practice standards—can be authority-based or research-based. They may be promulgated by practitioners, panels of professionals, or committees of senior experts. Many practice guidelines reflect the knowledge and experience of consumers as well as the consensus opinions of professionals. Some are based on and consistent with findings from systematic reviews, meta-analyses, and primary research evidence. Indeed, if the quality of the research-based evidence and the logic of the presentation are high enough, the latter may qualify as evidence-based practice guidelines. If not, view them

**BOX 4.2 • *Guide for Analyzing Authority-Based Information***

---

Title:

Is there a title or name of the publication, presentation, or communication? If so, what is it? Does the title accurately reflect the subject matter?

Author:

Is there an identifiable author? If so, who is the author? What are the author's credentials? What are the author's areas of expertise? What is the author's relevant experience? What are the author's related publications? With what agency, organization, association, or institute is the author affiliated? How may the author be contacted?

Form:

In what form is the information (written, print, audiovisual, digital, transcript of verbal interaction)? Is there a product that can be reviewed? If so, what is its quality?

Publisher or Producer:

Is the information published or produced? If so, who published or produced the product? What is the nature of the publisher or producer (self-published, for-profit, non-profit)? What is the reputation of the publisher or producer? How are materials chosen for publication or production? How may the publisher be contacted?

Date:

When was the information disseminated, revised, or updated? How old or recent is the product?

Sponsorship/Disclosure:

Who endorsed, supported, or funded the product? How may the sponsor be contacted? Are actual or potential conflicts of interest disclosed? How are actual or potential conflicts of interest managed?

Purpose:

What is the purpose of the product? How explicit are the goals or objectives? Who is the intended audience (reader or consumer)? Who is the target population?

Relevance:

Are the purposes and goals for the product pertinent to the topic of interest and the practice-effectiveness question?

Content:

What is the nature and quality of the content? Is the source of the information presented primary or secondary? How objective is the presentation? What perspectives are apparent? How scholarly is the product? How current is the material? How clear, specific, and precise is the information? How accurate is the material? What degree of breadth is reflected? What level of depth is apparent? How logical are the explicit or implicit arguments? How well-documented are the contents?

---

as forms of authority-based information, and evaluate their quality accordingly.

Analysis of authority-based materials involves evaluation of sources and contents according to the dimensions discussed earlier in this chapter. Indeed, because authoritative information appears in such varied forms under disparate auspices, you must rely heavily on your own logical reasoning and critical analysis. Box 4.2 and Tables 4.2, 4.3, and 4.4 may help you analyze authority-based publications.

## *Assessing Research-Based Evidence*

By now, you are well aware of the wide variety of information sources that may pertain to practice effectiveness. The prototypical source for evidence, however, is the research study. Typically published in a refereed journal or perhaps presented at a professional conference, the research paper is the predominant means by which scholars describe their studies and share their findings. Therefore, research articles published in professional journals are the primary sources of evidence of practice effectiveness.

There are numerous threats to internal and external validity that bear on the quality of research studies. Recognition of these threats requires knowledge about research methods, data collection, and statistical analysis. Consider, for example, Roth and Fonagy's description of the complex nature of therapeutic outcome research studies:

> At the outset, a clear distinction needs to be drawn between the *efficacy* of a therapy (the results it achieves in the setting of a research trial) and its *clinical effectiveness* (the outcome of the therapy in routine practice). Clinical trials are required to conform to a number of criteria to demonstrate reliability and validity (Cook & Campbell, 1979). In particular, they usually aim to achieve a high degree of *internal validity*. This can be defined as the extent to which a causal relationship can be inferred among variables, or where the absence of a relationship implies the absence of a cause. If internal validity is low, *statistical conclusional validity* is compromised, and the results of a study would be hard to interpret. However, achieving internal validity requires the use of techniques rarely seen in everyday practice, examples of which would be studying highly selected, diagnostically homogenous patient populations; randomizing the entry of these patients into treatments; and employing extensive monitoring of both patients' progress and the types of therapy used by therapists. All of this poses a threat to *external validity*—the extent to which we can infer that the causal relationship can be generalized. (Roth & Fonagy, 1996, p. 13)

The question of external validity that results from the primary use of randomized controlled trials (RCT) research is apparent in actual medical circumstances. A drug shown through several RCT studies to be 95 percent effective in treating a medical condition may be ineffective when applied to an individual patient, especially if the person does not reflect the characteristics of the studies' experimental samples. Nonetheless, in the absence of contradictory research findings or additional pertinent information, medical doctors would usually recommend a drug shown to be 95 percent effective rather than one shown to be 50 percent effective.

### *Validity and Reliability*

Validity refers to soundness, accuracy, truthfulness, legitimacy, relevance, and strength. As such, validity is an essential element of quality. A valid legal contract is based on legitimate law, agreed on through fair and proper processes, and supported by the facts. An invalid contract is inconsistent with current legal statutes, negotiated through improper, unfair, or illegal processes, or unsupported by the evidence. A valid argument is relevant to the context, communicated in an understandable fashion, and based on strong logic, solid evidence, or credible authority. An invalid argument is irrelevant, incoherent, illogical, unsupported, or undocumented. A valid test accurately indicates what it purports to measure. An invalid test measures something else. Similarly, valid information is relevant to the topic at hand, accurate or truthful, coherently presented, and strongly supported by logical argument, expert authority, or documented evidence. Invalid information is unrelated to the subject, false, inaccurate, incomplete or distorted, incoherent, illogical, or unsupported by documented evidence.

Reliability involves consideration of dependability, consistency, or predictability. A reliable train routinely works, arrives and departs at scheduled times, and regularly and predictably accomplishes its purpose of transporting people from one expected place to another. A reliable employee consistently arrives at or before the start of the workday, expends purposeful effort, and contributes meaningfully to the production of those goods or services that reflect the mission and goals of the organization. A reliable test consistently yields about the same results when the same substance, event, or process is examined repeatedly under similar or identical circumstances. Suppose, for example, that you provide a blood sample during a visit to your doctor. The sample is deposited into five separate vials or tubes. A laboratory then performs the same test for blood sugar levels on each vial at exactly the same time and under the same conditions. If the test is reliable, the results should indicate that the blood sugar levels are identical in each of the five samples.

Within the context of practice-effectiveness research, reliability typically refers to the degree to which we can trust that an assessment instrument or process accurately measures the phenomena under investigation. The reliability of assessment tools is extraordinarily important in that findings based on them often determine success or failure. Suppose, for instance, that researchers use a paper-and-pencil scale to assess the outcomes of a program intended to reduce violence in schools. If the scale is unreliable (the same individual responds quite differently under identical or similar circumstances), you cannot reasonably trust the results of the study.

If social workers adopt unreliable assessment tools in attempts to evaluate effectiveness, they may reach erroneous conclusions. For instance, in assessing a program intended to reduce violence, scores on a measurement instrument may indicate that the program works when it actually does not (false positive). Alternately, the outcome indicators may suggest that the program does not work when it actually does (false negative). Reliance upon findings derived from studies that use unreliable instruments can have devastating effects. Enormous amounts of time and money may be invested in programs that do not work or, worse, exacerbate problems. Based on false positive findings, an ineffective violence prevention program may be duplicated throughout the country. Parents and teachers may believe their children and students are better protected, and young people may feel safer when they are actually in greater danger than before the program was implemented. Conversely, false negative results may lead to the discontinuation of an effective practice or program. As a result, people who could have benefited from the service may never learn of its existence.

On the other hand, use of reliable instruments in well-designed research studies tends to decrease the proportion of false positive and false negative findings, and increase the number of true positives and true negatives. Accurate findings about the effectiveness of programs and practices, when properly disseminated to professionals and consumers, can contribute enormously to improved services and to a better quality of life for those persons who use them.

Most researchers and many social workers respect the fundamental principles of science and provide details about the participants, the manner in which they are selected, the research methods, the measurement tools, the intervention, and the findings. As a result, you usually have sufficient information to evaluate the quality of published research studies. They typically appear in professional journals where peer review is built into the process. In addition, once published, research-based journal articles are subject to the comments of readers, many of whom are expert practitioners and researchers in their own right.

In medicine, there is general consensus that randomized controlled or randomized clinical trial (RCT) studies represent the highest quality of research related to practice effectiveness. Such studies are considered a "gold standard" because RCT research designs control for many of the threats to validity inherent in other studies and approach the six characteristics of an ideal experiment (Grinnell, 1997). Grinnell suggests that in ideal experiments

1. The independent variable (the intervention, service, or treatment) occurs before the dependent variable (change in rate or severity of problem condition) in order to determine causality.
2. The independent variable is manipulated to establish change in the dependent variable (for example, one group receives an intervention while a control group receives a placebo condition; one group receives more of the intervention while another group receives less; one group receives an intervention while another group receives a different intervention).
3. The interdependent and dependent variables reflect a relationship so that changes in the former are associated with changes in the latter (for example, participants who receive a service for a longer period experience greater improvement than those served for a shorter period).
4. Potential "rival hypotheses" are controlled or eliminated (by managing exposure to or keeping constant other factors that could affect the dependent variable).
5. Participants in at least one control group are studied along with those in the experimental group.
6. Participants are randomly selected from a population and then randomly assigned to experimental or control groups (Grinnell, 1997, pp. 262–268).

Yegidis, Weinbach, and Morrison-Rodriquez (1999) suggest that good research designs are

1. Derived from comprehensive reviews of the research literature (reflect a genuine understanding of previous and contemporary research studies within the field)

2. Suited to the current level of knowledge (extend or advance current knowledge)
3. Coherent and consistent with their types and purposes (experimental studies attempt to determine causation through rigor, controls, and randomization, while exploratory studies attempt to learn about a phenomenon through open, flexible exploration)
4. Feasible or "do-able" (a manageable study that can be completed is superior to a perfect study that cannot be conducted)

Unlike medical physicians, social workers have yet to achieve consensus about what constitutes their gold standard for practice effectiveness. Indeed, debates about the best kinds of research for social work may be premature. The range of potential target client groups and service approaches; the variability in the amount of knowledge about different peoples, problems, and interventions; and the needs for additional knowledge are so great that good-quality practice-effectiveness research of all kinds should be welcome. How can we encourage the conduct of more research studies? may be a more pertinent question than What is the best kind of research study? Regardless of the nature of the research design, however, you must consider issues of validity in evaluating findings.

As Roth and Fonagy (1996) suggest, *internal validity* refers to the degree to which the research design establishes that the introduction of the independent variable (a social work intervention) alone can accurately be determined as the cause of change in the dependent variable (goal attainment or increase in empowerment as indicated by a predetermined measure). *External validity*, on the other hand, refers to the extent to which the research design allows for accurate generalization of findings to the population from which the sample was drawn.

In attempts to produce accurate findings, researchers consider and address various threats to validity that could endanger the quality of their research undertaking. At the conclusion of the study, researchers hope to determine that the independent variable (social work intervention) is or is not the only cause of change in the dependent variable (problem condition or goal). To the extent that such a determination is impossible, the study lacks internal validity. A study is more internally valid to the degree that alternative hypotheses can be ruled out or controlled. Therefore, researchers attempt to control for the influence of other variables that might support alternative explanations for the effects.

***Threats to Internal Validity*** Among the common threats to internal validity (Campbell & Stanley, 1966; Cook & Campbell, 1979; Grinnell, 1997; Isaac & Michael, 1971; Royse, 1995; Rubin & Babbie, 2001; Yegidis et al., 1999) are

*Nonequivalent or Flawed Selection and Assignment Processes:* While it is inevitable that participants in a study vary in several aspects, when the average characteristics of the experimental and control groups differ significantly it becomes impossible to determine whether the intervention or the different characteristics of the groups caused the effects. When nonequivalent groups are compared, the effects of the intervention cannot be decisively established. The most common way to control for this threat to internal validity is through the use of random sampling and random assignment. It is sometimes possible to match groups or identify how the groups do vary and compensate for those differences through statistical testing. However, such alternatives are not as strong as random assignment.

*History:* Events beyond the researcher's control may affect participants and the outcomes. Significant social or environmental events (wars, storms, floods, riots, sensational crimes) may occur during the time of the study (between beginning and ending, or pretest and posttest). When they do, the researcher may be unable to determine how much of the change was due to the intervention and how much was due to the historical events.

*Mortality/Attrition:* Participants' premature discontinuation from a study threatens the integrity of the research design and the validity of the findings. People who drop out are probably different from those who complete the program. Therefore, when people prematurely leave an experimental group or a control group, the groups may become less equivalent and perhaps less representative of the population. After all, it cannot be presumed that the process of dropping out is random or matched.

*Maturational Effects:* Changes that occur within participants during the time period of the study can affect outcomes. Consider, for instance, the nature of adolescence and how many alterations youngsters experience during those sometimes turbulent years. In general, time and aging influence participants in some ways. Because outcome scores may be affected by maturational changes, researchers attempt to control for their effects.

*Testing Effects:* Completing a pretest can, in itself, affect posttest scores. Participants might recall questions or topics covered in the pretest and score higher on the posttest. Some may feel anxious about taking the pretest but more relaxed about the posttest, while others are calm at first and tense at the end. The scores might differ because of the differential levels of anxiety.

*Instrumentation Effects:* If measurement instruments lack adequate validity or reliability or are administered improperly, or if mistakes are made in scoring, the results of the study may be questionable or even invalid.

*Statistical Regression:* There is a strong tendency for exceptionally high and exceptionally low scores to drift toward the average score. Therefore, some of the changes in subject scores that occur between pretest and posttest are probably the result of regression toward the mean.

*Reactive Effects:* The awareness that one is participating in a research study or the unusual nature of the research situation may, in itself, elicit a reaction from participants in the study. These "Hawthorne effects" or "placebo effects" may incorrectly be interpreted by researchers as the result of the intervention. The practice or research context and participants' expectations are often important causal factors. One way to control for these effects is to ensure that all experimental and control groups under study are treated equally except for the intervention.

*Intergroup Relations:* "Diffusion" or "imitation" may occur when experimental and control groups interact with one another and discuss aspects of the intervention or study. In a related process, "compensatory equalization" may occur when a researcher empathizes or sympathizes with the control groups that are "deprived of the beneficial treatment." The researcher may consciously or unconsciously compensate by providing additional or special attention or even by educating them about the intervention under study. "Compensatory rivalry" occurs when members of the control group compete with those in the experimental group to "win" the perceived contest.

*Causal Ambiguity:* Uncertainty may result when the time sequence of the independent and dependent variables is not clear. Under some circumstances, it can be difficult or impossible to determine whether the independent variable (program, service, intervention) affected the dependent variables or the dependent variables affected the independent variable. The researcher may be tempted to conclude that a program works when its effectiveness actually remains unknown. Rubin and Babbie (2001, pp. 299–300) discuss how a finding that clients who drop out of an antidrug program are more likely to abuse alcohol or drugs than those who finish might easily be misinterpreted. Researchers might conclude that completion of the program is effective in decreasing substance abuse. However, it might be that decreasing substance abuse leads to program completion.

*Interactional Effects:* Various threats can interact with one another to diminish the validity of a study. A common interactional threat is the combination of nonequivalent or flawed selection and maturational or historical effects.

**Threats to External Validity**    *External validity* refers to the degree to which a study's findings may validly be generalized to the larger population or to other contexts beyond the immediate situation of the study itself. Maximum external validity occurs when the participants selected for the study are representative of the population from which they are chosen and when the context for the intervention approximates the real-world conditions of the population. Such generalizations are difficult to establish through single-system research designs. It is much easier to do so through research designs that involve groups of participants.

Among the common threats to external validity (Campbell & Stanley, 1966; Grinnell, 1997; Royse, 1995; Rubin & Babbie, 2001; Yegidis et al., 1999) are

*Pretest-Intervention Interaction:* The pretest may, in effect, change the way participants react to the experimental intervention and score on the posttest. In a sense, the pretest may result in the group's becoming a nonrepresentative sample of the population. As a result, the findings may not reasonably be applied to the population.

*Selection-Intervention Interaction:* When random selection of participants does not occur, it becomes probable that the sample under study is not representative of the population from which it is selected. For example, suppose two social workers want to study incest survivors. They place advertisements for "incest survivors" in several newspapers. Although dozens of people respond to the ads, the social workers must assume that the respondents are not completely representative of the population of incest survivors. Incest survivors who respond to newspaper ads are probably different in some way from those who do not.

*Variable Specificity:* Research projects undertaken with a specific sample in a discrete place and time may not be generalizable to people at different times in different contexts. For example, interventions that work with a sample of upper-middle-class persons may not generalize to persons from a lower socioeconomic status—even though the problem or goal that is the focus of intervention might be similar among all participants.

*Reactivity:* External as well as internal validity can be affected by changes in attitude and behavior of participants that result from awareness that they are in a research study. These changes may move them from being representative to being nonrepresentative members of a population.

*Multiple-Intervention Effects:* If participants receive two or more interventions in sequence, the outcome of the first intervention may influence the results of the second. The results of the two interventions thus become combined. Consequently, it becomes difficult to distinguish which factors produced the changes.

*Researcher Bias:* People are likely to find what they expect or hope to discover. Researchers can knowingly or unknowingly influence a study to yield the results they anticipate or desire. For example, knowledge about which participants are in an experimental group and which are in a control group can lead a researcher to subtly reinforce or reward participants in the intervention cohort to "prove" that it works. In doing so, the participants may become unrepresentative samples of the population.

## Research Papers

Good-quality research papers published in professional-quality, peer-reviewed journals represent the preferred source for evidence of practice effectiveness. They are highly valued because they fall within the primary source, research-based category of information. In addition, they are selected through a peer-review process that generally serves to encourage better-quality research and more valid findings. Greenhalgh (1997) suggests that interesting, well-written manuscripts are frequently rejected for reasons such as:

1. Insignificant purpose, issue or topic (the goals of the study or the phenomena under investigation are relatively unimportant to the field)
2. Lack of originality (someone else previously conducted and published a similar study)
3. Failure to address the identified hypotheses or research questions
4. Application of an inappropriate research design

5. Flawed or compromised implementation
6. Insufficient sample size
7. Absence or inadequacy of controls
8. Inappropriate statistical processes or incorrect statistical analysis
9. Unsubstantiated conclusions (not supported by the presented evidence)
10. Unmanaged conflict of interest or bias
11. Poor preparation and editing (unscholarly or incoherent composition)

Despite the best efforts of researchers, reviewers, and editors, most studies reflect both strengths and weaknesses. A difficult and challenging endeavor, research is rarely, if ever, "perfect." Research papers—even those published in highly prestigious journals—reflect limitations, imperfections, and inconsistencies. Furthermore, reviewers and editors sometimes make mistakes. Occasionally, papers that should be accepted are rejected, while some that should be rejected are accepted and published. As you read more research articles and refine your abilities to understand and evaluate them, you will undoubtedly discover some published studies that contain flaws.

Most practice-effectiveness research studies fall into one of three general forms or categories: (1) experiments, (2) trials (clinical or controlled), and (3) surveys (Greenhalgh, 1997). Experiments are precise forms of research that occur within a highly structured and managed environment such as a laboratory. Trials are research projects that take place in clinics, agencies, or elsewhere in the real world. Clinical or controlled trials involve consenting humans who participate in research to determine the effectiveness of an agent or procedure, and to identify risks or adverse side-effects. Trials that are controlled through the random assignment of participants into experimental or treatment groups and control or placebo groups are preferred over uncontrolled trials. Uncontrolled trials involve more threats to internal validity. For example, when researchers use a convenience sample rather than a random sample of participants, they cannot be as certain that the findings are the result of the intervention as they could be if they adopted randomized selection and randomized assignment of participants to experimental and control groups.

A survey is an "observational or descriptive non-experimental study in which individuals are systematically examined for the absence or presence (or degree of presence) of characteristics of interest" (Guyatt, Sackett, & Sinclair, 1995, p. 690). Surveys are commonly used to determine consumer satisfaction with services and may provide indications of practice effectiveness. Evidence-based social workers value research-based survey data much more than authority-based opinions. When survey findings match the results of controlled trial studies, the convergence constitutes strong evidence.

In addition to experiments, trials, and surveys, other forms of research may add depth and breadth to the knowledge base of what works. Ethnographic studies, action research, focus groups, and single-system studies often contribute supplemental information about practice effectiveness.

Nathan and Gorman (1998) proposed a typology for the classification of research studies within psychology and psychotherapy. Their scheme represents a useful starting point to consider the differential quality of research studies, particularly those that involve practice effectiveness.

*Type One Studies:* These are the most rigorous and involve a randomized, prospective clinical trial. Such studies must involve comparison groups with random assignment, blinded assessments, clear presentation of exclusion and inclusion criteria, state-of-the-art diagnostic methods, adequate sample size to offer statistical power, and clearly described statistical methods.

*Type Two Studies:* These are clinical trials in which an intervention is made, but some aspect of the Type One study requirement is missing. For example, a trial in which a double-blind cannot be maintained; a trial in which two treatments are compared but the assignment is not randomized; and a trial in which there is a clear but not fatal flaw such as a period of observation that is felt to be too short to make full judgments on treatment efficacy. Such studies clearly do not merit the same consideration as Type One studies, but often make important contributions and generally should not be ignored.

*Type Three Studies:* These are clearly methodologically limited. Generally, Type Three studies are open treatment studies aiming at obtaining pilot data. They are highly subject to observer bias and can usually do little more than indicate if a treatment is worth pursuing in a more rigorous design. Also included in this category are case-control studies in which patients are identified and then information about treatment is obtained from them retrospectively. Such studies can, of course, provide a great deal of naturalistic information but are prone to all of the problems of uncontrolled data collection and retrospective recall error.

*Type Four Studies:* Reviews with secondary data analysis can be useful, especially if the data analytic techniques are sophisticated. Modern methods of meta-analysis attempt to account for the fact that, for example, negative studies tend to be reported at a substantially lower rate than positive outcome studies.

*Type Five Studies:* Reviews without secondary data analysis are helpful to give an impression of the literature but are clearly subject to the writer's opinion and sometimes are highly biased.

*Type Six Studies:* This encompasses a variety of reports that have marginal value, such as case studies, essays, and opinion papers. (Nathan & Gorman, 1998, pp. 19—20)

The American Psychiatric Association, in attempting to classify the quality of the supportive evidence contained in the references to its Clinical Practice Guidelines, uses a similar hierarchical rating system.

[A] *Randomized clinical trial.* A study of an intervention in which subjects are prospectively followed over time; there are treatment and control groups; subjects are randomly assigned to the two groups; both the subjects and the investigators are blind to the assignments.

[B] *Clinical trial.* A prospective study in which an intervention is made and the results of that intervention are tracked longitudinally; study does not meet standards for a randomized clinical trial.

[C] *Cohort or longitudinal study.* A study in which subjects are prospectively followed over time without any specific intervention.

[D] *Case-control study.* A study in which a group of patients and a group of control subjects are identified in the present and information about them is pursued retrospectively or backward in time.

[E] *Review with secondary analysis.* A structured analytic review of existing data, e.g., a meta-analysis or a decision analysis.

**TABLE 4.5**   *Comparison of Nathan and Gorman and the American Psychiatric Association Classification Schemes*

| Nathan and Gorman | American Psychiatric Association |
| --- | --- |
| Type 1: Randomized Controlled Trial | A: Randomized Controlled Trial |
| Type 2: Clinical Trial | B: Clinical Trial |
| Type 3: Methodologically Limited | C: Cohort or Longitudinal |
|  | D: Case Controlled |
| Type 4: Secondary or Meta-Analysis | E: Review with Secondary Analysis |
| Type 5: Reviews | F: Reviews without Secondary Analysis |
| Type 6: Case Studies, Opinion Pieces, and Essays | G: Other: Textbooks, Case Reports, Expert Opinion |

[F] *Review.* A qualitative review and discussion of previously published literature without a quantitative synthesis of the data.

[G] *Other.* Textbooks, expert opinion, case reports, and other reports not included above. (American Psychiatric Association, 2000a, References section, paras. 1–7)

Table 4.5 illustrates the classification typologies presented by Nathan and Gorman and by the American Psychiatric Association. You can readily observe the similarities among the two schemas.

Assessment of practice-relevant research papers involves consideration of the same factors outlined in Table 4.3 and 4.4. Indeed, identifying and evaluating these aspects are often quite straightforward because research publications tend to be organized and presented in a prescribed format. An *introductory section* includes discussion of the purpose and goals of the study, rationale and importance, background information, and specification of the research questions or hypotheses. In a *method section*, researchers identify the research design and discuss how they conducted the study, providing details about the investigative procedure. They describe the participants in terms of numbers and relevant characteristics, and discuss how they were selected and assigned. The intervention, procedure, instrument, or phenomenon under investigation is described in considerable detail. The assessment tools or processes are identified, and information about validity and reliability presented. In a *results section*, researchers discuss and illustrate the outcomes of the study. They present their findings—often using tables, graphs, figures, and statistics. They provide a rationale for the use of various statistical procedures and discuss issues such as statistical power, statistical significance, and effect size in relation to their results. In a *discussion section*, researchers examine and interpret the results in terms of the research questions or hypotheses, identify limitations, and explore the implications of their findings for theory building, practice, or further research. Finally, a detailed *reference section* includes documentation regarding the sources, including other relevant research studies, cited in the paper.

Researchers interested in effectiveness often conduct studies to determine the outcomes of practice models or programs, intervention methods, or service protocols. Some researchers study the effects of prevention practices and programs. Others attempt to determine the validity and reliability of diagnostic, assessment, or evaluation processes and instruments. Certain researchers investigate nonspecific relationship and contextual factors such as warmth, respect, and authenticity that may be associated with favorable outcomes. Others conduct research about characteristics of successful clients. There are so many variables involved in practice that researchers will never run out of things to study.

As you examine and evaluate research papers, consider questions such as: What is the topic or subject under investigation? What are the purposes or goals of the research study? What are the hypotheses or research questions? What kind of research design is used? Is the research design likely to test the stated hypotheses or produce answers to the research questions? What threats to internal and external validity are associated with the research design and procedures? Was the practice (independent variable) compared with another practice or a control, comparison, or placebo condition? How were outcomes measured or determined? What indicators or instruments were used? Do the measurement or evaluation instruments and processes match the topic under investigation? How valid and reliable are the measurement tools or procedures? Are they relevant to your practice-effectiveness question? Using the Nathan and Gorman (1998) or the American Psychiatric Association's (2000a) classification scheme, what type or level of study is evident in the study?

Also ask questions about the population being studied such as: Who are the participants in the study? What are their characteristics? How many are there? How were they recruited? How were they selected, and how were they assigned? Were participants randomly selected from a population or through some other process? Were participants randomly assigned to control or comparison groups in addition to one or more experimental groups? What were the sizes of the beginning and ending samples? What was the dropout or discontinuation rate? Were participants aware which service (experimental or control) they received? Where were the participants studied—in a controlled environment or in a real-world context? How similar are they to the client group that interests you? In particular, were they similar in characteristics such as race, ethnicity, gender, age, social circumstance, and physical and mental ability? Were they affected by problems and issues that are similar in nature, severity, and duration to those reflected by members of your target client group? Were the goals of service similar to those of your clientele?

Is the practice, program, service, or process under investigation clearly described in sufficient detail so that it could be reproduced or replicated? Is it relevant to your practice-effectiveness question? Did the intervention take place in artificial or in real-world circumstances? Were fidelity checks incorporated to ensure consistent implementation of the intervention? Were the experiences of participants in control or comparison groups described so that comparison with the experimental condition could be made?

In terms of results and discussion, consider questions such as: What are the findings? Have the researchers achieved their goals and answered their questions? How are the findings presented? Are the data presented in a complete and precise manner?

What statistical procedures were used? Were the selected statistics appropriate for the nature and quantity of data? Were the statistics calculated accurately? How were non-reported or missing data processed, and how were participants who discontinued counted? What statistical power is reflected? What significance levels are reported? What are the effect sizes? What do these findings actually mean? Are the presented findings supported by the evidence? Is the discussion about the results clear, coherent, and free from logical fallacies? Are the implications of and the limitations to the findings discussed in a fair, realistic, and balanced manner? How might the results relate to your practice-effectiveness question?

Assessment of research-based material requires understanding of research methods and statistics as well as application of logical reasoning. Box 4.3 may be used in conjunction with Tables 4.3 and 4.4 to facilitate evaluation. However, you may also need to refer to contemporary texts (Bloom, Fischer, & Orme, 2003; Weinbach, 2004; Yegidis & Weinbach, 2002) and consult experts in research and statistics. Evidence-based social workers should, however, have some direct understanding of "effect size" as it relates to practice effectiveness.

***Effect Size***    Effect size is a statistical indication of the difference between two groups. When the measurement scores of a treatment or experimental group are compared to those of a control or comparison group, the effect size statistic reveals the effectiveness of a service, treatment, or intervention. An especially useful indication of how well a practice works, the effect size (or the "size of the effect") is frequently reported in research papers. When omitted, however, the effect size may usually be calculated through the use of other commonly reported statistics.

Effect size may be calculated in several different ways. One common procedure is to subtract the mean (average) outcome score of the control or comparison group from the mean outcome score of the experimental or treatment group on the same measure, and then divide the result either by the standard deviation of the control group to produce Glass's Delta (Δ) or, as preferred by contemporary researchers (Rosenthal, 1991; Rosnow, Rosenthal, & Rubin, 2000), a pooled estimate of the average standard deviation of both groups combined. Calculation of effect size in this manner produces the Cohen's *d* statistic (Cohen, 1988).

*Effect Size = Mean (Experimental Group) − Mean (Control Group)/Pooled Standard Deviation*

Cohen originally suggested that effect sizes may be categorized as "small" (*d* = 0.2), "medium" (*d* = 0.5), and "large" (*d* = 0.8 or higher). An effect size of 1.0 or above reflects a considerable degree of impact or effectiveness.

For example, suppose a social worker wants to determine whether anger management combined with social communications skills training is more effective than anger management alone in reducing verbal and physical violence. There are thirty-two participants in all. Sixteen participants are randomly assigned to the combined approach and another sixteen to the single model group. Effectiveness is measured through self or collateral reports, and through an assessment scale that reflects a possible range of scores from 20 to 80. Higher scores suggest a lower potential for vio-

## BOX 4.3 • *Guide for Analyzing Research-Based Products*

Title:

What is the title of the research study? Does the title accurately reflect the subject matter?

Author:

Who is the author? What are the author's credentials? What are the author's areas of expertise? What is the author's relevant experience? What are the author's related publications? With what agency, organization, association, or institute is the author affiliated? How may the author be contacted?

Form:

In what form is the research-based information (written, print, audiovisual, digital, transcript of verbal interaction)? Is there a product that can be reviewed? If so, what is its quality?

Publisher or Producer:

Who published or produced the study? What is the nature and reputation of the publisher or producer? How are materials chosen for publication or production? How may the publisher be contacted?

Date:

When was the information disseminated, revised, or updated? How old or recent is the product? When was the study conducted and completed?

Sponsorship/Disclosure:

Who endorsed, supported, or funded the product? How may the sponsor be contacted? Are actual or potential conflicts of interest disclosed?

Purpose:

What are the purposes or goals for the study? How explicit are the goals or objectives? Are hypotheses or research questions specified? Who is the intended audience (practitioners, researchers, consumers, general public, or policymakers)?

Relevance:

Are the purposes and goals for the study pertinent to the topic of interest and the practice-effectiveness question?

Methodology:

What research design was used in this study? Who are the participants? Are they similar to the client or clients you hope to serve? How were participants recruited and selected for the study? How were participants assigned to different conditions (intervention, control)? How clearly were the different conditions described? What data were collected? How were the data collected? Were data collection processes likely to introduce bias? What measurement tools were used? How valid, reliable, and relevant are the measurement tools? How were dropouts or participants experiencing adverse consequences counted? Were all participants who began the intervention accounted for at the conclusion? Were measurements taken following the conclusion of the intervention? What statistical procedures were used? Where they properly selected and applied?

Findings:

What were the findings? Are the findings supported by the data? Do the findings address the research questions or hypotheses? Where the purposes of the study pursued and accomplished?

Content:

What is the nature and quality of the content? Is the source of the information presented primary or secondary? How objective is the presentation? What perspectives are apparent? How scholarly is the product? How current is the material? How relevant is the information to the practice-effectiveness question or query? How clear, specific, and precise is the information? How accurate is the material? What degree of breadth is reflected? What level of depth? How logical are the explicit or implicit arguments? How well-documented are the contents?

lence. Suppose the average outcome scores are 56.3 (SD = 4.53) for the combined group and 50.0 (SD = 4.58) for the anger management-alone group. The 6.3 point difference in the average scores suggests that the combined approach is more effective than the single model. Since you need only the average scores and the standard deviations to calculate effect size, you may do so easily as follows:

$$d = 56.3 - 50/4.58 = 6.3/4.58 = 1.38$$

The standard deviations for the two groups are almost identical. Therefore, when the effect size is calculated using the pooled standard deviation estimate, the result is the same ($d = 1.38$). Although the sample of thirty-two clients is small, an effect size of 1.38 is "large." If similar effects were obtained through additional studies, the social worker would have fairly credible evidence that the combined approach is more effective than the single model approach.

The calculation of effect size and strength of relationship for other forms of research studies may vary somewhat from Cohen's formula for comparison of group means described earlier. Indeed, several statistics may be used to represent findings about practice effectiveness. Among others, these include Cohen's $d$ and $\kappa$, Cramér's $V$, Kendall's $W$, Goodman-Kruskal's $\lambda$ and $\gamma$, Roy's $\theta$ and the Pillai-Barlett $V$ as well as $r^2$, $R^2$, $\eta^2$, $\phi^2$, and $\omega^2$ (American Psychological Association, 2001; Rosenthal & Rosnow, 1991).

Effect size estimates have become so important an indicator of effectiveness and relationship strength that the American Psychological Association now requires authors to report them in research papers submitted to their journals. Journal editors are urged to reject manuscripts that fail "to report effect sizes" (American Psychological Association, 2001, p. 5).

## Research Syntheses

Research syntheses involve the systematic and scientific analyses of a carefully selected and aggregated groups of published studies. As forms of original research, they are primary. However, they are also secondary because the data are aggregated from earlier research. Systematic reviews, such as those published by the Cochrane Collaboration, involve the careful application of precise protocols for the search, selection, and analysis of studies. In meta-analyses, researchers integrate original data, usually quantitative in nature, from carefully selected studies. Frequently, through the use of effect size estimates, the combined data from eligible research studies are statistically analyzed to yield general results or effects (Cook et al., 1992; Hunt, 1997; Rothman, Damron-Rodriguez, & Shenassa, 1994; Sutton, Abrams, Jones, Sheldon, & Song, 2000; Trull, Nietzel, & Main, 1988; Videka-Sherman, 1988, 1995).

Clearly, research-based systematic reviews and meta-analyses differ from typical secondary source material in that the nature of the search and analysis processes are explicated and systematic. The findings are original. Like other research studies, they may be replicated and verified or challenged. Therefore, high-quality systematic reviews and meta-analyses may be classified as primary source, research-based material. Such research syntheses are particularly valuable as evidence of practice effectiveness. Despite their obvious strengths, meta-analyses and systematic reviews must be as carefully scrutinized as other forms of evidence.

Researchers use the term "publication bias" (Dickersin, 1990; Stern & Simes, 1997) to describe the preference that journal editors and reviewers may give to studies that yield positive findings. Experienced scientists recognize that negative findings can be valuable, too. For example, when researchers discover that two interventions do not differ in their effectiveness, they may initially be somewhat disappointed because they hoped that one approach would be more effective than the other. Similarly, some journal editors may not be as impressed with the finding of "no significant difference" as they would be with one that reveals a significant difference. However, social workers and consumers might well celebrate the fact that two practices are about equally effective because it increases the range of possible interventions and improves the likelihood of matching a service to clients' personal and cultural characteristics. We may find that one approach is easier to apply or perhaps less expensive to consumers than another. Importantly, the findings also identify another intervention option if a practice approach proves to be ineffective with a particular client.

Some systematic reviewers, such as those in the Cochrane Collaboration, attempt to locate and evaluate unpublished studies to address the potential publication bias. These unpublished studies are considered along with the array of published studies. If their quality is sufficiently high to meet inclusion standards, they may be incorporated as evidence. You probably will not actively pursue unpublished studies in your search for evidence. However, realize the potential for publication bias. If and when you become a member of a team of evidence-based scholars, you may expand your searches to include unpublished studies as well.

Guyatt and colleagues (Guyatt, Sackett, & Sinclair, 1995) developed a hierarchical scheme that places a high value on systematic reviews and meta-analyses. Indeed, they consider them superior to individual randomized studies for the purpose of determining practice effectiveness. Greenhalgh (1997) summarizes that hierarchy as follows.

- Level 1: High-quality systematic reviews and meta-analyses
- Level 2: Randomized controlled studies with clear results
- Level 3: Randomized controlled studies with unclear results
- Level 4: Cohort studies
- Level 5: Case controlled studies

- Level 6: Cross-sectional surveys
- Level 7: Case reports

In efforts to evaluate evidence of practice-effectiveness for social work, the hierarchy proposed by Guyatt et al. (1995) holds considerable appeal. If high-quality systematic reviews or meta-analyses have been completed by reputable researchers and published in credible sources, and if the results are applicable to your target client groups, then you may build upon rather than duplicate those processes. In such circumstances, your primary responsibility is to check the quality and evaluate the reasonableness of their processes and conclusions.

Evaluation hierarchies facilitate assessment of factors such as research design, rigor, and the relative validity and reliability of findings. Indeed, sometimes classifications are used as criteria to determine which forms of evidence should be included and which should be excluded or rejected from consideration. Within evidence based medicine, such criteria are typically used as part of the search and analysis process so that studies that do not meet a certain standard of rigor are excluded from consideration. When a sufficient number of high-quality research studies are available, a rigorous definition of evidence helps ensure quality.

As mentioned earlier, the Society of Clinical Psychology of the American Psychology Association sponsored a review and analysis of evidence of the efficacy and effectiveness of various psychological treatments. The Division 12 Task Force on Psychological Interventions established two categories or levels of empirically supported treatments (ESTs): (1) well-established and (2) probably efficacious. The classification criteria are as follows (Chambless et al., 1998).

### *Well-Established Treatments*
I. At least two good between-group design experiments demonstrating efficacy in one or more of the following ways:
   A. Superior (statistically significantly so) to pill or psychological placebo or to another treatment
   B. Equivalent to an already established treatment in experiments with adequate sample sizes

*Or*

II. A large series of single case design experiments (n > 9) demonstrating efficacy

*These experiments must have:*
   A. Used good experimental designs and
   B. Compared the intervention to another treatment as in IA

*Further Criteria for Both I and II:*
III. Experiments must be conducted with treatment manuals.

IV. Characteristics of the client samples must be clearly specified.

V. Effects must have been demonstrated by at least two different investigators or investigating teams.

*Probably Efficacious Treatments*

I. Two experiments showing the treatment is superior (statistically significantly so) to a waiting-list control group

*Or*

II. One or more experiments meeting the well-established treatment criteria IA or IB, III, and IV, but not V

*Or*

III. A small series of single case design experiments (n > 3) otherwise meeting well-established treatment (Chambless et al., 1998, p. 4)

Systematic reviews of the research literature, such as those advocated by Archie Cochrane (1972, 1973, 1989) and conducted by participants in the Cochrane Collaboration (Clarke & Oxman, 2002), follow rigorous processes to locate, aggregate, and analyze studies that pertain to a topic of relevance for evidence-based medicine. High-quality systematic reviews are characterized by the following (Greenhalgh, 1997; Sutton et al., 2000).

- The purpose, goals, objectives, questions, processes, and methods of the systematic review are described in detail before the review is undertaken.
- A coherent, comprehensive strategy by which to search for all relevant studies is clearly outlined and respected.
- The eligibility criteria used to include or exclude studies from the review are explicitly stated and followed.
- The systematic processes for carefully extracting or abstracting and assembling data from selected studies are described and adopted.
- The criteria for evaluating the quality or validity of included studies' findings are outlined and respected.
- The data from the included studies are statistically synthesized (if possible) and analyzed.
- Plausible alternate analyses are considered.
- The outcomes of the review are precisely described.
- The strengths and limitations of the review process and results are critically evaluated and acknowledged.
- The implications of the results of the systematic review are discussed.

Systematic reviews conducted and published by the Cochrane Collaboration reflect these criteria (Cochrane Collaboration, 2001, p. 5). Cochrane reviews are incorporated within a database of systematic reviews for use by health care providers and policymakers as well as by interested consumers. Completion of exercises contained in this book leads to the preparation of a practice-effectiveness evidence report (PEER) that is similar to the reviews contained in the Cochrane Library. When finished, your PEER may not quite meet the high standards expected of a published journal article or Cochrane review. However, if you do a scholarly job, your evidence report may well contribute to improvements in the quality of service to clients.

Meta-analyses incorporate statistical techniques to process extracted data and "integrate the results of included studies" (Cochrane Collaboration, 2001, p. 16). They represent a sophisticated form of research synthesis that increases the precision of findings. Individual studies of social work-related concerns typically do not include large enough samples to warrant substantial confidence in the results. However, when several studies are aggregated through meta-analytic processes, the net sample size and confidence in the findings grow.

> Meta analysis allows the researcher to synthesize the data from multiple studies. In the event that the studies yield comparable effects, we are then able to report this effect. In the event that the effect varies among studies, we can attempt to track down the source of the variation. We could find that the effect varied by the quality of the study, or by the type of patient, or perhaps by the precise method used to administer treatment. Where the single study allowed the researcher to speculate about these possibilities and about the extent to which results could be generalized, the meta analysis often allows the researcher to address these issues empirically. (Borenstein & Rothstein, 1999, p. 15)

Numerous challenges emerge when multiple studies are assembled and synthesized, especially when the results are not uniformly positive or negative. Suppose, for instance, you locate ten eligible studies that meet your criteria for inclusion in a systematic review of the evidence of effectiveness of a particular practice model. Six studies obtained positive outcomes, two produced negative outcomes, and two were inconclusive. If you were to simply count the number of positive studies, notice that there are more of them than the number of negative studies, you might conclude that the practice model is effective because a majority of the studies obtained positive outcomes. However, such a conclusion might be quite misleading. Suppose, for example, that three of the six favorable studies included a small number of participants (for example, fewer than five persons in the treatment and control groups), while the two studies that reflected negative results involved more than a thousand participants. Obviously, the results of the studies with larger numbers of participants are less vulnerable to error than the smaller studies. Indeed, if two well-designed large-size studies obtained negative results, professionals would be ill-advised to apply the model in practice, and informed consumers would be unlikely to consent to such services.

Research syntheses (systematic reviews and meta-analyses) may be reviewed and evaluated like other research papers. Consider the *purpose* of the review or analysis. Identify the *participants* and the *practices* or *processes* (independent or experimental variables) under investigation, and the *design* of the review or analysis. Make note of the *criteria* used to select, include, or exclude studies from consideration and the *processes* by which the data are aggregated and analyzed. Identify the *measures* (dependent variables) used in the selected studies to evaluate change and the *meta-analytic processes* (statistics) used to obtain overall effects from the aggregated studies. Assess the *logical reasoning* reflected in the results and discussion sections, and consider whether the findings are supported by the data.

## *Practice Guidelines*

Practice guidelines range in quality and relevance as well as style and format. The most credible are based on the findings of well-designed research studies and disseminated by professional associations or published in refereed professional journals (Davenport, 1992; Field & Lohr, 1990; Howard & Jenson, 1999; Jackson, 1999; Kirk, 1999; Richey & Roffman, 1999; Rosen & Proctor, 2002; G. Steketee, 1999; Vandiver, 2002; Wambach, Haynes, & White, 1999; Williams & Lanigan, 1999). Practice guidelines may be quite theoretical and abstract (standards) or detailed and descriptive (manuals, protocols). They may match the characteristics of the clients and social problems with which you are concerned or, as is often the case, the guidelines may be targeted for a different clientele.

Earlier, you learned about the National Guideline Clearinghouse (http://www .guidelines.gov), which publishes a large and expanding array of resources related to evidence-based health care practice. The NGC has adopted precise criteria for inclusion of a clinical practice guideline within its database.

1.  The clinical practice guideline contains systematically developed statements that include recommendations, strategies, or information that assists physicians and/or other health care practitioners and patients make decisions about appropriate health care for specific clinical circumstances.

2.  The clinical practice guideline was produced under the auspices of medical specialty associations; relevant professional societies, public or private organizations, government agencies at the Federal, State, or local level; or health care organizations or plans. A clinical practice guideline developed and issued by an individual not officially sponsored or supported by one of the above types of organizations does not meet the inclusion criteria for NGC.

3.  Corroborating documentation can be produced and verified that a systematic literature search and review of existing scientific evidence published in peer reviewed journals was performed during the guideline development. A guideline is not excluded from NGC if corroborating documentation can be produced and verified detailing specific gaps in scientific evidence for some of the guideline's recommendations.

4.  The guideline is English language, current, and the most recent version produced. Documented evidence can be produced or verified that the guideline was developed, reviewed, or revised within the last five years. (National Guideline Clearinghouse, 2000b, Inclusion Criteria section, paras. 1–2)

As mentioned earlier, the American Psychiatric Association and several other professional organizations also publish practice guidelines. The American Psychiatric Association provides documentary evidence to support its guidelines and classifies practice recommendations according to three confidence levels.

I. Recommended with substantial clinical confidence
II. Recommended with moderate clinical confidence
III. May be recommended on the basis of individual circumstances. (American Psychiatric Association, 1998, Summary of Recommendations section, paras. 1–4)

Recognizing the potential impact upon consumers, several other organizations have attempted to improve the quality of practice guidelines. The most prominent include the European-based Appraisal of Guidelines for Research and Evaluation (AGREE) collaboration and the U.S. Agency for Healthcare Research and Quality (AHRQ), which sponsors the National Guidelines Clearinghouse (NGC).

AGREE's mission is to "improve the quality and effectiveness of clinical practice guidelines by establishing a shared framework for their development, reporting and assessment" (Appraisal of Guidelines Research and Evaluation, 2001, What Is AGREE? para 1). AGREE collaborators developed an instrument for assessing the quality of practice guidelines (Cluzeau et al., 2002) for use by policymakers, guideline developers, health care providers, and educators. The instrument for appraising guidelines, available on-line through the AGREE Web site at http://www .agreecollabaration.org, includes items related to the clarity and specificity of the scope and purpose of the guideline, the nature and extent of stakeholder involvement in the process of development, the scientific rigor through which supporting evidence was sought and incorporated, the clarity and precision of presentation, the consideration of issues related to application and implementation, and the management of potential biases and conflicts of interest.

In the United States, the AHRQ seeks to

> develop scientific evidence that enables health care decision makers—patients and clinicians, those who manage and purchase health care services, and policy makers—to make more informed health care choices. AHRQ accomplishes its mission by conducting, supporting, and disseminating scientific research designed to improve the outcomes, quality, and safety of health care, reduce its cost, broaden access to effective services, and improve the efficiency and effectiveness of the ways health care services are organized, delivered, and financed. (Agency for Healthcare Research and Quality, 2002, Agency Mission section, para. 1)

Like AGREE, AHRQ seeks to improve the quality of services through the evaluation, promotion, and application of evidence-based practice guidelines. Recognizing that guidelines, even those of excellent quality, may become dated or obsolete as new or better evidence appears, AHRQ regularly evaluates the validity and currency of guidelines and recommend their withdrawal, retention, or revision. In assessing the current validity of practice guidelines, AHRQ considers factors such as the development of new evidence about (1) interventions, (2) potential or actual risks and benefits, (3) outcomes, (4) application and implementation, (5) societal values and expectations, and (6) nature and extent of resources (Ortiz, Eccles, Grimshaw, & Woolf, 2002).

## *Grading the Evidence*

Analysis of the evidence leads to a general estimate of its quality. Guided by the practice-effectiveness question, the evidence may be authority based or research based and may, for example, relate to the effectiveness of assessment instruments, programs, processes, or services. Ideally, the evidence pertains to some aspect of practice. Therefore, you may provide an estimate of its value in the form of a practice quality rating (PQR). Table 4.6 contains a grading rubric that may be used as part of the evaluation process. Practice quality ratings appear in the form of letter grades, where A suggests a best practice based on strong, positive evidence, and F indicates a dangerous practice based on strong, negative evidence. In this context, positive evidence suggests that the practice may be safely and effectively used with clients. Negative evidence suggests that the practice is unsafe and potentially dangerous to clients.

## *Evaluating Evidence: Exercises*

The following exercises provide several opportunities to review and evaluate published materials. In addition to examining several published articles, you will also evaluate the quality of information collected in your own search for evidence of practice effectiveness. Word process your responses and label the computer file *EBSW Ch4 Evaluating Evidence Exercises*.

1. Go to the Web site of the Attention Deficit Disorder Association (ADDA) at http://www.adda.org. Locate the document entitled "Fact Sheet on Attention Deficit Hyperactive Disorder (ADHD/ADD)" at http://www.add.org/content/abc/factsheet.htm. Review and evaluate the quality of the Fact Sheet. Summarize your evaluation, and discuss the document's value as evidence.

2. Within the same Web site, find the document entitled "Guiding Principles for the Diagnosis and Treatment of Attention Deficit Hyperactive Disorder" (http://www.add.org/gp98.htm). Review and evaluate the document. Summarize your evaluation, and discuss the strengths and weaknesses of the guiding principles as evidence of practice effectiveness.

3. Go to the Research Navigator Web site at http://www.researchnavigator.com. Log in, and find the article entitled "Pay Attention to Girls with ADHD" by W. Eric Martin. The article was published in the November/December 2000 issue of the *Psychology Today* and is available on-line in full-text format through Research Navigator. (If you cannot easily locate it, select the **Helping Professions** database, enter the keyword *ADHD*, and click on the **Go** button to search for related articles.) Review and evaluate the quality of the article as

**TABLE 4.6** *Practice Quality Rating Rubric*

Use a scale where *A = Best Practice, B = Good Practice, C = Acceptable Practice, D = Questionable Practice, and F = Dangerous Practice*

| Grade | | | |
|---|---|---|---|
| A | Best Practice | Service of first choice, most frequently used except when its use conflicts with client personal or cultural values | Solid research-based evidence; randomized controlled and/or clinical trial studies along with other studies (e.g., case studies, consumer reports); strong expert or professional association endorsement, perhaps with practice guidelines or manualized protocol; consistent triangulated evidence demonstrates safety and effectiveness |
| B | Good Practice | Often used, for example, when client reflects preference, or when best practice is ineffective or inapplicable | Some research-based evidence; a few RCT studies, some clinical trial and several case studies and consumer reports; strong expert or professional association endorsement, perhaps with practice guidelines; most of evidence supports safety and effectiveness |
| C | Acceptable Practice | Sometimes used, for example, when client reflects strong preference, or when best or good practices are ineffective or inapplicable | Some research-based evidence; a few clinical trials and some case studies and consumer reports; some expert or professional association recommendation; evidence reflects few risks and some indication of effectiveness |
| D | Questionable Practice | Seldom used; service of last resort; attempted when better practices are ineffective or inapplicable | Lack of research-based evidence; a few case studies or consumer satisfaction reports; experts or professional association neutral; evidence reflects small risk and small potential for effectiveness |
| F | Dangerous Practice | Never used | Lack of research-based evidence or presence of research indicating negative outcomes; lack of case studies or consumer satisfaction reports, or presence of negative findings; experts or professional association recommend against its use; evidence reflects considerable risk and minimal indication of effectiveness |

evidence of practice effectiveness. Indicate whether you consider the information to be primary or secondary and authority based or research based, and summarize your evaluation.

4. Go to the Research Navigator Web site at http://www.researchnavigator.com. Log in, and find the article entitled "Research on the Long-Term Effects of Child Abuse" by G. A. Elam and D. M. Kleist. Published in the April 1999 issue of *Family Journal*, the paper is available on-line in full-text format through Research Navigator. Review and evaluate the quality of the article as evidence of practice effectiveness. Summarize your evaluation.

5. Go to the Research Navigator Web site at http://www.researchnavigator.com. Log in, and find the article entitled "A Meta-Analysis of Play Therapy Outcomes" by M. LeBlanc and M. Ritchie. Published in 2001 in *Counselling Psychology Quarterly*, the paper is available on-line in full-text format through Research Navigator. Review and evaluate the quality of the article as evidence of practice effectiveness. Summarize your evaluation.

6. Go to the Research Navigator Web site at http://www.researchnavigator.com. Locate the article entitled "Evidence-Based Treatment for Child ADHD: 'Real-World' Practice Implications" by Jason H. Edwards. Published in the April 2002 issue of the *Journal of Mental Health Counseling*, it is available on-line in full-text version through Research Navigator. Review and evaluate the quality of the article as evidence of practice effectiveness. Summarize your evaluation.

7. Go to the Research Navigator Web site at http://www.researchnavigator.com. Locate the article entitled "Practice Guidelines in Social Work: A Reply, or 'Our Glass is Half Full,'" by Janet B. W. Williams and John Lanigan. Published in the May 1999 issue of *Research on Social Work Practice*, the article is available on-line in full-text version through Research Navigator. Review and evaluate the quality of the article.

8. Log in to the Research Navigator databases at http://www.researchnavigator.com. Select the helping professions; health, nursing, and medical professions; and psychology databases, and search for the full-text article entitled "Psychosocial Interventions for Caregivers of People with Dementia: A Systematic Review" by D. D. Cooke et al. The article was published in 2001 in the journal *Aging & Mental Health*. First, scan the paper to learn about the organizational structure of a formal systematic literature review. Then carefully read the paper to understand its contents. Finally, evaluate the quality of the review using evaluation criteria discussed in this chapter. Word process your review and evaluation of the paper.

9. Log in to the Research Navigator databases at http://www.researchnavigator.com. Select the helping professions; health, nursing, and medical professions; and psychology databases, and search for the full-text article entitled "A Systematic Review of the Effectiveness of Psychosocial Interventions for Carers

of People with Dementia" by H. Pusey and D. Richards. The article was published in 2001 in the journal *Aging & Mental Health*. First, scan the paper to learn about the organizational structure of a formal systematic literature review. Then carefully read the paper to understand its contents. Finally, evaluate the quality of the review using evaluation criteria discussed in this chapter. Word process your review and evaluation of the paper, and discuss the differences and similarities between this paper and the one by Cooke et al. that you reviewed above.

 **10.** Go to the Research Navigator Web site at http://www.researchnavigator.com. Locate the article entitled "Meta-analysis of CBT for Bulimia Nervosa: Investigating the Effects Using DSM-III-R and DSM-IV Criteria" by A. Ghaderi and G. Andersson. Published in 1999 in the *Scandinavian Journal of Behaviour Therapy*, the article is available on-line in full-text version through Research Navigator. Review and evaluate the quality of the article.

 **11.** Go to the Research Navigator Web site at http://www.researchnavigator.com. Locate the article entitled "Child Sexual Abuse Prevention Programs: A Meta-analysis" by M. K. Davis and C. A. Gidycz. Published in 2000 in the *Journal of Clinical Child Psychology*, the article is available on-line in full-text version through Research Navigator. Review and evaluate the quality of the article.

 **12.** Go to the Cochrane Collaboration Library Web site at http://www.update-software.com/Cochrane/default.HTM. Click on **Abstracts of Cochrane Reviews.** Enter the keywords *conduct disorder delinquency*. Two or more review abstracts should appear. Click on the hyperlink entitled "Family and Parenting Interventions in Children and Adolescents with Conduct Disorder and Delinquency Aged 10–17 (Cochrane Review)" to access the abstract by Woolfenden, Williams, and Peat. Use the abstract to estimate the quality of the meta-analysis.

 **13.** Go to the Cochrane Collaboration Library Web site at http://www.update-software.com/Cochrane/default.HTM. Click on **Abstracts of Cochrane Reviews.** Enter the keywords *obesity children*. Several results should appear. Click on the hyperlink entitled "Interventions for Preventing Obesity in Children (Cochrane Review)" to access the abstract by Campbell, Waters, O'Meara, Kelly, & Summerbell. Use the abstract to estimate the quality of the meta-analysis.

 **14.** Go to the United States National Guideline Clearinghouse Web site at http://www.ngc.gov. Once there, search for practice guidelines that refer to the topic of childhood attention deficit hyperactive disorder (ADHD). Record the authors, titles, and sources of those guidelines. If you find more than one set of relevant guidelines, label them A, B, C, and so forth. You may use the compare guidelines feature of the National Guideline Clearinghouse to facilitate the comparison. Access and carefully read each of the guidelines. Classify them according to the Nathan and Gorman (1998), the American Psychiatric

Association (2000a), or the Guyatt typologies (Guyatt et al., 1995), and identify the guideline you determine reflects the best supporting evidence.

 **15.** Refer to the evidence-based practice-effectiveness question you prepared earlier. You have already searched for and collected materials related to your topic. Consider the nature and scope of the research-based information available to help you address your question. Based on the current state or level of knowledge development in this area, develop a definition of evidence and criteria for use in determining what forms of information to include or exclude from your analysis and evaluation. If the topical areas have been heavily researched, you may be able to define evidence in such a way that you can include only randomized controlled studies, systematic reviews, and meta-analyses in your review. In areas where research-based information is limited, you may need to include some authority-based and some research-based evidence. Word process your definition of evidence and the criteria you will use to include information within the review. Indicate what you plan to exclude as well.

 **16.** Apply your definition and your inclusion and exclusion criteria to the information you have discovered and collected. Prepare a bibliographic list of those materials you included and another one comprised of those you excluded from consideration.

 **17.** Sort through the information documents you included as evidence of practice effectiveness. Use a tabular format similar to the one in Table 3.3, Table of Practice-Effectiveness Research Studies, to summarize the sources of evidence. If you include authority-based information, revise the title of the table to read something like "Evidence of Practice Effectiveness."

 **18.** Apply the authority-based and research-based evaluation rubrics and other evaluation frameworks discussed in this chapter to each of the documents included as evidence. Prepare descriptive summaries of one or two paragraphs for each paper or other product.

## Synthesizing Evidence

Synthesizing evidence involves the integration of knowledge gained from your review and analysis of practice-effectiveness evidence in the form of reasoned conclusions and recommendations. A practice-effectiveness evidence report (PEER) is a formal means to summarize and synthesize the evidence. The PEER should be prepared as a research paper and reflect the characteristics of a high-quality review (Clark & Oxman, 2002, Section 2.1. It may be presented in a format similar to that outlined in Box 4.5.

The format is similar to the systematic reviews and meta-analyses you reviewed earlier. A title page serves as the cover and prominently displays the title of the PEER.

**Box 4.4 • *Format for a Practice-Effectiveness Evidence Report***

- Title Page
- Abstract and Keywords
- Introduction
  - Purpose
    - Evidence-Based Practice-Effectiveness Question
  - Background
  - Definition of Key Terms
- Search Strategy
  - Keywords and Search Strings
  - Sources
- Selection Criteria
  - Inclusion and Exclusion
  - Rationale
- Evidence of Practice Effectiveness
  - Description
  - Analysis
- Discussion and Recommendations
- References
- Bibliography and Suggested Resources
- Appendix—List of Evidence
  - Included
  - Excluded

The title should refer to the major elements of the evidence-based practice effectiveness question. Suppose, for example, that your question is, "What is the current best evidence regarding the effectiveness of assertive community treatment programs for adults affected by severe mental illness? You might develop a title such as "Assertive Community Treatment for Adults Affected by Severe Mental Illness: A Practice-Effectiveness Evidence Report." Include your name along with the names of other contributors. Identify academic and professional credentials, title, organizational affiliation, and contact information. Include the date, and provide guidelines for the acceptable use and distribution of the PEER.

If you complete the PEER as a course or academic program requirement, you may include a statement to that effect. For example, a social work student might include a phrase such as "Submitted in partial fulfillment of the requirements for the S685 Social Work Practice in Mental Health and Addictions Course."

A page header is positioned in the upper-right-hand corner of each page of the report. Along with the page number, a one- or two-word phrase that can identify the paper in case any pages are separated may be included (such as ACT PEER 1). A running head that captures the essence of the report is positioned below the page header (for example, ACT FOR ADULTS AFFECTED BY SEVERE MENTAL ILLNESS).

An *abstract* follows on the next page. The abstract should not exceed 120 words. It should include a clear description of the purpose of the report and summarize the most important aspects. Indicate that you conducted a review of published literature, briefly describe the search methodology, and identify the major results or recommendations.

Just below the abstract, provide a list of five to eight *keywords* that reflect the main elements of the report. You may use some of the keywords you used to search on-line catalogs and bibliographic databases. In addition to the terms that reflect your target client group, include terms such as *literature review*. Ask yourself, "If someone were searching for my report on a database, what words would help them locate it?" Choose keywords as if your report might be included along with published journal articles in a bibliographic database.

Below the keywords, credit sponsoring organizations or funding sources that provided support for production of the report. Acknowledge any real or potential conflicts of interest.

On the first page following the abstract, keywords, and acknowledgements, repeat the title of the paper and provide an *introduction* to the PEER. A section heading "Introduction" is not needed. Simply begin the introduction to the report beneath the title of the report. Within the introductory section, discuss the *purpose* of the project, and specify the evidence-based practice-effectiveness question that guided your efforts. Summarize how the report is organized. Present *background* information about and an overview of the topical areas. Identify and describe the special population as well as the social problem and practice issues that provided focus to the review. Provide *definitions of key terms* as used throughout the report.

If your practice-effectiveness question involves a specific target client group, a brief vignette may help illustrate the population and the social problem. Include information about the nature, extent, and effects of the social problem upon members of the special population. Demographic and statistical information serves to establish the significance of the problem. A brief summary of some of the needs and issues commonly faced by members of the target client group as they seek or receive services may provide context, as might some common client goals. Indeed, goal achievement is a powerful indication of practice effectiveness. Keep the goals for service in mind. Otherwise, you may identify practices that are effective in accomplishing goals other than those most important to clients.

A *search strategy* section follows the introduction. It is equivalent to the method or methodology section of a research paper. Describe your search plan, and summarize your search activities. Build on and edit those exercises you word processed in earlier chapters to complete this section. Identify *keywords*, synonyms, subject headings, and search strings used in the search. Refer to or perhaps include a final version of your table of keywords and synonyms. Use your search activities log to identify and describe the *sources* searched. Identify library catalogs, bibliographic databases, and journals examined in your search. Specify search engines and identify expert authorities, organizations, and governmental agencies contacted or electronically visited. Provide sufficient descriptive information so that potential readers can assess the nature, scope, and quality of your search processes. Be sure to acknowledge the weaknesses and limitations of the adopted search strategy.

A *selection criteria* section follows the search strategy. In this section, specify the criteria used to include and exclude materials from your review. Although evidence-based professionals prefer to determine the selection criteria prior to the search to reduce threats to the integrity of the process, the limited nature of the research knowledge base in some areas may require social workers to determine them after searching, collecting, and reviewing materials of various kinds and quality.

Describe the selection criteria in considerable detail, and provide a rationale for their choice. Common criteria include forms or types and quality of evidence (such as research studies, systematic reviews, meta-analyses), characteristics of participants (such as imprisoned African-American men), types of services (case management, cognitive behavioral group counseling), outcome indicators (standardized measures, questionnaires, surveys, frequency counts), or context (prisons, jails, residential facilities, schools, hospitals, urban neighborhoods).

Discuss how and at what point in the search or analysis process the criteria were applied. You may illustrate their application with one or two examples of excluded materials along with a brief explanation for their exclusion.

A section entitled "*Evidence of Practice Effectiveness*" includes identification and description of those materials that met the criteria for inclusion in the review and were incorporated in the analysis. If the outcomes of particular service approaches or programs were the focus of the review, provide summary descriptions of the models before presenting the effectiveness evidence. A table of evidence may be presented to provide a brief summary of the research-based or authority-based information used in the review.

Summarize the nature, kind, and extent of supportive evidence. Describe it in sufficient detail that readers may gain some sense of its quality and determine whether it indeed meets your selection criteria. Analysis of the evidence may be integrated in the descriptions or presented separately in a subsequent subsection. Evidence comes in many forms and reflects differential levels of validity, reliability, and relevance. Evaluate the quality of the evidence.

A *discussion and recommendations* section includes a summary synthesis of the evidence and the recommendations based on a clear and logical analysis of that evidence. First, present the results in coherent summary fashion. Numbers and percentages, and statistics such as effect sizes may be included. Then provide your recommendations in the form of a complete argument, rather than as a claim or assertion.

The major purpose of the PEER is to present an evidence-based recommendation that may guide other helping professionals. The recommendation should refer specifically to the practice-effectiveness question that guided the search and to the supporting evidence. Provide some indication of the degree of confidence you have in your recommendation.

Ideally, your analysis of the evidence results in the recommendation of a practice, program, approach, model, method, instrument, procedure, or perspective for service to members of the identified target client group. Indeed, the fundamental goal of the search for and analysis and synthesis of practice-effectiveness evidence is to determine what works for clients you serve. More precisely, you hope to determine what activity is most likely to be effective or reflects the greatest probability of yielding the best outcomes. Unfortunately, the available evidence does not always lead to an evidence-based best practice. Sometimes, the evidence is insufficient, contradictory, or of such low quality that you cannot reasonably identify a specific practice. The recommendation is based on and supported by the evidence information you collected, analyzed, and summarized. It is presented in the form of a reasoned argument. The argument contains a premise or proposition to be considered or proven, proof in the form of evidence, a logical rationale, and a recommendation that follows logically from the preceding statements.

If a proposition is offered without a supportive rationale or evidence, then it does not qualify as an argument or recommendation. It is simply a claim or unsubstantiated assertion (UA). Consider, for example, the following sentence: Assertive community treatment (ACT) is an effective model of practice for service to persons affected by serious mental illness. The statement may be true. However, it is not an argument because it does not contain a rationale or supportive evidence.

The following argument is presented in the form of a recommendation. Although incomplete, the passage illustrates several aspects of a practice-effectiveness recommendation:

> Programs of assertive community treatment (ACT) are supported by evidence of effectiveness for service to adults affected by severe and unstable forms of schizophrenia. Several randomized controlled trials (Nathan and Gorman Study Type 1; American Psychiatric Association Rating A; Guyatt et al. Level 2) and meta-analyses of RCTs (Nathan and Gorman Study Type 3; American Psychiatric Association Rating E; Guyatt et al. Level 1) support the use of ACT services for adult men and women of diverse racial and ethnic characteristics when compared to standard care on outcome indications of contact with and support from mental health providers, number of admissions to and days of hospitalization, housing, employment, and satisfaction with services (for example, Audini, Marks, Lawrence, Connolly, & Watts, 1994; Bond, Miller, Krumwied, & Ward, 1988; Bond et al., 1990; Bush, Langford, Rosen, & Gott, 1990; Chandler, Meisel, McGowen, Mintz, & Madison, 1996; Drake et al., 2001; Drake et al., 2000; Ford et al., 2001; Herinckx, Kinney, Clarke, & Paulson, 1997; Lehman & Steinwachs, 1998a, 1998b; Marshall & Lockwood, 2002; Mueser, Bond, Drake, & Resnick, 1998; Schaedle, McGrew, Bond, & Epstein, 2002; Scott & Dixon, 1995). In addition, the National Alliance for the Mentally Ill (NAMI) recommends ACT (National Alliance for the Mentally Ill, 1998); the American Psychiatric Association suggests that assertive community treatment and assertive outreach be considered for patients with schizophrenia (American Psychiatric Association, 1997a); the University of York (UK) NHS Centre for Reviews and Dissemination National Health (2000) and the Surgeon General (U.S. Department of Health and Human Services, 1999) refer to the effectiveness of assertive community treatment in service to persons with severe mental illness.
>
> Clear and descriptive practice manuals (Allness & Knoedler, 1998; Stein & Santos, 1998) promote understanding and implementation of the model. Tools and procedures for monitoring fidelity are also available (McGrew, Bond, Dietzen, & Salyers, 1994).
>
> Based upon this review of the evidence of practice effectiveness, ACT programs warrant an A practice quality rating.

A well-prepared recommendation addresses the previously identified dimensions (credibility of included authors, researchers, and sources; quality of evidence; validity and reliability of findings; relevance to the target client group; consistency with professional values, ethics, and experience; compatibility with client's personal and cultural values; and support by the overall quality of evidence). Of course, not all reviews and analyses lead to favorable recommendations. Some practices may be deemed unsafe or dangerous, while others may lack sufficient evidence to justify any recommendation.

As a courtesy, social workers should routinely share their evidence reports with agency administrators and colleagues. Social workers serving as contributing members of practice research network communities or journal clubs would also normally receive copies. If you believe your PEER is of professional quality and the recommendations credible, you may provide a copy to relevant researchers and practitioners. You might also present summary analyses of the practice-effectiveness data at professional conferences, on appropriate Web sites, or as manuscripts submitted to scholarly journals. There are also evidence-based clearinghouses and collaborations (Cochrane, Campbell, NASW PRN) that may be interested in your work.

## Synthesizing Evidence: Exercises

The following exercises provide opportunities to refine your learning about synthesizing evidence. You will view a few more examples of systematic reviews or meta-analyses to familiarize yourself with common ways to organize and present the results of scholarly reviews of evidence. In addition, you will complete a final version of a PEER based on your own search for evidence of practice effectiveness.

Word process and save your responses to a computer file labeled *EBSW Ch4 Synthesizing Exercises*. The PEER should be word processed as a formal paper and saved in a separate file. You could label it with your surname and the word PEER along with the version number (for example, *Johnson PEER Draft 01*)

1. Describe the essential components of a practice-effectiveness evidence report.

2. Log in to the Research Navigator databases at http://www.researchnavigator .com. Select the helping professions; health, nursing, and medical professions; and psychology databases, and search for the full-text article entitled "Family Treatment of Preschool Behavior Problems" by J. Corcoran. Published in 2000 in *Research on Social Work Practice*, the full-text version may be accessed on-line through Research Navigator. First, scan the paper to learn about the organizational structure of a formal systematic literature review. Then carefully read the paper to understand its contents. Finally, evaluate the quality of the review using evaluation criteria discussed in this chapter. Word process your review and evaluation of the paper.

3. Use Corcoran's article and other systematic reviews and meta-analyses you reviewed while completing exercises as a general guide to prepare a PEER based on the results of your own search and analysis of evidence of practice effectiveness. Use the format suggested in this chapter.

4. Most authors prepare several drafts in efforts to improve the quality of the finished product. At least two draft versions are usually needed before the report is of sufficient quality. As you complete each draft, share it with colleagues for critical feedback. Use their commentary to improve the report.

## Notes

1. *The Publication Manual of the American Psychological Association,* 5th ed., is an excellent guide for the preparation of professional-quality papers.

# 5

# *Applying and Evaluating*

The application and evaluation phase of evidence-based social work involves the implementation of a recommended practice in service to one or more relevant clients and the evaluation of its effectiveness. If you are fortunate enough to identify a best (A level) practice (see Table 4.6) through your search, discovery, and evaluation of relevant information, and if you have the informed consent of an appropriate client, you provide the evidence-based service. If you cannot determine a best practice, then you and your clients may consider a good (B level) practice. If a good practice is unsupported by the evidence, you may weigh the suitability of an acceptable (C level) practice. Obviously, dangerous (F level) practices should be avoided, and questionable (D level) practices may be considered only in extraordinary circumstances. In the absence of evidence-based practices, you and your clients must rely on traditional, customary, or usual services that reflect authority-based support. Of course, there should be a written service plan, preferably based on an evidence-based practice guideline or practice manual, and the process and outcomes of service delivery should be documented and evaluated. Indeed, ideographic research about your service to clients is a hallmark of evidence-based social work.

In this chapter, you will explore the tasks and functions associated with the application phase of evidence-based social work. You will learn to implement an evidence-based practice and evaluate its effectiveness.

## *Applying*

The processes of searching, reviewing, analyzing, and synthesizing evidence of practice effectiveness typically produce useful information about what works. They often lead to the identification of best or good practices. Whenever possible, try to locate or, if necessary, create a manualized outline of the planned service so that its application can be clearly understood and evaluated. *Manualization* refers to the process of converting practice guidelines, principles, standards, or protocols into clear, descriptions of procedures, processes, and activities that may be replicated by others. In a sense, a practice manual is an expanded version of a service or treatment plan that contains detailed and explicit descriptions of the processes and actions to be taken by the service provider and the consumer.

During your search for evidence of effectiveness, you may have located practice guidelines, treatment manuals, service plans, or intervention protocols. Several practice manuals already exist, especially in the areas of health, mental health, and child and family services. Some are available in book or monograph form, while others appear in professional journals or association reports. For example, Bourke and Van Hasselt (2001) published a research paper that includes a treatment manual to guide leadership of a social problem-solving skills training program for incarcerated offenders (available in full-text form through Research Navigator). The authors provide a manualized overview of the practice, a description of goals (for example, improve social skills, anger control, cognitive coping skills, tension management, problem-solving abilities, empathic understanding, interpersonal verbal and nonverbal skills), a discussion of the stages of service, and the strategies of intervention. Because treatment is manualized, it allows helping professionals to clearly understand the nature of the service and, if applicable, apply it in service to their own clients. Practices that lack clear descriptions of goals, processes, and procedures cannot readily be adopted or adapted by other professionals.

Fortunately, many practices have already been manualized, and several more are under development. If the manual is clearly based on and congruent with the evidence of practice effectiveness; consistent with professional values, ethics, and experience; compatible with the client's personal and cultural values; and suitable for service to or for your clients, you may implement the practice as described—assuming, of course, that you have clients' informed consent.

Sometimes evidence-based practice manuals are developed for use with a very specific special population (for example, adult female European-Americans affected by extreme grief brought on by the unexpected death of a child). Others focus more on the problem or issue of concern rather than the characteristics of the served population. If the evidence suggests that the approach would likely be effective for your clients, you may adapt the manual to match their personal and cultural characteristics while maintaining the core components of the practice.

Of course, evidence-based practice manuals do not yet exist for all client groups affected by all social problems. In such circumstances, you may need to rely on authority-based practice guidelines or standards. Health, mental health, and child and family service professionals have considerable experience in the development of expert consensus guidelines. Such guidelines sometimes include considerable descriptive detail. For example, the editors of the *Journal of Clinical Psychiatry* regularly publish a series of expert consensus guidelines as supplements (March, Frances, Carpenter, & Kahn, 1997; McEvoy, Scheifler, & Frances, 1999). Each contains information about the processes by which consensus is determined as well as useful content about how to implement the practice principles. However, since the guidelines result from the opinions of experts in the field, they lack the same quality or level of evidence that would result from numerous randomized controlled trials and systematic reviews. Nonetheless, the quality of such authority-based evidence is usually quite good and often includes reference to research-based evidence as well.

Obviously, clients should be provided with sufficient information about the safety and effectiveness of potential practices to enable them to make informed decisions about their participation. In discussing possible services with clients, social workers may cite authoritative evidence associated with expert consensus guidelines along with whatever research-based support is available.

Social workers and other helping professionals may participate collaboratively to complete systematic reviews and meta-analyses of the practice-effectiveness literature, and develop manualized practice guidelines through involvement in practice research networks (PRNs), journal clubs, or practice effectiveness evidence report (PEER) groups. Through modern electronic communication, groups of scholarly professionals interested in similar target client groups and practice models may plan search activities and exchange annotated bibliographies, literature reviews, and evidence reports. As they apply evidence-based practices with their clients and collect ideographic information about effectiveness, they may share that data with their colleagues as well.

High-quality practice manuals and guidelines enable professionals to implement programs, practices, and services in a systematic manner. Since they are written in clear and descriptive language, other social workers can understand what is involved and, if warranted, use the practice with clients of their own. As practice-relevant research studies increasingly reveal information about effectiveness, the development and use of descriptive protocols or manuals enable providers to remain faithful to the evidence (Wilson, 1966). Practice integrity, or treatment fidelity, is a major issue in service delivery. In this context, there are two major forms of practice infidelity. In one form, the practice protocol is not implemented in the same manner in which its effectiveness was determined. In the other, the practice is not applied consistently with different clients over time.

When professionals first learn about an effective practice, they may read voraciously and enthusiastically seek specialized training and supervision. They often faithfully implement the practice precisely and consistently for some time. After a while, however, practitioners may inadvertently violate major features of the effective service so that client outcomes begin to suffer.

Scott Henggeler and his colleagues researched the effects of treatment fidelity in regard to multisystemic therapy (MST) with adolescent offenders and their families. In a large multiple-site study, they found that higher degrees of fidelity with the MST protocol were significantly associated with more favorable outcomes. Lower fidelity was associated with higher rates of rearrest and incarceration (Henggeler, Melton, Brondino, Scherer, & Hanley, 1997). Other studies have produced similar results (Detrich, 1999; Gresham, 1989; Gresham, Gansle, & Noell, 1993; Gresham, Gansle, Noell, Cohen, & Rosenblum, 1993; Gresham, MacMillan, Beebe-Frankenberger, & Bocian, 2000; Henggeler, 1999; Henggeler, Schoenwald, Liao, Letourneau, & Edwards, 2002; Henggeler, Schoenwald, & Pickrel, 1995; Moncher & Prinz, 1991; Rosen, 1999; Schoenwald, Henggeler, Brondino, & Rowland, 2000; Startup & Shapiro, 1993).

Absolute fidelity in evidence-based practice is, of course, neither possible nor desirable. Social workers must consider the unique values, needs, and cultural characteristics of the client system and adapt the protocol accordingly. One hundred percent fidelity is not required to ensure favorable outcomes. Rather, the worker must remain faithful to the major elements of the practice approach. Some adjustments in minor aspects of the model are inevitable. Be extremely cautious, however, before making substantial modifications. If you do so, you may turn an evidence-based practice into a psychosocial experiment for which the client may not have provided consent.

Although most practice manuals guide the actions of service providers, manuals for clients can be useful as well. Containing resources, exercises, and other materials intended to educate and encourage progress, client manuals or workbooks can supplement professional expertise. Indeed, client materials not only increase the likelihood of practice fidelity, but they may also add potency to the services themselves.

There are dozens of practice manuals currently available to providers and consumers. Some authors have published or edited books that contain collections of treatment manuals. For example, Craig LeCroy published a *Handbook of Child and Adolescent Treatment Manuals* (1994); Vincent B. Van Hasselt and Michel Hersen published both the *Sourcebook of Psychological Treatment Manuals for Adult Disorders* (1996) and the *Handbook of Psychological Treatment Protocols for Children and Adolescents* (1998). Other treatment manuals in book form include the *Clinical Handbook of Psychological Disorders: A Step-By-Step Treatment Manual* (Barlow, 2001), *Cognitive Processing Therapy for Rape Victims: A Treatment Manual* (Resick & Schnicke, 1993), and the *Motivational Enhancement Therapy Manual: A Clinical Research Guide for Therapists Treating Individuals with Alcohol Abuse and Dependence* (Miller, 1995).

Some organizations and certain publishers have begun to offer series of specialized practice manuals. For example, the National Institute on Drug Abuse (NIDA) publishes several treatment manuals related to cocaine abuse (Budney & Higgins, 1998; Carroll, 1998; Mercer & Woody, 1999). In their Best Practices for Therapy™ series, New Harbinger Publications markets empirically based protocols for the treatment of conditions such as generalized anxiety (White, 1999a, 1999b), panic and agoraphobia (Zuercher-White, 1999a, 1999b), obsessive-compulsive disorder (G. S. Steketee, 1999a, 1999b), specific phobia (Bourne, 1998a, 1998b), anger (Deffenbacher & McKay, 2000a, 2000b), depression (Emery, 1999, 2000), and posttraumatic stress disorder (Smyth, 1999a, 1999b).

> Empirically based treatment protocols combine the results of carefully designed and replicable scientific studies into a step-by step, session-by-session treatment plan. Effective protocols save time, increase the probability of obtaining good results, make it easier to train and supervise new therapists, and satisfy the needs of third parties to know that the proposed treatment follows the best available practices. . . .
>
> Each protocol will be accompanied by its own client manual, containing all the client education materials, worksheets, and skill building assignments that the client will need. The protocols are designed to be user-friendly, and a consistent format and structure will be used throughout the entire Best Practices for Therapy™ series. (New Harbinger Publications, 2001, para. 1 and 2)

The Psychological Corporation® (PsychCorp®) also offers a series of empirically supported treatments called TherapyWorks® (http://www.psychcorp.com/catalogs /paipc/psy105cpri.htm). Each product contains both a therapist's guide and a client's workbook.

> The Psychological Corporation is proud to offer the *TherapyWorks*® line of empirically-supported treatments. Based on years of research comparing the effectiveness of various psychotherapies, *TherapyWorks* programs are recognized in American Psychological Association Clinical Division Task Force reports as effective forms of treatments for specific disorders. *TherapyWorks* systematic treatment programs describe treatment protocols in detail to allow trained clinicians to administer them in the same method in which they were proven effective so as to ensure positive results. (The Psychological Corporation, para. 1)

Among the treatment manuals marketed in the TherapyWorks series are those that address anxiety and panic (Barlow & Craske, 2000; Craske Barlow & Meadows, 2000), rape induced posttraumatic stress disorder (Rothbaum & Foa, 2000a, 2000b), social anxiety (Hope, Heimberg, Turk, & Juster, 2000), obsessive-compulsive disorder (Kozak & Foa, 1998a 1998b), depression (Gilson & Freeman, 2000; Weissman, 2000), drug or alcohol problems (Daley & Marlatt, 1998a, 1998b), specific phobias (Craske, Antony, & /Barlow, 1998; Craske, Barlow, & Antony, 1998), and eating disorders (Agras & Apple, 1999a, 1999b).

In the absence of relevant evidence-based practice manuals, you may sometimes need to prepare versions to guide your services to clients. Obviously, you cannot create book-length practice manuals for each target client group. However, you can extend and elaborate on a service or treatment plan to provide additional descriptive detail in the form of a manualized practice outline. Provide sufficient descriptions so that the approach can be replicated. As the evidence grows and the precise nature and form of effective practice approaches become clearer, experts in the field will produce more extensive manuals. You can further that process by contributing ideographic information gained from services provided to or for your own clients.

In preparing manualized practice outlines, you may also refer to a series entitled Practice*Planners*® published by John Wiley and Sons (http://www.practiceplanners .wiley.com). They offer treatment planners, progress note planners, homework planners, and document sourcebooks. The treatment planners contain written treatment goals, objectives, and interventions related to major problems or issues within the topical area. The may be adapted or edited to better fit the needs of the client and the circumstances, as well as the practice-effectiveness evidence.

Among the planners are those that address psychotherapy with children (Jongsma, Peterson, & McInnis, 2000b), adolescents (Jongsma, Peterson, & McInnis, 2000a), adults (Jongsma & Peterson, 1999), and older adults (Frazer & Jongsma, 1998); therapy with couples (O'Leary, Heyman, & Jongsma, 1998), families (Dattilio & Jongsma, 2000), and groups (Paleg & Jongsma, 1999); services to persons in crisis (Kolski, Avriette, & Jongsma, 2001) and those with severe and persistent mental illness (Berghuis & Jongsma, 2000), mental retardation and developmental disability

(Slaggert, Jongsma, & Berghuis, 2000), addictions (Perkinson & Jongsma, 2001), personality disorders (Bockian & Jongsma, 2001), and special education needs (Winkelstern & Jongsma, 2001); school counseling and school social work (Knapp & Jongsma, 2002); crisis counseling (Kolski, Avriette, & Jongsma, 2001), rehabilitation psychology (Rusin & Jongsma, 2001), behavioral medicine (DeGood, Crawford, & Jongsma, 1999), employment assistance (Oher, Conti, & Jongsma, 1998), and continuum of care (Stout & Jongsma, 1997); services to juveniles in justice and residential care (McInnis, Dennis, Myers, Sullivan, & Jongsma, 2002); and social work and human services (Wodarski, Rapp-Paglicci, Dulmus, & Jongsma, 2000). Many of the topics also have homework planners and planners for maintaining progress notes. The homework planners contain numerous tasks and activities that clients may complete between meetings.

Outlines of practice manuals or treatment protocols are not standardized. They appear in many different forms. However, the outline in Box 5.1 contains dimensions that should apply to most circumstances. You may adapt the outline to best meet the needs of your target client groups and practice context.

Practice manuals reflect qualitatively different levels of evidentiary support and consistency with evidence of practice effectiveness. There are several reasons for these variations. The most evidence-based manuals are virtually identical to those used in the research studies that established the practice's effectiveness. You may appropriately adopt these manuals when the characteristics of your clients match those of the participants in the research studies (your clients come from the same population group and reflect the same social problem as the research participants).

Social workers implement evidence-based practice approaches by following the principles and processes outlined in practice or program manuals, or sometimes in the research protocols. As a professional rather than a technician, you must make ethical judgments and respect the idiosyncratic needs and circumstances of your clients. While adhering as much as possible to the fundamental elements of the manualized practice approach, you must respect clients' personal and cultural values.

This process is complex and warrants careful consideration of several factors. Research findings (Bond, Becker, Drake, & Vogler, 1997; Bond, Evans, Salyers, Williams, & Kim, 2000; Detrich, 1999; Henggeler et al., 1997; Henggeler et al., 2002; Orwin, 2000; Teague, Bond, & Drake, 1998) suggest that fidelity to an evidence-based practice is a key element in determining effective outcomes. If you abandon the program or practice guidelines too easily, your actions may inadvertently contribute to diminished effectiveness. If, on the other hand, you fail to respect clients' individual needs, characteristics, and circumstances, you may negatively affect their motivation. Negotiating these complexities requires critical thinking and professional judgment.

Evidence-based practice manuals do not exist for all populations and all problems. On occasion, you may need to adapt a manualized practice to address the needs of your clients, and sometimes you may have to create your own. Of course, creation of new or changes to existing manuals raise questions about practice fidelity. This is a major reason to conduct ideographic evaluation of the outcomes of your professional activities. In departing from an evidence-based practice, you and your clients essentially engage in practice experiments. As a consequence, you have a special obligation

**BOX 5.1  •  *Practice Manual Outline Format***

- Introduction and Overview
  - Target client group (identify the special population affected by a social problem that seeks or needs the service)
  - Evidence-based practice approach (identify the practice approach that you selected through your review and analysis of the evidence)
- Practice Approach
  - Principles and guidelines (describe the principles, core concepts, and practice guidelines that inform application and implementation of the practice approach)
  - Relevant problems or issues (describe the problems or issues commonly experienced by members of the target client group)
  - General goals (describe the goals that clients typically pursue through the practice approach)
  - Recruitment and selection of clients (describe how potential clients are recruited and selected for participation in the service; identify the criteria used to include and exclude potential clients)
  - Legal and ethical issues (discuss the laws, policies, and ethical principles that relate to the use of the evidence-based practice approach with the identified target client group)
  - Documentation and supervision (describe how records are maintained, supervision provided, and fidelity with the practice approach monitored)
- Phase I: Preparing
  - Orientation and preparing processes (describe how selected clients are oriented to and prepared for the service; identify the resources needed to implement the service)
  - Pretesting processes (describe the pretests used prior to the beginning of service)
- Phase II: Beginning (describe the beginning stages of the service; identify steps, processes, and activities)
- Phase III: Exploring (describe the processes through which clients are encouraged to discuss and elaborate upon themselves, the problems or issues of concern, and their situation or circumstances)
- Phase IV: Assessing (describe the processes through which an assessment of the person-problem-situation occurs)
- Phase V: Contracting
  - Problem-definition (describe the processes by which the problems or issues for work are clarified and defined)
  - Goal-Setting (describe the processes by which specific goals for work are determined)
  - Service Planning (describe the processes by which the practice approach is used to address the problems and pursue the goals)
- Phase VI: Working and Evaluation
  - Practice strategies, activities, and techniques (describe the strategies, activities, and techniques used to address problems and pursue goals)
  - Means by which progress toward achievement of general and specific goals is evaluated (describe the processes and instruments used to evaluate progress toward problem resolution and goal attainment)

*(continued)*

## BOX 5.1  Continued

- Phase VII: Ending
  - Posttesting (describe how the pretest instrument completed during the preparing phase is completed again as a posttest)
  - Saying good-bye (discuss the processes by which service activities are concluded and the involved participants say good-bye)
  - Follow-up testing (discuss when and how the instrument used as a pretest and posttest is completed again as a follow-up test)

to evaluate service effects, protect clients from harm, and determine if the outcomes are beneficial.

## Evaluating

Professional social workers evaluate the effectiveness of their professional activities as a normal part of service delivery. By itself, nomothetic information is insufficient. You also require ideographic evidence that your practices are effective for the clients you actually serve. To determine effectiveness, you may use traditional forms of evaluation (such as goal assessment scales or client feedback). However, try to incorporate valid and reliable instruments or indicators such as those used in the nomothetic research studies of practice effectiveness. Whenever possible, adopt practice-evaluation designs (such as single-system or small group designs) that decrease or manage threats to internal and external validity.

Suppose, for example, you begin to serve a single parent who became housebound during the past two years. She experiences panic attacks at the thought of leaving her home. She does not have a physical condition or disability that could account for the intense anxiety. Rather, she appears to meet the DSM-IV criteria for panic disorder with agoraphobia. She has two children, ten and twelve years of age, who want her to accompany them to sporting and recreational events, parent-teacher meetings, and visits to the doctor. She reports that the panic attacks and agoraphobic symptoms began about the time her spouse left the state with another woman. She has not heard from him since. The elder child has recently begun to manifest some of the same symptoms of extreme anxiety when leaving the home. The younger child has become quite unmanageable. He plays in the neighborhood and often refuses to return home when called by his mother. He seems to understand that she will not leave the house to come after him.

You review and analyze the relevant nomothetic evidence of practice effectiveness (Bakker, van Balkom, Spinhoven, Blaauw, & van Dyck, 1998; Barlow & Cerny, 1988; Barlow & Craske, 2000; Barlow, Craske, Cerny, & Klosko, 1989; Boyer, 1995; Chambless & Gillis, 1993; Clark, 1989, 1996; Craske, Antony, and Barlow, 1998;

Craske & Barlow, 2001; Craske Barlow, & Meadows, 2000; Gould, Otto, & Pollack, 1995; Milrod & Busch, 1996; Oehrberg et al., 1995; Oei, Llamas, & Devilly, 1999; Trull Nietzel, & Main, 1988; van Balkom et al., 1997; van Balkom, Nauta, & Bakker, 1995). Based on your analysis, you conclude that a cognitive or cognitive-behavioral approach with exposure is likely to be effective for your client, particularly if combined with certain antidepressant medications (serotonin reuptake inhibitors). You discuss the evidence with the client and consider the approach. She indicates that she would like to try CBT with exposure to meet the needs of her children and enhance the quality of her own life. With the client's permission, you telephone her medical doctor to schedule a visit and discuss the possibility of obtaining a prescription. You also adopt a practice manual prepared by Barlow and Craske (Barlow & Craske, 2000; Craske & Barlow, 2001; Craske Barlow, & Meadows, 2000), although Zuercher-White (1999a, 1999b) and Leahy and Holland (2000) have solid evidence-based manuals as well. Barlow and Craske refer to their protocol as panic control treatment (PCT).

In conjunction with the client, you also agree on several measures of outcome effectiveness. A key indicator is a panic attack record in which the client records the date and time of the episode, stimulus factors or triggers, degree of fear on a 9-point subjective rating scale (0 = none and 8 = extreme), and identification of panic-related symptoms (Barlow & Craske, 2000; Craske & Barlow, 2001). The client also maintains a daily mood record to record general ratings of the overall degree of anxiety, depression, and worry about panic. Each of these three aspects of mood is rated on 9-point scales (0 – 8).

As a supplement to the PCT model, you might ask the client to maintain a record of excursions outside the home. This record (adapted from Leahy & Holland, 2000, p. 92) enables the client to record (1) the date and time of each excursion, (2) the subjective level of anxiety (0 – 8) prior to the excursion, (3) the expectations in anticipation of the excursion and the degree of confidence in their validity (0 – 100 percent), (4) physiological sensations during the excursion, (5) subjective level of anxiety (0 – 8) during the excursion, and (6) a brief summary of the excursion including its duration, the distance from the home, and the circumstances.

Various inventories may be used to complement the self-monitoring measures. Depending on the individual nature of their symptoms, clients may be asked to complete one or two of the following instruments: the Beck Anxiety Inventory (Beck, Epstein, Brown, & Steer, 1988), the Fear Questionnaire, agoraphobia subscale (Marks & Mathews, 1978), the Mobility Inventory (Chambless, Caputo, Gracely, Jasin, & Williams, 1985), the Panic Attack Symptoms Questionnaire (Clum, Broyles, Borden, & Watkins, 1990), the Anxiety Sensitivity Index (Reiss, Peterson, Gursky, & McNally, 1986), the Body Sensations Questionnaire (Chambless, Caputo, Bright, & Gallagher, 1984), the Agoraphobia Cognitions Questionnaire (Chambless et al., 1984), the Albany Panic and Phobia Questionnaire (Rapee, Craske, & Barlow, 1995), or the Anxiety Control Questionnaire (Rapee, Craske, Brown, & Barlow, 1996).

The identification and selection of assessment instruments for use with manualized practices vary according to several factors. The major considerations involve the client's needs, problems, issues, abilities, and, of course, personal and cultural values.

The instruments should, of course, measure changes in the problem conditions or the goals for service. If at all possible, try to adopt tools that have been used in the practice-effectiveness research studies themselves.

Be aware that some states limit the use of certain psychological instruments to designated professionals (such as psychologists or university professors). If so, you may wish to consult with a suitable licensed professional in your agency, university, or community. Also, many instruments are copyrighted and require permission from the author or publisher. Others are offered commercially and require a fee for use. Despite these constraints, the use of standardized measures as a dimension of evidence-based social work is extremely important. It is especially useful when you can consider your clients' results on instruments that have been used in practice-effectiveness research studies.

When feasible, ask clients to complete the selected instruments prior to implementation of the intervention plan and periodically (weekly or twice-monthly) during the course of your work together. In addition to narrative progress notes in which you and the client record observations, experiences, themes, and issues, graph scores on the measures so that you may track them in a manner consistent with the principles and procedures of single-system design research (Alter & Evans, 1990; Bloom, 1995; Blythe & Rodgers, 1993; Corcoran, 1993; Hersen & Barlow, 1976).

> · Single-system design offers an alternative to the unsystematic case study as a means of documenting and evaluating a client's progress (Kazdin, 1982). Other names for this methodology include time-series research, $N = 1$, ideographic research, single-organism research, nomothetic research, single-case design, and single-subject design. Note that the "system" can be a client or a client unit. (Blythe, 1995, p. 2164)

As a professional social worker, your primary responsibility is to help clients. Therefore, evaluation of progress toward mutually agreed upon goals is an essential element of service. To increase the likelihood of obtaining effective outcomes and contribute to the generation of practice-effectiveness knowledge, you may also estimate the degree of treatment fidelity or integrity. Standardized measures of fidelity exist for a few protocols (Bond et al., 1997; Bond et al., 2001; Schoenwald et al., 2000; Teague, Bond, & Drake, 1998). However, most have yet to develop systematic means for determining the consistency with which an evidence-based protocol is applied. Under such circumstances, use the major components of the practice as guidelines upon which to estimate fidelity. For example, in the case of a practice approach that combines cognitive-behavioral and exposure interventions, you could determine the relative proportion of time or effort you and the client invest in cognitive-behavioral and exposure activities. If practice activities that involve neither cognitive-behavioral or exposure represent a substantial percentage of your work together, you may begin to question the fidelity of the practice.

Whenever possible, try to collect information prior to the initiation of the intervention. Baseline scores help strengthen the value of data generated during and following the intervention. When you can compare preintervention scores with postintervention scores through single-system research, you can estimate the effect of the intervention. Similarly, follow-up scores from measures taken some time after completion of the intervention (one month, three months, six months) provide information about the durability of the outcomes.

Graphic representations of data help clarify their meaning to clients who may not understand the implications of numbers alone. They also aid in communicating information about practice effectiveness to colleagues. Simple charts may be easily generated through the use of popular spreadsheet programs. Most programs have a means to convert numerical data into graphic form (see Figure 5.1 for an illustrative example).

Fidelity to the essential aspects of a manualized practice is essential if you hope to contribute to the body of knowledge about its effectiveness. Obviously, you and your clients are personally invested in the results. Clients hope to resolve the issues confronting them, and you hope to help them do so. This is your first priority and the primary purpose for generating ideographic information. The same data, however, may also contribute to the general practice-effectiveness knowledge base if your application of the practice conforms to manualized guidelines, and you share your results with other practitioners and researchers. Social workers and other providers may maximize their knowledge-generation activities by adopting common practice manuals for appropriate target client groups, collecting single-system information about outcomes, and pooling the data. The power of the evidence is enhanced when several workers contribute ideographic results that can be aggregated and analyzed (see Figure 5.2).

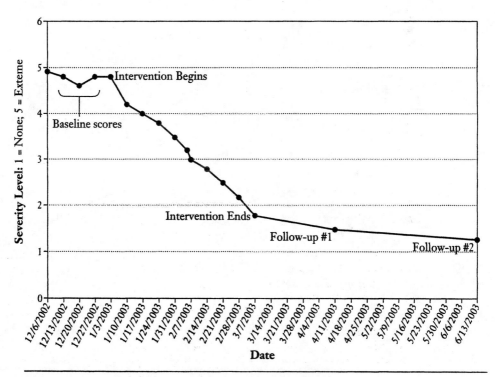

**FIGURE 5.1**  *Client Scores on Body Sensations Questionnaire*

You might join an electronic community of social workers who serve a similar target client group and use the same standardized measures to evaluate progress. In the contemporary world, it matters little where you practice. You might work in a town or city almost anywhere in North America or indeed in the world. You may communicate with colleagues via e-mail to share approaches, experiences, and assessment data.

Consider the size of the data set you could generate if twenty colleagues each contributed common standardized pre-, post-, and follow-up scores of ten similar clients. With very little effort, you could produce outcome data regarding the effectiveness of service to a target client group of some two hundred clients. Through such collaboration, a small group of social workers and other helping professionals can efficiently convert single-system ideographic into nomothetic information.

In sharing practice-effectiveness data, social workers must respect the rights of their clients and agencies. You should refer to the code of ethics for general guidance about the dissemination of ideographic practice-effectiveness research findings. This is not as complicated as it might initially seem. Assessment data is usually generated as a natural part of service, securely maintained within a client's case record, and protected by the sponsoring agency. Such information is an appropriate and essential part of normal service delivery. However, if you wish to share outcome data with people outside the agency, you must take additional steps to safeguard the people who might be affected by its dissemination. Extra caution is required whenever you share client

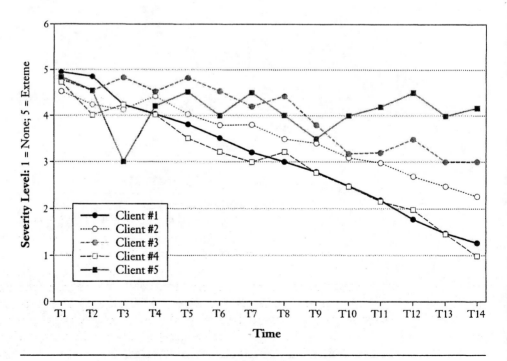

**FIGURE 5.2**   *Five Clients: Scores on Body Sensations Questionnaire*

scores electronically via e-mail, on Web sites, at professional conferences, or in professional journal articles.

The ideographic information generated from service to clients is, in effect, the property of various stakeholders in the process. Clients themselves obviously have a say in how data they provide or produce may be used. This is especially important when narrative information about them is conveyed. Clients have a right to anonymity and privacy, but they also should be informed about what will be shared, with whom, and in what form. Essentially, clients must grant permission for the information to be used in the specified manner.

The programs and agencies that employ social workers also have a say in data generated during the course of service to clients. Consult with agency administrators about policies and procedures for acceptable use. Sometimes boards of directors may need to provide consent as well. In general, you may anticipate that most managers and directors will applaud the collection, analysis, and dissemination of practice-effectiveness information, especially if they are assured that clients' rights are fully protected.

Social workers affiliated with universities, large hospitals, and certain other settings must comply with federal guidelines to protect human participants in research studies. Sometimes named Institutional Review Board or Human Subjects Review, an office usually provides guidance to researchers and processes requests.

## *Applying and Evaluating: Exercises*

The following exercises represent opportunities to strengthen learning about the application and evaluation processes of evidence-based social work. Word process your responses and label the computer file *EBSW Ch5 Applying and Evaluating Exercises.*

1. Describe the essential aspects of the application and evaluation processes of evidence-based social work.

2. Go to the Web site of the U.S. National Library of Medicine at http://www .nlm.nih.gov. Click on the hyperlinked icon to access the search page of the Medline/PubMed bibliographic database (http://www.ncbi.nlm.nih.gov/entrez/query.fcgi). Enter the search string *social OR psychosocial,* and click on **Go.** Make note of the number of citations returned. While looking at the first page of returns, click on the **Limits** button just beneath the search window that contains the phrase "social OR psychosocial." Under the **Limited to** section, you should notice a window entitled **Publication Types.** Click on the down arrow to reveal a drop-down menu. Click on **Practice Guideline** to limit the search to publications of that particular type. Move your cursor back up to the search window, and click on **Go.** Note the number of citation returns. Glance through the reference titles and make note of those articles that might apply to social workers. You could check the select box adjacent to each relevant citation and use the copy and paste functions of your Internet browser and word processor to record them to a computer file.

3. Go the National Guidelines Clearinghouse at http://www.guidelines.gov. Enter the search string *social OR psychosocial* in the search window. Before clicking the **Submit** button, select **All Results** from the **Results (per page)** drop-down menu. Now click **Submit**. Make note of the number of results. Glance through the titles, and record those guidelines that might apply to social workers. You could check the select box adjacent to each relevant citation and use the copy and paste functions of your Internet browser and word processor to record them to a computer file.

4. Go the National Guidelines Clearinghouse at http://www.guidelines.gov. Enter the string *case management substance abuse* in the search window. After you click the **Submit** button, a list of citations should appear. Among the first several should be one entitled "Substance Abuse Treatment for Persons with Child Abuse and Neglect Issues" and another identified as "Comprehensive Case Management for Substance Abuse Treatment." Click on either hyperlinked title to review a brief summary of the guideline. Scroll to the bottom of the brief summary to locate the section labeled Guideline Availability. Below that should be a hyperlinked reference to the National Library of Medicine Health Services/Technology Assessment Text (HSTAT) Web site that maintains an electronic copy of the guideline. Click on that link to go to the front page of either "TIP 36: Substance Abuse Treatment for Persons with Child Abuse and Neglect Issues" or "TIP 27: Comprehensive Case Management for Substance Abuse Treatment." Adjacent to the heading Table of Contents is a **View** button. Click on that button to access the interactive table of contents for the complete practice guideline. Read each section of the guideline by clicking on the chapter title. Start with the front matter and proceed through the entire document. When finished, prepare a short essay to explore how the guideline might be used in service to a relevant client. Incorporate a brief discussion of the potential benefits as well as the possible risks associated with application of this particular guideline in actual practice.

5. Login to the Research Navigator Web site at http://www.researchnavigator .com. Select the helping professions, nursing, health, and medicine, and psychology bibliographic databases. Search for and locate "A Brief Behavioral Activation Treatment for Depression: Treatment Manual" by C.W. Lejuez, D. R. Hopko, and S. D. Hopko, published in the April 2001 issue of the journal *Behavior Modification* and available in full-text version through Research Navigator. The authors describe a treatment manual for use by depressed clients. Read the article. When finished, prepare a short essay to explore how the manual might be used in service with a depressed client. Incorporate a brief discussion of the potential benefits as well as the possible risks associated with application of this particular guideline in actual practice.

**6.** Go to Library of Congress on-line catalog at http://catalog.loc.gov. Choose **Basic Search,** enter the string *treatment manual* in the **Search Text** window, and select **Title** in the **Search Type** window. Click on the **Begin Search** button. Scan the resulting book citations. Make note of those that might be of use to social workers. Be sure to highlight those that might relate to your own practice-effectiveness question. After that, follow the same process with the search string *practice guideline*, again making note of those books that might be of use to social workers and especially those that might pertain to your practice-effectiveness question. Finally, conduct the two searches with the same strings, but this time select **Keyword** as the **Search Type.** Make note of the different number of hits when searching keywords rather than titles.

**7.** Refer back to your own practice-effectiveness project. If you have not yet identified a relevant evidence-based practice guideline or manual, use the search skills processes you have learned to locate one. Be sure to look for books as well as articles and reports. If you cannot find one that matches your target client group, locate a good-quality practice manual for service for persons affected by another social problem. Record the complete reference for the manual.

**8.** Refer to the format for a practice manual outline (Box 5.1) presented earlier in this chapter. Use the outline to prepare an abbreviated summary of a practice manual for service to members of the client group you selected. If you located an appropriate evidence-based practice manual or guideline, you may use it as a source. If such documents are unavailable, create an abbreviated practice manual from the evidence of practice effectiveness you have discovered. Take up to five double-spaced pages to prepare the practice manual summary.

# *Epilogue*

Congratulations! You have reached the end of *The Evidence-Based Social Work (EBSW) Skills Book*. Completion of the exercises acquainted you with the skills and processes associated with EBSW. You learned to formulate a practice-effectiveness question, search for relevant information, analyze and evaluate its quality, synthesize the evidence, and prepare a practice-effectiveness evidence report as a basis for the application of evidence-based practices in service to clients.

You now recognize that evidence appears in diverse forms and reflects various levels of quality. You learned to distinguish authority-based from research-based information, and primary from secondary source material, and you became acquainted with literature reviews, systematic reviews, and meta-analyses as well as practice guidelines and manualized practices.

You also realize that evidence is not enough. In applying evidence of what works, you must incorporate the ethical principles of the profession and respect the wisdom derived from practice experience. Furthermore, you must carefully consider the implications of evidence for the particular characteristics, values, cultural experience, and choices of the people you serve. Nomothetic evidence of effectiveness does not guarantee that a practice will produce positive outcomes with each and every client. Ideographic evaluation is required to determine whether what works generally also works for the real people you serve.

You may agree that evidence-based social work has enormous potential to contribute to the development of the profession and, more importantly, help improve the quality and effectiveness of services to clients. There are, however, obstacles to the acceptance and application of EBSW by social workers.

One obstacle involves the history and culture of the profession. Although social work educational programs in the United States have offered social work degrees for about a hundred years, a culture of research and scholarship has not truly accompanied the growth of the profession. As most social workers know, the origins of the profession in this country were associated with the charity organization society and settlement house movements around the beginning of the twentieth century. The earliest educational efforts involved agency-based training programs. In apprenticeships, novice social workers learned under the direct tutelage and supervision of more-experienced practitioners. Professional knowledge was fundamentally authority based in nature.

In the first decades of the profession, there were, of course, few practice-related research studies that could inform and guide program development and service delivery. As university-based social work education programs emerged during the early 1900s, classroom instruction supplemented agency-based training. The contemporary social work practicum experience, requiring more than four hundred hours at the BSW and nine hundred or more at the MSW level, reflects the continued importance placed on practical learning in agency-based settings under the supervision and instruction of experienced social workers. Reflecting the profession's special value for knowledge gained through experience and wisdom acquired from seasoned social workers, field practicums are highly prized by students and faculty alike. In a sense, they continue the apprenticeship legacy of a century ago and undoubtedly contribute greatly to the socialization and development of social work students. Unfortunately, schools and departments of social work do not typically place as high a value on research-based knowledge and research activities as important aspects of professional education.

According to the Bureau of Labor Statistics, there are nearly 750,000 educated social workers employed in the United States. The overwhelming majority of social workers do not engage in research activities, and a surprisingly small proportion regularly read the results of practice-effectiveness research studies. In earlier decades, authority-based information was often the only kind available to guide practice. Social workers had to rely on unsubstantiated theoretical approaches, their own practice experiences, and the advice of colleagues. This is no longer the case. In the twenty-first century, the nature and scope of research-based knowledge is enormous and is growing exponentially. Furthermore, the emergence of the World Wide Web, electronic bibliographic databases, sophisticated search processes, and publication of full-text articles and books makes such knowledge readily accessible to the vast majority of social workers and indeed to consumers of their services.

Numerous social work leaders and scholars have advocated for the development of a new kind of social work professional—one who is both researcher and practitioner. David Austin (1992), Peg Hess and Ed Mullin (1995), Eileen Gambrill (1997, 1999; 2001), Joel Fischer (1981, 1984, 1993), and several other prominent social workers have called for a change in the culture of the profession. Sometimes called "scientist-practitioners" (Bloom & Fischer, 1982) or "practitioner-researchers" (Hess & Mullen, 1995), contemporary social workers are envisioned as critically thinking, scholarly professionals interested in and capable of carefully reviewing and evaluating research studies, applying relevant findings in service delivery, and conducting small-scale practice-relevant research studies of their own services in their own agencies. Such practitioner-researchers are quite different from the historical conception of social workers as well-intentioned, caring people who are more artistic than scientific, and more intuitive or ideological than academic or analytical. Rather, they are scholarly social workers who seek out research-based knowledge and embrace research as a fundamental aspect of practice.

Growth and acceptance of evidence-based principles in social work may be impeded by an antiresearch theme that occasionally emerges from some professionals who suggest, in effect, that "nothing can be known for sure, so why bother with research studies. And those statistics! They are simply mysterious numbers and symbols. Nobody can understand them. Everybody knows you can find or create statistics to prove anything!"

Another obstacle may be recognized in statements such as "All clients are unique. Research studies are irrelevant to my practice activities. I need to develop individualized assessments and plans for each client. I cannot possibly base my service on research about the effectiveness of services to groups of other people. Social work is individually focused."

A variation may appear as "The relationship with clients is more important than anything else. I focus on developing and maintaining good rapport. Knowledge about specific techniques and practice approaches, and findings from research studies may be nice to know, but they are not as important as the person-to-person relationships we have with clients."

A social worker might say, "I don't have time to read the journals. I'm too busy trying to help clients. It's all I can do to serve the dozens of clients I have, and then the paperwork! You can't imagine the amount of documentation that's required for each service I provide. How can I possibly find the time and energy to read, too?"

Another might observe, "Almost every time I read a research paper that identifies a best practice, I run across another one that suggests that a different approach is best. It's simply too hard to analyze the studies and determine which one is more credible. To be honest, it takes too much thought. I'd rather work with people all day long than try to figure out which research study is best."

Such statements, of course, are common among highly stressed, overworked, underpaid professional social workers who fulfill incredibly responsible roles and functions in their efforts to serve people in need. It is indeed difficult to imagine how social workers could do much more than they do now. Asking them to search for, discover, analyze, and apply evidence of practice effectiveness would simply be too much. Requesting that they prepare a practice-effectiveness evidence report might put them over the edge!

As future social workers, you probably already recognize the challenges associated with personal and social change. Unless faced with life-threatening crises, human systems tend to reflect considerable inertia. Generally quite useful, such forces contribute to continuity, equilibrium, and predictability. When the established patterns and processes match contemporary needs, demands, and circumstances, forces of inertia work well. However, in times of change, adherence to old ways often becomes problematic. At some point, the negative effects of established practices become so apparent or severe that change appears desirable or perhaps tolerable. Many social workers and large numbers of organizations increasingly recognize they must be ready to learn, unlearn, and relearn almost continuously to address the numerous complex social problems affecting clients and society. Schools and departments of social work are also changing. Promulgated by the Council on Social Work Education, new Educational Policy and Accreditation Standards, effective in 2002, encourage programs to make changes to better prepare students for contemporary practice. In effect, social work programs must become evidence based in their evaluation of program effectiveness. Encouraged to adopt best practices in education and assess student outcomes, programs are expected to use evidence in processes of continuous quality improvement.

Experienced social workers who develop evidence-based skills and expend the extra effort to seek, read, and reflect upon practice-relevant research exemplify openness to change. Their colleagues may learn from their example. The profession's hope, however, rests in you and other social work students and the social work teachers who help you learn and grow. If you become critically thinking, scholarly, and evidence based during your academic studies and your practicum experiences, you may continue to do so after graduation, when you provide professional-quality help to people who deserve the most effective services available.

# References

Abel, E. M. (2000). Psychosocial treatments for battered women: A review of the empirical research. *Research on Social Work Practice, 10*(1), 55–77.

Agency for Healthcare Research and Quality. (2002). *Guidelines for ensuring the quality of information disseminated to the public.* Retrieved December 18, 2002, from http://www.dhhs.gov/infoquality/AHRQinfo.htm.

Agras, W. S., & Apple, R. F. (1999a). *Overcoming eating disorders client workbook: A cognitive behavioral treatment for bulimia nervosa and binge-eating disorder.* San Antonio, TX: TherapyWorks: The Psychological Corporation.

Agras, W. S., and Apple, R. F. (1999b). *Overcoming eating disorders: A cognitive behavioral treatment for bulimia nervosa and binge-eating disorder: Therapist guide.* San Antonio, TX: TherapyWorks: The Psychological Corporation.

Allness, D. J., and Knoedler, W. H. (1998). *The PACT model of community-based treatment for persons with severe and persistent mental illnesses: A manual for PACT start-up.* Arlington, VA: National Alliance for the Mentally Ill.

Alter, C., and Evans, W. (1990). *Evaluating your practice: A guide to self-assessment.* New York: Springer.

American Psychiatric Association. (1993a). *American Psychiatric Association practice guidelines for major depressive disorder in adults.* Washington, DC: Author.

American Psychiatric Association. (1993b). *American Psychiatric Association practice guidelines for eating disorders.* Washington, DC: Author.

American Psychiatric Association. (1995a). *American Psychiatric Association practice guideline for the treatment of patients with substance use disorders: Alcohol, cocaine, opiods.* Washington, DC: Author.

American Psychiatric Association. (1995b). American Psychiatric Association practice guideline for psychiatric evaluation of adults. *American Journal of Psychiatry, 152*(11, Supplement).

American Psychiatric Association. (1996a). *American Psychiatric Association practice guidelines.* Washington, DC: Author.

American Psychiatric Association. (1996b). American Psychiatric Association practice guideline for the treatment of patients with nicotine dependence. *American Journal of Psychiatry, 153*(10, Supplement).

American Psychiatric Association. (1997a). *American Psychiatric Association practice guideline for the treatment of patients with schizophrenia.* Washington, DC: Author.

American Psychiatric Association. (1997b). American Psychiatric Association practice guideline for the treatment of patients with Alzheimer's disease and other dementias of late life. *American Journal of Psychiatry, 154*(5, Supplement).

American Psychiatric Association. (1998). *American Psychiatric Association practice guidelines for the treatment of patients with panic disorder.* Retrieved February 2, 2002, from http://www.psych.org/clin_res/pg_panic.cfm.

American Psychiatric Association. (2000a). *American Psychiatric Association practice guideline for the treatment of patients with eating disorders.* Retrieved February 2, 2002, from http://www.psych.org/clin_res/guide.bk42301.cfm.

American Psychiatric Association. (2000b). *American Psychiatric Association practice guidelines for the treatment of patients with major depression.* Retrieved February 2, 2002, from http://www.psych.org/clin_res/Depression2e.book.cfm.

American Psychiatric Association. (2000c). *American Psychiatric Association practice guidelines for the treatment of patients with HIV/AIDS.* Retrieved February 2, 2002, from http://www.psych.org/clin_res/hivaids32001.cfm.

American Psychiatric Association. (2001). *American Psychiatric Association practice guidelines for the treatment of patients with borderline personality disorder.* Retrieved February 2, 2002, from http://www.psych.org/clin_res/borderline.index.cfm.

American Psychological Association. (2001). *Publication manual of the American Psychological Association* (5th ed.). Washington, DC: Author.

American Sociological Association. (1997). *American Sociological Association style guide* (2nd ed.). Washington, DC: American Sociological Association.

Antony, M. M., & Barlow, D. H. (Eds.). (2002). *Handbook of assessment and treatment planning for psychological disorders.* New York: Guilford.

Appraisal of Guidelines Research and Evaluation. (2001). *Introduction to the AGREE collaboration.* Retrieved November 18, 2002, from http://www.agreecollaboration.org/.

Appraisal of Guidelines Research and Evaluation. (2002). *AGREE instrument.* Retrieved December 18, 2002, from http://www.agreecollaboration.org/.

Audini, B., Marks, I. M., Lawrence, R. E., Connolly, J., & Watts, V. (1994). Home-based versus outpatient/in-patient care for people with serious mental illness. Phase II of a controlled study. *British Journal of Psychiatry, 165,* 204–210.

Austin, D. (1992). Findings of the NIMH task force on social work research. *Research on Social Work Practice, 2*(3), 311–322.

Azrin, N. H., & Besalel, V. B. (1979). *A parent's guide to bedwetting control.* New York: Pocket Books.

Badke, W. B. (1990). *The survivor's guide to library research: A simple, systematic approach to using the library and writing research papers.* Grand Rapids, MI: Zondervan Publishing.

Bakker, A., van Balkom, A. J., Spinhoven, P., Blaauw, B. M., & van Dyck, R. (1998). Follow-up on the treatment of panic disorder with or without agoraphobia: A quantitative review. *Journal of Nervous and Mental Disease, 186*(7), 414–419.

Barker, R. J. (1997). *[CD-ROM]. The social work dictionary* (3rd ed.). Washington, DC: NASW Press.

Barlow, D. H. (Ed.). (2001). *Clinical handbook of psychological disorders: A step-by-step treatment manual* (3rd ed.). New York: Guilford.

Barlow, D. H. (Ed.). (2002). *Anxiety and its disorders: The nature and treatment of anxiety and panic* (2nd ed.). New York: Guilford.

Barlow, D. H., & Cerny, J. A. (1988). *Psychological treatment of panic.* New York: Guilford.

Barlow, D. H., & Craske, M. G. (2000). *Mastery of your anxiety and panic: MAP-3: Client workbook* (3rd ed.). San Antonio, TX: TherapyWorks: The Psychological Corporation.

Barlow, D. H., Craske, M. G., Cerny, J. A., & Klosko, J. S. (1989). Behavioral treatment of panic disorder. *Behavior Therapy, 20,* 261–282.

Baucom, D. H., & Epstein, N. (1990). *Cognitive-behavioral marital therapy.* New York: Brunner/Mazel.

Beasley, D. (2000). *Beasley's guide to library research.* Toronto: University of Toronto Press.

Beck, A. T., Epstein, N., Brown, G., & Steer, R. A. (1988). An inventory for measuring clinical anxiety: Psychometric properties. *Journal of Consulting and Clinical Psychology, 56,* 893–897.

Beck, A. T., Rush, A. J., Shaw, B. F., & Emery, G. (1979). *Cognitive therapy of depression.* New York: Guilford.

Beebe, L. (Ed.). (1997). *An author's guide to social work journals* (4th ed.). Washington, DC: NASW Press.

Beers, M. H., & Berkow, R. (1999). *Merck manual of diagnosis and therapy.* Retrieved June 25, 2002, from http://www.merck.com/pubs/mmanual/.

Berghuis, D. J., & Jongsma, A. E., Jr. (2000). *The severe and persistent mental illness treatment planner.* New York: Wiley.

Berkow, R. (2000). *Merck manual of medical information—home edition.* Retrieved June 25, 2002, from http://www.merck.com/pubs/mmanual_home/.

Blanchard, E. B., & Andrasik, F. (1985). *Management of chronic headache: A psychological approach.* Elmsford, NY: Pergamon Press.

Bloom, M. (1995). Primary prevention overview. In R. L. Edwards (Ed.), *Encyclopedia of social work* (19th ed., Vol. 3, pp. 1895–1905). Washington, DC: NASW Press.

Bloom, M., & Fischer, J. (1982). *Evaluating practice: Guidelines for the accountable professional.* Englewood Cliffs, NJ: Prentice Hall.

Bloom, M., Fischer, J., & Orme, J. (2003). *Evaluating practice: Guidelines for the accountable professional* (4th ed.). Boston: Allyn & Bacon.

Blythe, B. (1992). Should undergraduate and graduate social work students be taught to conduct empirically-based practice? Yes! *Journal of Social Work Education, 28*(3), 260–263.

Blythe, B. J. (1995). Single-system design. In R. L. Edwards (Ed.), *Encyclopedia of social work* (19th ed., Vol. 3, pp. 2164–2168). Washington, DC: NASW Press.

Blythe, B. J., & Briar, S. (1985). Developing empirically based models of practice. *Social Work, 30*(6), 483–488.

Blythe, B. J., & Rodgers, A. Y. (1993). Evaluating our own practice: Past, present, and future trends. *Journal of Social Service Research, 18,* 101–119.

Bockian, N. R., & Jongsma, A. E., Jr. (2001). *The personality disorders treatment planner.* New York: Wiley.

Bolner, M. S., Dantin, D. B., & Murray, R. C. (1991). *Library research skills handbook*. Dubuque, IA: Kendall/Hunt.

Bond, G. R., Becker, D. R., Drake, R. E., & Vogler, K. M. (1997). A fidelity scale for the individual placement and support model of supported employment. *Rehabilitation Counseling Bulletin, 40,* 265–284.

Bond, G. R., Evans, L., Salyers, M. P., Williams, J., & Kim, H. K. (2000). Measurement of fidelity in psychiatric rehabilitation. *Mental Health Services Research, 2,* 75–87.

Bond, G. R., Miller, L. D., Krumwied, R. D., & Ward, R. S. (1988). Assertive case management in three CMHCs: A controlled study. *Hospital and Community Psychiatry, 39,* 411–418.

Bond, G. R., Vogler, K. M., Resnick, S. G., Evans, L. J., Drake, R. E., & Becker, D. R. (2001). Dimensions of supported employment: Factor structure of the IPS fidelity scale. *Journal of Mental Health, 10*(4), 383–393.

Bond, G. R., Witheridge, T. F., Dincin, J., Wasmer, D., Webb, J., & De Graaf-Kaser, R. (1990). Assertive community treatment for frequent users of psychiatric hospitals in a large city: A controlled study. *American Journal of Community Psychology, 18,* 865–891.

Borenstein, M., & Rothstein, H. (1999). *Comprehensive meta analysis: A computer program for research synthesis [Manual]*. Englewood, NJ: Biostat.

Bourke, M. L., & Van Hasselt, V. B. (2001). Social problem-solving skills training for incarcerated offenders: A treatment manual. *Behavior Modification, 25*(2), 163–186.

Bourne, E. J. (1998a). *Overcoming specific phobia: Client manual*. Oakland, CA: New Harbinger.

Bourne, E. J. (1998b). *Overcoming specific phobia: Therapist protocol*. Oakland, CA: New Harbinger.

Bowen, G. L., Martin, B. R., & Nelson, J. P. (2002). A community capacity response to family violence in the military. In A. R. Roberts & G. J. Greene (Eds.), *Social workers' desk reference* (pp. 551–557). New York: Oxford University Press.

Boyer, W. (1995). Serotonin uptake inhibitors are superior to imipramine and alprazolam in alleviating panic attacks: A meta-analysis. *International Clinical Psychopharmacology, 10,* 45–49.

Brewer, M. B., & Collins, B. E. (Eds.). (1981). *Scientific inquiry and the social sciences*. San Francisco: Jossey-Bass.

Briar, S. (1990). *Empiricism in clinical practice: Present and future*. Silver Spring, MD: NASW Press.

Brown, T., O'Leary, T., & Barlow, D. H. (1994). Generalized anxiety disorder. In D. H. Barlow (Ed.), *Clinical handbook of psychological disorders* (2nd ed.). New York: Guilford.

Brown, T. A., O'Leary, T. A., & Barlow, D. H. (2001). Generalized anxiety disorder. In D. H. Barlow (Ed.), *Clinical handbook of psychological disorders: A step-by-step treatment manual* (3rd ed.). New York: Guilford.

Budney, A. J., & Higgins, S. T. (1998). *Manual 2: A community reinforcement approach: Treating cocaine addition*. Washington, DC: National Institute on Drug Abuse, U.S. Department of Health and Human Services, National Institutes of Health.

Bush, C. T., Langford, M. W., Rosen, P., & Gott, W. (1990). Operation outreach: Intensive case management for severely psychiatrically disabled adults. *Hospital and Community Psychiatry, 41,* 647–649.

Buttell, F. (2002). Group intervention models with domestic violence offenders. In A. R. Roberts & G. J. Greene (Eds.), *Social workers' desk reference* (pp. 714–717). New York: Oxford University Press.

Campbell Collaboration. (2001). *About the Campbell Collaboration*. Retrieved April 21, 2003, from http://www.campbellcollaboration.org/FraAbout .html.

Campbell, D. T., Cook, T. D., & Cook, T. H. (1979). *Quasi-experimentation*. Chicago: Rand McNally.

Campbell, D. T., & Stanley, J. C. (1966). *Experimental and quasi-experimental designs for research*. Chicago: Rand McNally.

Carlson, B. E., & Maciol, K. (1997). Domestic violence: Gay men and lesbians. In R. L. Edwards (Ed.), *Encyclopedia of social work* (19th, 1997 Supplement ed., pp. 101–111). Washington, DC: NASW Press.

Carroll, K. M. (1998). *Manual 1: A cognitive-behavioral approach: Treating cocaine addition*. Washington, DC: National Institute on Drug Abuse, U.S. Department of Health and Human Services, National Institutes of Health.

Chalk, R., King, P.A., National Research Council, & Institute of Medicine (Eds.). (1998). Violence in families: Assessing prevention and treatment programs. Washington, DC: National Academy Press.

Chambless, D. L., Baker, M. J., Baucom, D. H., Beutler, L.E., Calhoun, K. S., Crits-Christoph, P., Daiuto, A., DeRubeis, R., Detweiler, J., Haaga, D. A., Johnson, S. B., McCurry, S., Mueser, K. T., Pope, K. S., Sanderson, W. C., Shoham, V., Stickle, T., Williams, D. A., Woody, S. R. (1998). An update on empirically validated therapies, II. *Clinical Psychologist, 51*(1), 3–16.

Chambless, D. L., Caputo, G. C., Bright, P., & Gallagher, R. (1984). Assessment of fear in agoraphobics: The Body Sensations Questionnaire and the Agoraphobic Cognitions Questionnaire. *Journal of Consulting and Clinical Psychology, 52,* 1090–1097.

Chambless, D. L., Caputo, G., Gracely, S., Jasin, E., & Williams, C. (1985). The Mobility Inventory for agoraphobia. *Behaviour Research and Therapy, 23,* 35–44.

Chambless, D. L., & Gillis, M. M. (1993). Cognitive therapy of anxiety disorders. *Journal of Consulting and Clinical Psychology, 61,* 248–260.

Chambless, D. L., & Hollon, S. D. (1998). Defining empirically supported therapies. *Journal of Consulting and Clinical Psychology, 66*(1), 7–19.

Chambless, D. L., Sanderson, W. C., Shoham, V., Johnson, S. B., Pope, K. S., Crits-Christoph, P., et al. (1996). An update on empirically validated therapies. *Clinical Psychologist, 49*(2), 5–18.

Chandler, D., Meisel, J., McGowen, M., Mintz, J., & Madison, K. (1996). Client outcomes in two model capitated integrated service agencies. *Psychiatric Services, 47,* 175–180.

Cheetham, J. (1992). Evaluating social work effectiveness. *Research on Social Work Practice, 2*(3), 265–287.

Chicago Editorial Staff. (1993). *The Chicago manual of style: The essential guide for writers, editors, and publishers* (14th ed.). Chicago: University of Chicago Press.

Clark, D. M. (1989). Anxiety states: Panic and generalized anxiety. In K. Hawton, P. Salkovskis, J. Kirk & D. M. Clark (Eds.), *Cognitive behavior therapy for psychiatric problems: A practical guide.* (pp. 52–96). Oxford: Oxford University Press.

Clark, D. M. (1996). Panic disorder: From theory to therapy. In P. M. Salkovskis (Ed.), *Frontiers of cognitive therapy* (pp. 318–344). New York: Guilford.

Clarke, M., & Oxman, A. D. (Eds.). (2002). *Cochrane reviewers handbook 4.1.5 [updated April 2002]. In the Cochrane Library, Issue 2, 2002.* Oxford, UK: Update Software: Updated Quarterly.

Clum, G. A., Broyles, S., Borden, J., & Watkins, P. L. (1990). Validity and reliability of the Panic Attack Symptoms and Cognition Questionnaire. *Journal of Psychopathology and Behavioral Assessment, 12,* 233–245.

Cluzeau, F. A., Burgers, J. S., Brouwers, M., Grol, R., Mäkelä, M., Littlejohns, P., et al. (2002). Development and validation of an international appraisal instrument for assessing the quality of clinical practice guidelines: The AGREE project. *Quality and Safety in Health Care, 11*(4).

Cochrane, A. L. (1972). *Effectiveness and efficiency: Random reflections on the health service.* London: Nuffield Provincial Hospitals Trust.

Cochrane, A. L. (1973). Debate over effectiveness and efficiency. Reply to Professors Sanazaro, Williamson, and Hart. *International Journal of Health Service, 3*(3), 507–509.

Cochrane, A. L. (1989). Archie Cochrane in his own words. Selections arranged from his 1972 introduction to "Effectiveness and Efficiency: Random Reflections on the Health Services" 1972. *Control Clinical Trials, 10*(4), 428–433.

The Cochrane Collaboration. (2001). *The Cochrane reviewers' handbook glossary.* Oxford: The Cochrane Collaboration.

Cohen, J. A. (1988). *Statistical power analysis for the behavioral sciences* (2nd ed.). Hillsdale, NJ: Lawrence Earlbaum Associates.

Cook, T. D., & Campbell, D. T. (Eds.). (1979). *Quasi-experimentation: Design and analysis issues for field settings.* Chicago: Rand McNally.

Cook, T. D., Cooper, H., Cordray, D. S., Hartmann, H., Hedges, L., Light, R. J., et al. (1992). *Meta-analysis for explanation: A casebook.* New York: Russell Sage Foundation.

Cooke, D. D., McNally, L., Mulligan, K. T., Harrison, M. J. G., & Newman, S. P. (2001). Psychosocial interventions for caregivers of people with dementia: A systematic review. *Aging and Mental Health, 5*(2), 120–135.

Corcoran, J. (2000). Family treatment of preschool behavior problems. *Research on Social Work Practice, 10*(5), 547–589.

Corcoran, K., & Fischer, J. (1987). *Measures for clinical practice: A sourcebook.* New York: The Free Press.

Corcoran, K. J. (1993). Practice evaluation: Problems and promises of single-system designs in clinical practice. *Journal of Social Service Research, 18,* 147–159.

Cournoyer, B. R., & Powers, G. T. (2002). Evidence-based social work: The quiet revolution continues. In A. R. Roberts & G. J. Greene (Eds.), *Social workers' desk reference* (pp. 798–807). New York: Oxford University Press.

Cournoyer, B. R., & Stanley, M. J. (2002). *The social work portfolio: Planning, assessing and documenting lifelong learning in a dynamic profession.* Pacific Grove, CA: Brooks/Cole.

Craske, M. G., Antony, M. M., & Barlow, D. H. (1998). *Mastery of your specific phobia: Therapist guide.* San Antonio, TX: TherapyWorks: The Psychological Corporation.

Craske, M. G., & Barlow, D. H. (2001). Panic disorder and agoraphobia. In D. H. Barlow (Ed.), *Clinical handbook of psychological disorders: A step-by-step treatment manual* (3rd ed., pp. 1–59). New York: Guilford.

Craske, M. G., Barlow, D. H., & Antony, M. M. (1998). *Mastery of your specific phobia: Client workbook*. San Antonio, TX: TherapyWorks: The Psychological Corporation.

Craske, M. G., Barlow, D. H., & Meadows, E. A. (2000). *Mastery of your anxiety and panic: MAP-3: Therapist guide for anxiety, panic, and agoraphobia* (3rd ed.). San Antonio, TX: TherapyWorks: The Psychological Corporation.

CSWE. (2001). *Educational policies and accreditation standards*. Retrieved January 23, 2002, from http://www.cswe.org/epas.htm.

Daley, D. C., & Marlatt, G. A. (1998a). *Managing your drug or alcohol problem: Client workbook*. San Antonio, TX: TherapyWorks: The Psychological Corporation.

Daley, D. C., & Marlatt, G. A. (1998b). *Managing your drug or alcohol problem: Therapist guide*. San Antonio, TX: TherapyWorks: The Psychological Corporation.

Dattilio, F. M., & Jongsma, A. E., Jr. (2000). *The family therapy treatment planner*. New York: Wiley.

Davenport, J. (1992). Continuing social work education: The empirical base and practice guidelines. *Journal of Continuing Social Work Education, 5*(3), 27–30.

Davies, M. (2000). *The Blackwell encyclopaedia of social work*. Oxford: Blackwell.

Davies, M. (Ed.). (2002). *The Blackwell companion to social work* (2nd ed.). Malden, MA: Blackwell.

Davis, L. V. (1989). Empirical clinical practice from a feminist perspective: A response to Ivanoff, Robinson, and Blythe. *Social Work, 34*(6), 557–558.

Davis, L. V. (1995). Domestic violence. In R. L. Edwards (Ed.), *Encyclopedia of social work* (19th ed., Vol. 1, pp. 780–789). Washington, DC: NASW Press.

Davis, M. K., & Gidycz, C. A. (2000). Child sexual abuse prevention programs: A meta-analysis. *Journal of Clinical Child Psychology, 29*(2), 257–265.

Deaton, W. S., & Hertica, M. (2001a). *Growing Free: A manual for survivors of domestic violence*. New York: Haworth Maltreatment and Trauma Press.

Deaton, W. S., & Hertica, M. (2001b). *A therapist's guide to Growing Free: A manual for survivors of domestic violence*. New York: Haworth Maltreatment and Trauma Press.

Deffenbacher, J., & McKay, M. (2000a). *Overcoming situational and general anger: Client manual*. Oakland, CA: New Harbinger.

Deffenbacher, J., & McKay, M. (2000b). *Overcoming situational and general anger: Therapist protocol*. Oakland, CA: New Harbinger.

DeGood, D. E., Crawford, A. L., & Jongsma, A. E., Jr. (1999). *The behavioral medicine treatment planner*. New York: Wiley.

Delaney, J. (1987). *Learning legal reasoning: Briefing, analysis and theory*. Bogota, NJ: John Delaney Publications.

Detrich, R. (1999). Increasing treatment fidelity by matching interventions to contextual variables within the educational setting. *School Psychology Review, 28*(4), 608–621.

Dickersin, K. (1990). The existence of publication bias and risk factors for its occurrence. *Journal of American Medical Association, 263*(10), 1385–1389.

Drake, R. E., Goldman, H. H., Leff, H. S., Lehman, A. F., Dixon, L., Mueser, K. T., et al. (2001). Implementing evidence-based practices in routine mental health service settings. *Psychiatric Services, 52*(2), 179–182.

Drake, R. E., Mueser, K. T., Torrey, W. C., Miller, A. L., Lehman, A. F., Bond, G. R., Goldman, H. H. & Leff, H. S. (2000). Evidence-based treatment of schizophrenia. *Current Psychiatry Report, 2*(5), 393–397.

Edwards, R. L. (Ed.). (1995). *Encyclopedia of social work* (19th ed.). Washington, DC: NASW Press.

Edwards, R. L. (Ed.). (1997). *Encyclopedia of social work* (19th, 1997 Supplement ed.). Washington, DC: NASW Press.

Elam, G. A., & Kleist, D. M. (1999). Research on the long-term effects of child abuse. *Family Journal, 7*(2), 154–161.

Emery, G. (1999). *Overcoming depression: Therapist protocol*. Oakland, CA: New Harbinger.

Emery, G. (2000). *Overcoming depression: Client manual*. Oakland, CA: New Harbinger.

Engel, S. M. (1990). *With good reason: An introduction to informal fallacies*. New York: St. Martin's Press.

Fairburn, C. G. (1985). Cognitive-behavioral treatment for bulimia. In D. M. Garner & P. E. Garfinkel (Eds.), *Handbook of psychotherapy for anorexia nervosa and bulimia*. New York: Plenum.

Fairburn, C. G., & Brownell, K. D. (Eds.). (2002). *Eating disorders and obesity: A comprehensive handbook* (2nd ed.). New York: Guilford.

Fairburn, C. G., & Wilson, G. T. (Eds.). (1993). *Binge eating: Nature, assessment, and treatment*. New York: Guilford.

Fall, K. A., Howard, S., & Ford, J. E. (1999). *Alternatives to domestic violence: A homework manual for battering intervention groups*. Philadelphia: Accelerated Development.

Field, M. J., & Lohr, K. N. (Eds.). (1990). *Clinical practice guidelines: Directions for a new program.* Washington, DC: National Academy.

Fink, A. (1998). *Conducting research literature reviews: From paper to the Internet.* Thousand Oaks, CA: Sage.

Fischer, J. (1981). The social work revolution. *Social Work, 26*(3), 199–207.

Fischer, J. (1984). Revolution, schmevolution: Is social work changing or not? *Social Work, 29,* 74–75.

Fischer, J. (1993). Empirically-based practice: The end of an ideology? *Journal of Social Service Research, 18*(1), 19–64.

Fischer, J., & Corcoran, K. (1994). *Measures for clinical practice: A sourcebook* (2nd ed.). New York: The Free Press.

Foa, E. B., & Franklin, M. E. (2001). Obsessive-compulsive disorder. In D. H. Barlow (Ed.), *Clinical handbook of psychological disorders: A step-by-step treatment manual* (3rd ed.). New York: Guilford.

Ford, R., Barnes, A., Davies, R., Chalmers, C., Hardy, P., & Muijen, M. (2001). Maintaining contact with people with severe mental illness: 5-year follow-up of assertive outreach. *Social Psychiatry Psychiatric Epidemiology., 36*(9), 444–447.

Forehand, R., & McMahon, R. J. (1981). *Helping the noncompliant child: A clinician's guide for parent training.* New York: Guilford.

Forgatch, M., & Patterson, G. R. (1987). *Parents and adolescents living together—Part 2: Family problem solving.* Eugene, OR: Castalia Publishing.

Foxx, R. M., & Azrin, N. H. (1989). *Toilet training in less than a day.* New York: Simon & Schuster.

Fraser, M. (1995). Violence overview. In R. L. Edwards (Ed.), *Encyclopedia of social work* (19th ed., Vol. 3, pp. 2453–2460). Washington, DC: NASW Press.

Fraser, M., Taylor, M. E., Jackson, R., & O'Jack, J. (1991). Social work and science: Many ways of knowing? *Social Work Research and Abstracts, 27*(4), 5–15.

Frazer, D. W., & Jongsma, A. E., Jr. (1998). *The older adult psychotherapy treatment planner.* New York: Wiley.

Friedland, D. J. (Ed.). (1998). *Evidence-based medicine: A framework for clinical practice.* New York: Lange Medical Books/McGraw-Hill.

Friend, C., & Mills, L. G. (2002). Domestic violence and child protective services: Risk assessments. In A. R. Roberts & G. J. Greene (Eds.), *Social workers' desk reference* (pp. 679–684). New York: Oxford University Press.

Gambrill, E. (1994). What's in a name? Task-centered, empirical, and behavioral practice. *Social Service Review, 68*(4), 578–599.

Gambrill, E. (1997). Social work education: Current concerns and possible futures. In M. Reisch & E. Gambrill (Eds.), *Social work in the 21st century* (pp. 317–327). Thousand Oaks, CA: Pine Forge Press.

Gambrill, E. (1999). Evidence-based practice: An alternative to authority-based practice. *Families in Society, 80*(4), 341–350.

Gambrill, E. (2001). Social work: An authority-based profession. *Research on Social Work Practice, 11*(2), 166–176.

Garner, D. M., & Garfinkel, P. E. (Eds.). (1997). *Handbook of treatment for eating disorders* (2nd ed.). New York: Guilford.

Gerdes, K. E., & Edmonds, R. M. (1996). A statewide survey of licensed clinical social workers' use of practice evaluation procedures. *Research on Social Work Practice, 6*(1), 27–40.

Ghaderi, A., & Andersson, G. (1999). Meta-analysis of CBT for bulimia nervosa: Investigating the effects using DSM-III-R and DSM-IV criteria. *Scandinavian Journal of Behaviour Therapy, 28*(2), 79–87.

Gibaldi, J. (1999). *MLA handbook for writers of research papers* (5th ed.). New York: Modern Language Association of America.

Gibbs, L., & Gambrill, E. (1996). *Critical thinking for social workers: A workbook.* Thousand Oaks, CA: Pine Forge Press.

Gibbs, L. E. (2002). How social workers can do more good than harm: Critical thinking, evidence-based clinical reasoning, and avoiding fallacies. In A. R. Roberts & G. J. Greene (Eds.), *Social workers' desk reference* (pp. 752–756). New York: Oxford University Press.

Gilson, M., & Freeman, A. (2000). *Overcoming depression: A cognitive therapy approach for taming the depression beast: Client workbook.* San Antonio, TX: TherapyWorks: The Psychological Corporation.

Glazer, A., Glock, M. H., & Page, F. E. (1997, June). *Current bibliographies in medicine 97-3: Domestic violence assessment by health care practitioners.* Bethesda, MD: United States Department of Health and Human Services, Public Health Service, National Institutes of Health, National Library of Medicine.

Gondolf, E. W., & White, R. J. (2001). Batterer program participants who repeatedly reassault. *Journal of Interpersonal Violence, 16*(4), 361–381.

Gottman, J. M., & DeClaire, J. (2001). *The relationship cure: A five-step guide for building better connections with family, friends, and lovers.* New York: Crown Publishers.

Gottman, J. M., & Silver, N. (1999). *The seven principles for making marriage work.* New York: Crown Publishers.

Gould, R. A., Otto, M. W., & Pollack, M. H. (1995). A meta-analysis of treatment outcome for panic disorder. *Clinical Psychology Review, 15*(8), 819–844.

Greenhalgh, T. (1997). *How to read a paper: The basics of evidence based medicine.* London: BMJ Publishing.

Gresham, F. M. (1989). Assessment of treatment integrity in school consultation and prereferral intervention. *School Psychology Review, 18,* 37–50.

Gresham, F. M., Gansle, K. R., & Noell, G. H. (1993). Treatment integrity in applied behavior analysis with children. *Journal of Applied Behavior Analysis, 26,* 257–263.

Gresham, F. M., Gansle, K. R., Noell, G. H., Cohen, S., & Rosenblum, S. (1993). Treatment integrity in school-based intervention studies: 1980–1990. *School Psychology Review, 22,* 254–272.

Gresham, F. M., MacMillan, D. L., Beebe-Frankenberger, M. E., & Bocian, K. M. (2000). Treatment integrity in learning disabilities intervention research: Do we really know how treatments are implemented? *Learning Disabilities Research and Practice, 15*(4), 198–206.

Grinnell, R. M. (1997). *Social work research and evaluation: Quantitative and qualitative approaches* (5th ed.). Itasca, IL: F. E. Peacock.

Guyatt, G. H., Sackett, D. L., & Sinclair, J. C. (1995). Users' guide to the medical literature IX. A method for grading health care recommendations. *Journal of the American Medical Association, 274,* 1800–1804.

Hecker, J. E., & Thorpe, G. L. (1992). *Agoraphobia and panic: A guide to psychological treatment.* Boston: Allyn & Bacon.

Henderson, H. (Ed.). (2000). *Domestic violence and child abuse sourcebook.* Detroit, MI: Omnigraphics.

Henggeler, S. W. (1999). Multisystemic treatment of substance-abusing and dependent delinquents: Outcomes, treatment fidelity, and transportability. *Mental Health Services Research, 1*(3), 171–184.

Henggeler, S. W., Melton, G. B., Brondino, M. J., Scherer, D. G., & Hanley, J. H. (1997). Multisystemic therapy with violent and chronic juvenile offenders and their families: The role of treatment fidelity in successful dissemination. *Journal of Consulting and Clinical Psychology, 65*(5), 821–833.

Henggeler, S. W., Schoenwald, S. K., Liao, J. G., Letourneau, E. J., & Edwards, D. L. (2002). Transporting efficacious treatments to field settings: The link between supervisory practices and therapist fidelity in MST programs. *Journal of Clinical Child and Adolescent Psychology, 31*(2), 155–167.

Henggeler, S. W., Schoenwald, S. K., & Pickrel, S. G. (1995). Multisystemic therapy: Bridging the gap between university- and community-based treatment. *Journal of Consulting and Clinical Psychology, 63,* 709–717.

Herinckx, H. A., Kinney, R. F., Clarke, G. N., & Paulson, R. I. (1997). Assertive community treatment versus usual care in engaging and retaining clients with severe mental illness. *Psychiatric Services, 48,* 1297–1306.

Hersen, D. H., & Barlow, M. (1976). *Single case experimental designs.* New York: Pergamon Press.

Hess, P. M., & Mullen, E. J. (Eds.). (1995). *Practitioner-researcher partnerships: Building knowledge from, in, and for practice.* Washington, DC: NASW Press.

Heyes, C., & Huyll, D. L. (Eds.). (2001). *Selection theory and social construction: The evolutionary naturalistic epistemology of Donald T. Campbell.* Albany, NY: State University of New York Press.

Holosko, M. J., & Leslie, D. (1998). Obstacles to conducting empirically based practice. In J. S. Wodarski & B. A. Thyer (Eds.), *Handbook of empirical social work practice: Social problems and practice issues* (Vol. 2, pp. 433–451). New York: Wiley.

Hooper-Briar, K., & Lawson, H. (Eds.). (1996). *Expanding partnerships for vulnerable children and families.* Washington, DC: Council on Social Work Education.

Hope, D. A., Heimberg, R. G., Turk, C. L., & Juster, H. R. (2000). *Managing social anxiety: A cognitive-behavioral therapy approach: Client workbook.* San Antonio, TX: TherapyWorks: The Psychological Corporation.

Howard, M. O., & Jenson, J. M. (1999). Clinical practice guidelines: Should social work develop them? *Research on Social Work Practice, 9*(3), 283–301.

Hudson, W. W. (1990). *Partner abuse scales.* Temple, AZ: Walmyr Publishing.

Humphreys, C. (2002). Domestic violence. In M. Davies (Ed.), *Blackwell companion to social work* (2nd ed., pp. 36–42). Oxford: Blackwell Publishing.

Hunt, M. (1997). *How science takes stock: The story of meta-analysis.* New York: Russell Sage Foundation.

INFOMINE Scholarly Internet Resources Collections. (1994). *About INFOMINE.* Retrieved July 5, 2002, from http://infomine.ucr.edu/about/index.php.

Institute for the Advancement of Social Work Research. (2000). *The mission of IASWR.* Retrieved April 8, 2002, from http://www.cosw.sc.edu/iaswr/.

Institute for Clinical Systems Improvement. (2001). *Health care guideline: Domestic violence.* Bloomington, MN: Author.

Institute of Medicine. (Ed.). (1990). *Clinical practice guidelines: Directions for a new program.* Washington, DC: National Academy Press.

Isaac, N. E., & Enos, V. P. (2001, September). *National Institute of Justice research brief: Documenting domestic violence: How health care providers can help victims.* Washington, DC: United States Department of Justice, Office of Justice Programs, National Institute of Justice.

Isaac, S., & Michael, W. B. (1971). *Handbook in research and evaluation.* San Diego, CA: EdITS Publishers.

Ivanoff, A., Blythe, B. J., & Briar, S. (1987). The empirical clinical practice debate. *Social Casework: The Journal of Contemporary Social Work, 68*(5), 290–298.

Ivanoff, A., Robinson, E. A. R., & Blythe, B. J. (1987). Empirical clinical practice from a feminist perspective. *Social Work, 32,* 417–423.

Jackson, V. H. (1999). Clinical practice guidelines: Should social work develop them? *Research on Social Work Practice, 9*(3), 331–338.

Jacobson, N. S., & Margolin, G. (1979). *Marital therapy: Strategies based on social learning and behavior exchange principles.* New York: Brunner/Mazel.

Jayaratne, S., & Levy, R. L. (1979). *Empirical clinical practice.* New York: Columbia University Press.

Jongsma, A. E., Jr., & Peterson, L. M. (1999). *The complete adult psychotherapy treatment planner.* New York: Wiley.

Jongsma, A. E., Jr., Peterson, M., & McInnis, W. P. (2000a). *The adolescent psychotherapy treatment planner* (2nd ed.). New York: Wiley.

Jongsma, A. E., Jr., Peterson, M., & McInnis, W. P. (2000b). *The child psychotherapy treatment planner* (2nd ed.). New York: Wiley.

Kaplan, S. J. (Ed.). (1996). *Family violence: A clinical and legal guide.* Washington, DC: American Psychiatric Press.

Keefe, F. J., Beaupre, P. M., & Gil, K. M. (1997). Group therapy for patients with chronic pain. In R. J. Gatchel & D. C. Turk (Eds.), *Psychological treatments for pain: A practitioner's handbook.* New York: Guilford Press.

Khan, K. S., Popay, J., & Kleijnen, J. (2001). Stage I: Planning the review. Phase 2: Development of a review protocol. In K. S. Khan, G. ter Riet, J. Glanville, A. J. Sowden, & J. Kleijnen (Eds.), *Undertaking systematic reviews of research on effectiveness: CRD's guidance for those carrying out or commissioning reviews* (2nd ed.). York, UK: National Health Service Centre for Reviews and Dissemination, University of York.

Kirk, S. A. (1999). Good intentions are not enough: Practice guidelines for social work. *Research on Social Work Practice, 9*(3), 302–311.

Kirk, S. A., Osmalov, M., & Fischer, J. (1976). Social workers involvement in research. *Social Work, 21*(2), 121–132.

Klein, W. C., Bloom, M., & Chandler, S. M. (1994). *Is there an ethical responsibility to use practice methods with the best empirical evidence of effectiveness?* Boston: Allyn and Bacon.

Klerman, G. L., Weissman, M. M., Rounsaville, B. J., & Chevron, E. S. (1984). *Interpersonal psychotherapy of depression.* New York: Basic Books.

Knapp, S. E., & Jongsma, A. E., Jr. (2002). *The school counseling and school social work treatment planner.* New York: Wiley.

Kolski, T. D., Avriette, M., & Jongsma, A. E., Jr. (2001). *The crisis counseling and traumatic events treatment planner.* New York: Wiley.

Koocher, G. P., Norcross, J. C., & Hill S. S., III. (Eds.). (1998). *Psychologists' desk reference.* New York: Oxford University Press.

Kozak, M., & Foa, E. B. (1998a). *Mastery of obsessive-compulsive disorder: A cognitive-behavioral approach.* San Antonio, TX: TherapyWorks: The Psychological Corporation.

Kozak, M., & Foa, E. B. (1998b). *Mastery of obsessive-compulsive disorder: Client workbook.* San Antonio, TX: TherapyWorks: The Psychological Corporation.

Kozloff, M. A. (1979). *A program for families of children with learning and behavior problems.* New York: Wiley.

Kutchins, H. (1998). Does the fiduciary relationship guarantee a right to effective treatment? *Research on Social Work Practice, 8*(5), 615–622.

Last, J. M. (Ed.). (2001). *A dictionary of epidemiology.* New York: Oxford University Press.

Leahy, R. L., & Holland, S. J. (2000). *Treatment plans and interventions for depression and anxiety disorders.* New York: Guilford.

LeBlanc, M., & Ritchie, M. (2001). A meta-analysis of play therapy outcomes. *Counselling Psychology Quarterly, 14*(2), 149–164.

LeCroy, C. W. (Ed.). (1994). *Handbook of child and adolescent treatment manuals.* New York: Free Press.

Lehman, A. F., & Steinwachs, D. M. (1998a). Initial results from the Schizophrenia Patient Outcomes Research Team (PORT) client survey. *Schizophrenia Bulletin, 24*(1), 11–20.

Lehman, A. F., & Steinwachs, D. M. (1998b). Translating research into practice: The Schizophrenia Patient Outcomes Research Team (PORT) treatment recommendations. *Schizophrenia Bulletin, 24*(1), 1–10.

Lehmann, P., & Rabenstein, S. (2002). Children exposed to domestic violence: Assessment and treatment protocols. In A. R. Roberts & G. J.

Greene (Eds.), *Social workers' desk reference* (pp. 673–679). New York: Oxford University Press.

Lewis, B. Y. (1985). The wife abuse inventory: A screening device for identification of abused women. *Social Work, 30,* 32–35.

Ley, D. J., Jr. (2001). *Effectiveness of a court-ordered domestic violence treatment program: A clinical utility study.* Unpublished Ph.D., University of New Mexico, Albuquerque.

Liebert, R. M., & Houts, A. C. (1985). *Bedwetting: A guide for parents and children.* Springfield, IL: Charles C Thomas.

MacMillan, H. L., & Canadian Task Force on Preventive Health Care. (2000). Preventive health care, 2000 update: Prevention of child maltreatment. *Canadian Medical Association Journal, 163*(11), 1451–1458.

Mann, T. (1998). *The Oxford guide to library research.* New York: Oxford University Press.

March, J. S., Frances, A., Carpenter, D., & Kahn, D. A. (1997). The expert consensus guideline series: Treatment of obsessive-compulsive disorder. *Journal of Clinical Psychiatry, 58*(Supplement 4).

Marks, I. M., & Mathews, A. M. (1978). Brief standard self-rating for phobic patients. *Behaviour Research and Therapy, 17,* 263–267.

Marshall, L. L. (1992). Development of the Severity of Violence against Women Scales. *Journal of Family Violence, 7,* 103–121.

Marshall, M., & Lockwood, A. (2002). Assertive community treatment for people with severe mental disorders [Systematic Review]. *Cochrane Database of Systematic Reviews*(2).

Mathews, D. J. (1995). *Foundations for violence-free living: A step-by-step guide to facilitating men's domestic abuse groups.* Saint Paul, MN: Amherst H. Wilder Foundation.

Maxwell, C. D., Garner, J. H., & Fagan, J. A. (2001, July). *National Institute of Justice research brief: The effects of arrest on intimate partner violence: New evidence from the spouse assault replication program.* Washington, DC: United States Department of Justice, Office of Justice Programs, National Institute of Justice.

McClennen, J. C., & Gunther, J. (Eds.). (1999). *A professional's guide to understanding gay and lesbian domestic violence: Understanding practice interventions.* Lewiston, NY: E. Mellen.

McCue, M. L. (1995). *Domestic violence: A reference handbook.* Santa Barbara, CA: ABC-CLIO.

McEvoy, J. P., Scheifler, P. L., & Frances, A. (1999). The expert consensus guideline series: Treatment of schizophrenia 1999. *Journal of Clinical Psychiatry, 60*(Supplement 11), 1–80.

McGrew, J. H., Bond, G. R., Dietzen, L., & Salyers, M. (1994). Measuring the fidelity of implementation of a mental health program model. (Special Section: New Methods in Mental Health Research). *Journal of Consulting and Clinical Psychology, 62*(4), 270–279.

McInnis, W. P., Dennis, W. D., Myers, M. A., Sullivan, K. O. C., & Jongsma, A. E., Jr. (2002). *The juvenile justice and residential care treatment planner.* New York: Wiley.

Meichenbaum, D. (1985). *Stress inoculation training.* New York: Pergamon Press.

Mercer, D. E., & Woody, G. E. (1999). *Manual 3: An individual drug counseling approach to treat cocaine addiction: The Collaborative Cocaine Treatment Study model.* Washington, DC: National Institute on Drug Abuse, U.S. Department of Health and Human Services, National Institutes of Health.

Miller, W. R. (1995). *Motivational enhancement therapy manual: A clinical research guide for therapists treating individuals with alcohol abuse and dependence.* Washington, DC: U.S. Government Printing Office.

Milrod, B., & Busch, F. (1996). Long-term outcome of panic disorder treatment: A review of the literature. *Journal of Nervous and Mental Disease, 184*(12), 723–730.

Moncher, F. J., & Prinz, R. J. (1991). Treatment fidelity in outcome studies. *Clinical Psychology Review, 11,* 247–266.

Mooney, L. A., Knox, D., & Schacht, C. (1997). *Understanding social problems.* Minneapolis/St. Paul, MN: West.

Moore, B. N., & Parker, R. (1995). *Critical thinking* (4th ed.). Mountain View, CA: Mayfield.

Mueser, K. T., Bond, G. R., Drake, R. E., & Resnick, S. G. (1998). Models of community care for severe mental illness: A review of research on case management. *Schizophrenia Bulletin, 24*(1), 37–74.

Murphy, L. L., Impara, J. C., & Plake, B. S. (Eds.). (2002). *Tests in print VI.* Lincoln, NE: University of Nebraska Press.

Myers, L. L., & Thyer, B. A. (1997). Should social work clients have the right to effective treatment? *Social Work, 42*(3), 288–299.

NASW. (1999). *Code of ethics of the National Association of Social Workers.* Washington, DC: National Association of Social Workers.

NASW. (2000). *Announcing NASW's Practice Research Network!* Retrieved February 25, 2002, from http://www.socialworkers.org/naswprn/default.htm.

Nathan, P. E., & Gorman, J. M. (Eds.). (1998). *A guide to treatments that work.* New York: Oxford University Press.

National Alliance for the Mentally Ill. (1998, October 6). *NAMI announces major national initiative to promote a treatment program with 25-year successful track record*. Retrieved July 15, 2002, from http://www.nami.org/pressroom/981006215423.html.

National Guideline Clearinghouse. (2000a). *About the National Guideline Clearinghouse*. Retrieved February 3, 2002, from http://www.guidelines.gov/FRAMESETS/static_fs.asp?view=about.

National Guideline Clearinghouse. (2000b). *Inclusion criteria*. Retrieved February 3, 2002, from http://www.guidelines.gov/FRAMESETS/static_fs.asp?view=about.inclusion.

National Library of Medicine. *MeSH browser*. Retrieved August 17, 2002, from http://www.ncbi.nlm.nih.gov/entrez/meshbrowser.cgi?term=%22child+abuse%22&retrievestring=&mbdetail=y.

National Library of Medicine. (2002, April 25). *MeSH vocabulary*. Retrieved May 18, 2002, from http://www.nlm.nih.gov/bsd/pubmed_tutorial/m1009.html

New Harbinger Publications. (2001). *Best practices for therapy series*. Retrieved July 18, 2002, from http://www.newharbinger.com/shproto.htm.

NHS Centre for Reviews and Dissemination. (2000). Psychosocial interventions for schizophrenia. *Effective Health Care: Bulletin of the University of York NHS Centre for Reviews and Dissemination, 6*(3), 1–8.

Oehrberg, S., Christiansen, P. E., Behnke, K., Borup, A. L., Severin, B., Soegaard, J., et al. (1995). Paroxetine in the treatment of panic disorder: A randomised, double-blind, placebo-controlled study. *British Journal of Psychiatry, 167,* 374–379.

Oei, T. P., Llamas, M., & Devilly, G. J. (1999). The efficacy and cognitive processes of cognitive behaviour therapy in the treatment of panic disorder with agoraphobia. *Behavioural and Cognitive Psychotherapy, 27*(1), 63–88.

Oher, J. M., Conti, D. J., & Jongsma, A. E., Jr. (1998). *The employee assistance treatment planner.* New York: Wiley.

O'Leary, K. D., Heyman, R. E., & Jongsma, A. E., Jr. (1998). *The couples psychotherapy treatment planner.* New York: Wiley.

Ortiz, E., Eccles, M., Grimshaw, J., & Woolf, S. (2002). *Current validity of clinical practice guidelines. Technical review 6 (AHRQ Publication No. 02–0035)*. Rockville, MD: Agency for Healthcare Research and Quality.

Orwin, R. G. (2000). Assessing program fidelity in substance abuse health services research.

*Addiction, 95*(11, Supplement 3), 309–328.

Paleg, K., & Jongsma, A. E., Jr. (1999). *The group therapy treatment planner*. New York: Wiley.

Parrillo, V. N. (2002). *Contemporary social problems* (5th ed.). Boston: Allyn & Bacon.

Patterson, G. R., & Forgatch, M. (1987). *Parents and adolescents living together—Part 1: The basics.* Eugene, OR: Castalia Publishing.

Patterson, G. R., Reid, J. B., Jones, R. R., & Conger, R. E. (1975). *A social learning approach to family interaction* (Vol. 1). Eugene, OR: Castalia Publishing.

Paul, R. (1993). *Critical thinking: What every person needs to survive in a rapidly changing world* (3rd ed.). Santa Rosa, CA: Foundation for Critical Thinking.

Penka, C., & Kirk, S. (1991). Practitioner involvement in clinical evaluation. *Social Work, 36,* 1513–1518.

Perkinson, R. R., & Jongsma, A. E., Jr. (2001). *The addiction treatment planner* (2nd ed.). New York: Wiley.

Petrosino, A., Turpin-Petrosino, C., & Buehler, J. (2002a). "Scared Straight" and other juvenile awareness programs for preventing juvenile delinquency (Cochrane Review Abstract). *The Cochrane Library, 2002.*

Petrosino, A., Turpin-Petrosino, C., & Buehler, J. (2002b). "Scared Straight" and other juvenile awareness programs for preventing juvenile delinquency (Cochrane Review). *The Cochrane Database of Systematic Reviews*(2).

Plake, B. S., & Impara, J. C. (Eds.). (2001). *The fourteenth mental measurements yearbook.* Lincoln, NE: Buros Institute of Mental Measurements.

Pomeroy, E. C., Rubin, A., & Walker, R. J. (1995). Effectiveness of a psychoeducational and task-centered group intervention for family members of people with AIDS. *Social Work Research, 19*(3), 142–153.

Powers, G. T. (1999). Scholarly product rating inventory. Indianapolis, IN: Indiana University School of Social Work.

The Psychological Corporation. *TherapyWorks*. Retrieved July 28, 2002, from http://www.psyccorp.com/catalogs/paipc/psy105cpri.htm.

Pusey, H., & Richards, D. (2001). A systematic review of the effectiveness of psychosocial interventions for carers of people with dementia. *Aging and Mental Health, 5*(2), 107–120.

Rapee, R. M., Craske, M. G., & Barlow, D. H. (1995). Assessment instrument for panic disorder that includes fear of sensation-producing activities: The Albany Panic and Phobia Questionnaire. *Anxiety, 1,* 114–122.

Rapee, R. M., Craske, M. G., Brown, T. A., & Barlow, D. H. (1996). Measurement of perceived control over anxiety-related events. *Behavior Therapy, 27,* 279–293.

Rapp-Paglicci, L. A., Roberts, A. R., & Wodarski, J. S. (Eds.). (2002). *Handbook of violence.* New York: Wiley.

Raw, S. D. (1998). Who is to define effective treatment for social work clients? *Social Work, 43*(1), 81–87.

Reid, W. J. (1992). *Task strategies: An empirical approach to clinical social work.* New York: Columbia University Press.

Reid, W. J. (1994). The empirical practice movement. *Social Service Review, 68*(2), 165–184.

Reiss, S., Peterson, R., Gursky, D., & McNally, R. (1986). Anxiety sensitivity, anxiety frequency, and the predictions of fearfulness. *Behaviour Research and Therapy, 24,* 1–8.

Rennison, C. M., & Welchans, S. (2002). *Bureau of Justice Statistics special report: Intimate partner violence.* Retrieved August 18, 2002, from http://www.ojp.usdoj.gov/bjs/pub/pdf/ipv.pdf.

Resick, P. A., & Schnicke, M. K. (1993). *Cognitive processing therapy for rape victims: A treatment manual.* Thousand Oaks, CA: Sage.

Richey, C., Blythe, B., & Berlin, S. (1987). Do social workers evaluate their practice? *Social Work Research and Abstracts, 23*(23), 14–20.

Richey, C. A., & Roffman, R. A. (1999). On the sidelines of guidelines: Further thoughts on the fit between clinical guidelines and social work practice. *Research on Social Work Practice, 9*(3), 311–322.

Roberts, A. R. (Ed.). (2002). *Handbook of domestic violence intervention strategies: Policies, programs, and legal remedies.* Oxford: Oxford University Press.

Roberts, A. R., & Greene, G. J. (Eds.). (2002). *Social workers' desk reference.* New York: Oxford University Press.

Rosen, A., & Proctor, E. K. (2002). Standards for evidence-based social work practice: The role of replicable and appropriate interventions, outcomes, and practice guidelines. In A. R. Roberts & G. J. Greene (Eds.), *Social workers' desk reference* (pp. 743–751). New York: Oxford University Press.

Rosen, G. M. (1999). Treatment fidelity and research on eye movement desensitization and reprocessing (EMDR). *Journal of Anxiety Disorders, 13*(1–2), 173–184.

Rosenberg, G., & Holden, G. (1992). Social work effectiveness: A response to Cheetham. *Research on Social Work Practice, 2*(3), 288–296.

Rosenthal, R. (1991). *Meta-analytic procedures for social research.* Newbury Park, CA: Sage.

Rosenthal, R., & Rosnow, R. L. (1991). *Essentials of behavioral research: Methods and data analysis* (2nd ed.). New York: McGraw Hill.

Rosnow, R. L., Rosenthal, R., & Rubin, D. B. (2000). Contrasts and correlations in effect-size estimation. *Psychological Science: A Journal of the American Psychological Society, 11*(6), 446–453.

Roth, A., & Fonagy, P. (Eds.). (1996). *What works for whom? A critical review of psychotherapy research.* New York: Guilford.

Rothbaum, B. O., & Foa, E. B. (2000a). *Reclaiming your life after rape: A cognitive-behavioral therapy for PTSD.* San Antonio, TX: TherapyWorks: The Psychological Corporation.

Rothbaum, B. O., & Foa, E. B. (2000b). *Reclaiming your life after rape: A cognitive-behavioral therapy for PTSD: Client workbook.* San Antonio, TX: TherapyWorks: The Psychological Corporation.

Rothman, J., Damron-Rodriguez, J., & Shenassa, E. (1994). Systematic research synthesis: Conceptual integration methods of meta-analysis. In J. R. E. Thomas (Ed.), *Intervention research: Design and development for human service* (pp. 133–154). Binghamton, NY: Haworth Press.

Royse, D. (1995). *Research methods in social work* (2nd ed.). Chicago: Nelson-Hall.

Rubin, A., & Babbie, E. (2001). *Research methods for social work* (4th ed.). Belmont, CA: Wadsworth.

Rusin, M. J., & Jongsma, A. E., Jr. (2001). *The rehabilitation psychology treatment planner.* New York: Wiley.

Sackett, D. L., Straus, S. E., Richardson, W. S., Rosenberg, W., & Haynes, R. B. (2000). *Evidence-based medicine: How to practice and teach EBM* (2nd ed.). New York: Churchill Livingstone.

Salkovskis, P. M., & Clark, D. M. (1991). Cognitive treatment of panic disorder. *Journal of Cognitive Psychotherapy, 3,* 215–226.

Sanders, M. R., & Dadds, M. R. (1993). *Behavioral family intervention.* Needham Heights, MA: Allyn & Bacon.

Sanderson, W. C., & Woody, S. R. (1995). Manuals for empirically validated treatments: A project of the Task Force on Psychological Interventions. *The Clinical Psychologist, 48*(4), 7–11.

Saunders, D. G. (1995). Domestic violence: Legal issues. In R. L. Edwards (Ed.), *Encyclopedia of social work* (19th ed., Vol. 1, pp. 789–795). Washington, DC: NASW Press.

Schaedle, R., McGrew, J. H., Bond, G. R., & Epstein, I. (2002). A comparison of experts' perspectives on assertive community treatment and intensive case management. *Psychiatric Services, 53*(2), 207–210.

Schinke, S. P., & Nugent, W. R. (1994). *Are some research methodologies inherently more worthy of professional endorsement than others?* Boston: Allyn and Bacon.

Schoenwald, S. K., Henggeler, S. W., Brondino, M. J., & Rowland, M. D. (2000). Multisystemic therapy: Monitoring treatment fidelity. *Family Process, 39*(1), 83–104.

Scott, J. E., & Dixon, L. B. (1995). Assertive community treatment and case management for schizophrenia. *Schizophrenia Bulletin, 21*(4), 657–668.

Sheldon, B., & Chilvers, R. (2000). *Evidence-based social care: A study of prospects and problems.* Dorset, England: Russell House.

Shermer, M. (1997). *Why people believe weird things: Pseudoscience, superstition, and other confusions of our time.* New York: W. H. Freeman Company.

Siegel, D. (1984). Defining empirically based practice. *Social Work, 29*(4), 325–337.

Siegel, D. H. (1985). Effective teaching of empirically based practice. *Social Work Research and Abstracts, 21*(1), 40–48.

Singer, M. I., & Hussey, D. L. (1995). Adolescents: Direct practice. In R. L. Edwards (Ed.), *Encyclopedia of social work* (19th ed., Vol. 1, pp. 40–48). Washington, DC: NASW Press.

Slaggert, K., Jongsma, A. E., Jr., & Berghuis, D. J. (2000). *The mental retardation and developmental disability treatment planner.* New York: Wiley.

Slavin, R. E. (1986). Best-evidence synthesis: An alternative to meta-analytic and traditional reviews. *Educational Researcher, 15*, 5–11.

Smyth, L. (1999a). *Overcoming post-traumatic stress disorder: Client manual.* Oakland, CA: New Harbinger.

Smyth, L. (1999b). *Overcoming post-traumatic stress disorder: Therapist protocol.* Oakland, CA: New Harbinger.

Society for Social Work and Research. (2000). *About SSWR.* Retrieved April 8, 2002, from http://www.sswr.org/home.htm.

Startup, M., & Shapiro, D. A. (1993). Therapist treatment fidelity in prescriptive vs. exploratory psychotherapy. *British Journal of Clinical Psychology, 32*, 443–456.

Stein, L. I., & Santos, A. B. (1998). *Assertive community treatment of persons with severe mental illness.* New York: Norton.

Steketee, G. (1993). *Treatment of obsessive compulsive disorder.* New York: Guilford.

Steketee, G. (1999). Yes, but cautiously. *Research on Social Work Practice, 9*(3), 343–347.

Steketee, G. S. (1999a). *Overcoming obsessive-compulsive disorder: Client manual.* Oakland, CA: New Harbinger.

Steketee, G. S. (1999b). *Overcoming obsessive-compulsive disorder: Therapist protocol.* Oakland, CA: New Harbinger.

Stern, J. M., & Simes, R. J. (1997). Publication bias: Evidence of delayed publication in a cohort study of clinical research projects. *British Medical Journal, 315*, 640–645.

Stout, C. E., & Jongsma, A. E., Jr. (1997). *The continuum of care treatment planner.* New York: Wiley.

Straus, M. A. (1979). Measuring intrafamily conflict and violence: The Conflict Tactics (CT) Scales. *Journal of Marriage and the Family, 39*, 75–88.

Straus, M. A. (1990). The Conflict Tactics (CT) Scale and its critics: An evaluation and new data on validity and reliability. In *Physical violence in American families: Risk factors and adaptations to violence in 8,145 families* (pp. 49–73). New Brunswick, NJ: Transaction.

Straus, M. A., Hamby, S. L., Boney-McCoy, S., & Sugarman, D. B. (1996). The revised Conflict Tactics Scales (CTS2): Development and preliminary psychometric data. *Journal of Family Issues, 17*, 283–316.

Substance Abuse and Mental Health Services Administration Center for Substance Abuse Treatment. (2000). *Substance abuse treatment for persons with child abuse and neglect issues: Treatment improvement protocol (TIP) series 36.* Rockville, MD: Department of Health and Human Services.

Sutton, A. J., Abrams, K. R., Jones, D. R., Sheldon, T. A., & Song, F. (2000). *Methods for meta-analysis in medical research.* New York: Wiley.

Teague, G. B., Bond, G. R., & Drake, R. E. (1998). Program fidelity in assertive community treatment: Development and use of a measure. *American Journal of Orthopsychiatry, 68*, 216–232.

Teare, R., & Sheafor, B. W. (1995). *Practice-sensitive social work education.* Washington, DC: Council on Social Work Education.

Temple University Department of Psychology Social Phobia Program. (n.d.). *Cognitive behavioral group therapy for social phobia.* Philadelphia: Author.

Thyer, B. A. (1996). Forty years of progress toward empirical clinical practice? *Social Work Research, 20*(2), 77–82.

Thyer, B. A., & Myers, L. L. (1999). On science, antiscience, and the client's right to effective treatment. *Social Work, 44*(5), 501–505.

Thyer, B. A., & Strean, H. S. (1992). Should social workers be well trained in behavioral principles? In E. D. Gambrill & R. Pruger (Eds.), *Controversial issues in social work* (pp. 79–91). Boston: Allyn and Bacon.

Thyer, B. A., & Wodarski, J. S. (Eds.). (1998). *Handbook of empirical social work practice* (Vol. 1). New York: Wiley.

Toulmin, S. (2001). *Return to reason*. Cambridge: Harvard University Press.

Trull, T. J., Nietzel, M. T., & Main, A. (1988). The use of meta-analysis to assess the clinical significance of behavior therapy for agoraphobia. *Behavior Therapy, 19*, 527–538.

Turabian, K. L., Grossman, J., & Bennett, A. (1996). *A manual for writers of term papers, theses, and dissertations* (6th ed.). Chicago: University of Chicago Press.

Turk, C. L., Heimberg, R. G., & Hope, D. A. (2001). Social anxiety disorder. In D. H. Barlow (Ed.), *Clinical handbook of psychological disorders: A step-by-step treatment manual* (3rd ed.). New York: Guilford.

Turk, D. C., Meichenbaum, D., & Genest, M. (1983). *Pain and behavioral medicine: A cognitive-behavioral perspective*. New York: Guilford.

Turner, S. M., Beidel, D. C., & Cooley, M. (1997). *Social effectiveness therapy: A program for overcoming social anxiety and phobia*. Toronto: Multi-Health Systems.

Tutty, L. (1990). The response of community mental health professionals to client's rights: A review and suggestions. *Canadian Journal of Community Mental Health, 9*(1), 1–24.

U.S. Department of Health and Human Services. (1999). *Mental health: A report of the surgeon general*. Rockville, MD: Department of Health and Human Services, Substance Abuse and Mental Health Services Administration, Center for Mental Health Services, National Institutes of Health, National Institute of Mental Health.

United States National Library of Medicine. (2000, February 1). *Fact sheet: Medical subject headings (MeSH®)*. Retrieved May 16, 2002, from http://www.nlm.nih.gov/pubs/factsheets/mesh.html.

van Balkom, A. J., Bakker, A., Spinhoven, P., Blaauw, B. M., Smeenk, S., & Ruesink, B. (1997). A meta-analysis of the treatment of panic disorder with or without agoraphobia: A comparison of psychopharmacological, cognitive-behavioral, and combination treatments. *Journal of Nervous and Mental Disease, 185*(8), 510–516.

van Balkom, A. J., Nauta, M. C., & Bakker, A. (1995). Meta-analysis on the treatment of panic disorder with agoraphobia: Review and re-examination. *Clinical Psychology and Psychotherapy, 2*(1), 1–14.

Vandiver, V. L. (2002). Step-by-step practice guidelines for using evidence-based practice and expert consensus in mental health settings. In A. R. Roberts & G. J. Greene (Eds.), *Social workers' desk reference* (pp. 731–738). New York: Oxford University Press.

Van Hasselt, V. B., & Hersen, M. (Eds.). (1996). *Sourcebook of psychological treatment manuals for adult disorders*. New York: Plenum.

Van Hasselt, V. B., & Hersen, M. (Eds.). (1998). *Handbook of psychological treatment protocols for children and adolescents*. Mahwah, N.J.: Erlbaum.

Videka-Sherman, L. (1988). Meta-analysis of research on social work practice in mental health. *Social Work, 33*, 325–338.

Videka-Sherman, L. (1995). Meta-analysis. In R. L. Edwards (Ed.), *Encyclopedia of social work* (19th ed., Vol. 2, pp. 1711–1720). Washington, DC: NASW Press.

Wambach, K. G., Haynes, D. T., & White, B. W. (1999). Practice guidelines: Rapprochement or estrangement between social work practitioners and researchers. *Research on Social Work Practice, 9*(3), 322–331.

Weiberg, N. (1992). Commentary on "Social Work and Science: Many Ways of Knowing?" *Social Work Research and Abstracts, 28*(2), 21–23.

Weinbach, R. W. (2004). *Statistics for social workers* (6th ed.). Boston: Allyn & Bacon.

Weissman, M. M. (2000). *Mastering depression through interpersonal psychotherapy: Patient workbook*. San Antonio, TX: TherapyWorks: The Psychological Corporation.

Weissman, M. M., Markowitz, J. C., & Klerman, G. L. (2000). *Comprehensive guide to interpersonal psychotherapy*. New York: Basic Books.

West Group. (1999). *Federal rules of evidence: 1999–2000 edition*. St. Paul, MN: Author.

White, J. R. (1999a). *Overcoming generalized anxiety disorder: Client manual: A relaxation, cognitive restructuring, and exposure-based protocol for the treatment of GAD*. Oakland, CA: New Harbinger.

White, J. R. (1999b). *Overcoming generalized anxiety disorder: Therapist protocol*. Oakland, CA: New Harbinger.

Williams, J. B. W., & Lanigan, J. (1999). Practice guidelines in social work: A reply, or "Our glass is half full." *Research on Social Work Practice, 9*(3), 338–343.

Wilson, G. T. (1966). Manual-based treatments: The clinical application of research findings. *Behavioral Research and Therapy, 34*, 295–314.

Wilson, K. J. (1997). *When violence begins at home: A comprehensive guide to understanding and ending domestic abuse*. Alameda, CA: Hunter House Publishers.

Winkelstern, J. A., & Jongsma, A. E., Jr. (2001). *The special education treatment planner*. New York: Wiley.

Witkin, S. L. (1992a). Empirical clinical practice or Witkin's revised views: Which is the issue? *Social Work, 37*(5), 465–468.

Witkin, S. L. (1992b). Should empirically-based practice be taught in BSW and MSW programs? No! *Journal of Social Work Education, 28*(3), 265–269.

Witkin, S. L. (1993). The right to effective treatment and the effective treatment of rights: Rhetorical empiricism and the politics of research. *Social Work, 43*(1), 75–81.

Wodarski, J. S., Rapp-Paglicci, L. A., Dulmus, C., & Jongsma, A. E., Jr. (2000). *The social work and human services treatment planner*. New York: Wiley.

Woody, S. R., & Sanderson, W. C. (1998). Manuals for empirically supported treatments: 1998 update. *The Clinical Psychologist, 51*(1), 17–21.

Yegidis, B. L., & Weinbach, R. W. (2002). *Research methods for social workers* (4th ed.). Boston: Allyn and Bacon.

Yegidis, B. L., Weinbach, R. W., & Morrison-Rodriquez, B. (1999). *Research methods for social workers* (3rd ed.). Boston: Allyn and Bacon.

Zuercher-White, E. (1999a). *Overcoming agoraphobia and panic disorder: Client manual*. Oakland, CA: New Harbinger.

Zuercher-White, E. (1999b). *Overcoming agoraphobia and panic disorder: Therapist protocol*. Oakland, CA: New Harbinger.

# Index

Abel, E. M., 87
Abrams, K. R., 162, 164
Agency for Healthcare Quality and
    Research (AHQR), 8, 103, 167
Agras, W. S., 10, 183
Allness, D. J., 176
Alter, C., 188
American Psychiatric Association, 5,
    156–157, 157–158, 166
American Psychological Association, 5, 10,
    163–164
American Sociological Association (ASA),
    27
Analyzing in EBSW, 17, 118–178
    authority-based evidence, 123, 146–147
    evidence evaluation, 17–18, 118–172
    grading evidence, 168
    research-based evidence, 123, 148–167
    synthesizing evidence, 172–178
Andrasik, F., 10
Antony, M. M., 10, 183, 186
Anxiety Disorders Association of
    America, 5
Apple, R. F., 10, 183
Applying and evaluating in EBSW, 17–18,
    179–193
    applying, 17–18, 179–183, 191–193
    evaluating, 17–18, 186–193
Appraisal Guidelines for Research and
    Evaluation (AGREE), 167
Assessment tools
    formulating questions about, 30
    types of, 187
Audini, B., 176
Austin, D., 195
Authority-based evidence, 123, 146–147
Avriette, M., 183, 184
Azrin, N. H., 10

Babbie, E., 151, 153
Badke, W. B., 50
Baker, M. J., 10, 163, 164
Bakker, A., 186, 187
Barker, R. J., 25
Barlow, D. H., 10, 182, 183, 186, 187
Barlow, M., 188
Barnes, A., 176

Baucom, D. H., 10, 163, 164
Beasley, D., 50
Beaupre, P. M., 10
Beck, A. T., 10, 187
Becker, D. R., 184, 188
Beebe, L., 129
Beebe-Frankenberger, M. E., 181
Beers, M. H., 74
Behnke, K., 187
Beidel, D. C., 10
Bennett, A., 57
Berghuis, D. J., 183, 184
Berkow, R., 74
Berlin, S., 2
Besalel, V. B., 10
Beutler, L. E., 10, 163, 164
Bibliographic databases, 42–43, 53, 85–100
Bibliographic reference lists, 68–71, 92–96
Blaauw, B. M., 186, 187
Blanchard, E. B., 10
Bloom, M., 2, 159, 188, 195
Blythe, B. J., 2, 3, 5, 188
Bocian, K. M., 181
Bockian, N. R., 184
Bolner, M. S., 41, 50
Bond, G. R., 176, 184, 188
Boney-McCoy, S., 68
Books, 42, 71–74
    practice guidelines and standards, 73,
        146, 166–167
    practice handbooks and manuals, 71,
        72, 179–186
Boolean logic, 52–55
Borden, J., 187
Borenstein, M., 165
Borup, A. L., 187
Bourke, M. L., 180
Bourne, E. J., 182
Bowen, G. L., 68
Boyer, W., 186
Brewer, M. B., 13
Briar, S., 3, 5
Bright, P., 187
Brondino, M. J., 181, 184, 188
Brouwers, M., 121, 167
Brown, G., 187
Brown, T., 10

Brown, T. A., 187
Brownell, K. D., 10
Broyles, S., 187
Budney, A. J., 182
Buehler, J., 101, 102
Burgers, J. S., 121, 167
Busch, F., 187
Bush, C. T., 176
Buttell, F., 68

C2-SPECTR, 103
Calhoun, K. S., 10, 163, 164
Cambridge Scientific Abstracts, 93
Campbell, D. T., 13, 151, 153
Campbell Collaboration, 13–14, 102–103
Caputo, G. C., 187
Carlson, B. E., 68
Carpenter, D., 180
Carroll, K. M., 182
Centers for Disease Control (CDC), 25
Centre for Evidence-Based Social Services
    (CEBSS), 14
Cerny, J. A., 10, 186
Chalmers, C., 176
Chambless, D. L., 10, 163, 164, 186, 187
Chandler, D., 176
Chandler, S. M., 2
Cheetham, J., 5
Chevron, E. S., 10
Chilvers, R., 2
Christiansen, P. E., 187
Clark, D. M., 10, 186
Clarke, F. N., 176
Clarke, M., 164, 172
Classification of source, 121–124
ClinicalTrials database, 104
Clum, G. A., 187
Cluzeau, F. A., 121, 167
Cochrane, A. L., 164
Cochrane Collaboration, 9, 13, 101–103,
    119, 161–165
Cohen, J. A., 159
Cohen, S., 181
Collins, B. E., 13
Combined Health Information Database
    (CHID), 104
Conger, R. E., 10

Connolly, J., 176
Contents of evidence
  contents cards for, 57–63
  evaluating, 130–146
  source versus, 131
Conti, D. J., 184
Cook, T. D., 13, 151, 162
Cook, T. H., 13
Cooley, M., 10
Cooper, H., 162
Corcoran, J., 188
Corcoran, K., 30
Cordray, D. S., 162
Council on Social Work Education
  (CSWE), 1–2, 196
Cournoyer, B. R., 2, 4
Craske, M. G., 10, 183, 186, 187
Crawford, A. L., 184
Crits-Christoph, P., 10, 163, 164

Dadds, M. R., 10
Daiuto, A., 10, 163, 164
Daley, D. C., 183
Damron-Rodriguez, J., 118, 162
Dantin, D. B., 41, 50
Database searches
  bibliographic databases, 42–43, 53,
    85–100
  Boolean logic in, 52–55
  nature of databases, 51–52
Dattilio, F. M., 183
Davenport, J., 166
Davies, M., 68
Davies, R., 176
Davis, L. V., 5, 68
Deaton, W. S., 69
DeClaire, J., 10
Deffenbacher, J., 182
DeGood, D. E., 184
De Graaf-Kaser, R., 176
Delaney, J., 6
Dennis, W. D., 184
DeRubeis, R., 10, 163, 164
Detrich, R., 181, 184
Detweiler, J., 10, 163, 164
Devilly, G. J., 187
Dewey Decimal Classification (DDC),
  35–36
Dickersin, K., 162
Dictionaries, 66
Dietzen, L., 176
Dincin, J., 176
Dissertations, 42, 74–76
Dixon, L. B., 176
Documentation
  of search activities, 50, 55–63
Drake, R. E., 176, 184, 188
Dulmus, C., 184

EBSCO Publishing Services, 87–88, 95

EBSW. *See* Evidence-based social work
  (EBSW)
Eccles, M., 167
Edmonds, R. M., 2
Educational Resources Information
  Center (ERIC), 93
Edwards, J. L., 181, 184
Edwards, R. L., 34, 68
Effect size, 159–161
Emery, G., 10, 182
Empirically based practice (EBP), 3–4
Encyclopedias, 64–69
Engel, S. M., 143
Enos, V. P., 109
Epidemiology, 25
Epstein, I., 176
Epstein, N., 10, 187
Evaluation tools
  formulating questions about, 30
  types of, 187
Evans, L., 184
Evans, L. J., 188
Evans, W., 188
Evidence, 5–14
  defined, 3
  evaluating, 17–18, 118–172
  grading, 168, 169
  legal, 6–7
  medical, 7–9
  in psychology, 9–10
  in social work, 11–14
Evidence-based collaborations, 101–112
  Campbell Collaboration, 13–14,
    102–103
  Cochrane Collaboration, 9, 13,
    101–103, 119, 161–165
Evidence-based medicine (EBM), x, 3, 41,
  95, 101, 163, 164
Evidence-Based Practice Centers (EPC), 8
Evidence-based social work (EBSW), 1–20
  analyzing in, 17, 118–178
  applying in, 17–18, 179–186, 191–193
  in contemporary practice, 18–19
  defined, 4
  effectiveness of, 4–5
  evaluating in, 17–18, 186–193
  evidence as term, 3
  evidence types, 5–14
  nature of, 3–4
  phase overview, 15–18
  questioning in, 15–16, 21–48
  searching in, 16–17, 49–117
Evidence evaluation, 17–18, 118–172
  authority-based evidence, 123, 146–147
  contents of evidence, 130–146
  grading evidence, 168, 169
  research-based evidence, 123, 148–167
  source of evidence, 121–130
Evidence synthesis, 172–178
Expanded Academic ASAP, 87–88

External validity, 151, 153–154

Fagan, J. A., 109
Fairburn, C. G., 10
Fall, K. A., 70
False negative, 120
False positive, 120
FedStats, 108
Field, M. J., 166
FINDARTICLES, 97
Fink, A., 50
FirstGov, 108
Fischer, J., 1, 2, 3, 30, 159, 195
Foa, E. B., 10, 183
Fonagy, P., 148, 151
Ford, J. E., 70
Ford, R., 176
Forehand, R., 10
Forgatch, M., 10
Foxx, R. M., 10
Frances, A., 180
Franklin, M. E., 10
Fraser, M., 5, 68
Frazer, D. W., 183
Freeman, A., 183
Friedland, D. J., 20n
Friend, C., 68

Gallagher, R., 187
Gambrill, E., 3, 18, 143, 195
Gansle, K. R., 181
Garfinkel, P. E., 10
Garner, D. M., 10
Garner, J. H., 109
Genest, M., 10
Gerdes, K. E., 2
Gibaldi, J., 57
Gibbs, L., 143
Gil, K. M., 10
Gillis, M. M., 186
Gilson, M., 183
Glazer, A., 109
Glock, M. H., 109
Goldman, H. H., 176
Gondolf, E. W., 114–115
Gorman, J. M., 10, 155–158,
  171, 176
Gott, W., 176
Gottman, J. M., 10
Gould, R. A., 187
Government resources, 101–112
Gracely, S., 187
Grading evidence, 168, 169
Green, G. J., 68
Greenhalgh, T., 121, 155, 162, 164
Gresham, F. M., 181
Grimshaw, J., 167
Grinnell, R. M., 150, 151, 153
Grol, R., 121, 167
Grossman, J., 57

Guidelines, practice, 8–9, 73, 103, 146, 166–167
Gunther, J., 69
Gursky, D., 187
Guyatt, G. H., 121, 155, 162, 163, 172, 176

Haaga, D. A., 10, 163, 164
Hamby, S. L., 68
Handbooks, 71, 72, 179–186
Hanley, J. H., 181, 184
Hardy, P., 176
Hartmann, H., 162
Haynes, D. T., 166
Haynes, R. B., 20n
HealthFinder, 109
Health Services/Technology Assessment Text (HSTAT), 104
Hecker, J. E., 10
Hedges, L., 162
Heimberg, R. G., 10, 183
Henderson, H., 69
Henggeler, S. W., 181, 184, 188
Herinckx, H. A., 176
Hersen, D. H., 188
Hersen, M., 182
Hertica, M., 69
Hess, P. M., 195
Heyes, C., 13
Heyman, R. E., 183
Higgins, S. T., 182
Hill, S. S., III, 10
Holden, G., 6
Holland, S. J., 187
Hollon, S. D., 10
Holosko, M. J., 2
Hooper-Briar, K., 74
Hope, D. A., 10, 183
Houts, A. C., 10
Howard, M. O., 166
Howard, S., 70
Hudson, W. W., 68
Humphreys, C., 68
Hunt, M., 162
Hussey, D. L., 34
Huyll, D. L., 13

Ideographic dimensions of evidence, 4, 18
Impara, J. C., 30
Incidence rate, 25
INFOMINE Scholarly Internet Resources, 114
INFOTRIEVE, 97
INGENTA, 95–97
Institute for the Advancement of Social Work Research (IASWR), 11
Internal validity, 151–153
Inventories, 187
Isaac, N. E., 109, 151
Ivanoff, A., 5

Jackson, R., 5
Jackson, V. H., 166
Jacobson, N. S., 10
Jasin, E., 187
Jayartne, S., 3
Jenson, J. M., 166
Johnson, S. B., 10, 163, 164
Jones, D. R., 162, 164
Jones, R. R., 10
Jongsma, A. E., Jr., 183, 184
Journals, 42, 76–81, 86–87
Juster, H. R., 183

Kahn, D. A., 180
Kaplan, S. J., 69
Keefe, F. J., 10
Keywords, 16
  generating, 34–41
  planning searches based on, 41–48, 50
Khan, K. S., 119
Kim, H. K., 184
Kinney, R. F., 176
Kirk, S. A., 2, 19, 166
Kleijnen, J., 119
Klein, W. C., 2
Klerman, G. L., 10
Klosko, J. S., 186
Knapp, S. E., 184
Knoedler, W. H., 176
Knox, D., 26
Kolski, T. D., 183, 184
Koocher, G. P., 10
Kozak, M., 10, 183
Kozloff, M. A., 10
Krumwied, R. D., 176
Kutchins, H., 2

Langford, M. W., 176
Lanigan, J., 166
Last, J. M., 25
Lawrence, R. E., 176
Lawson, H., 74
Leahy, R. L., 187
LeCroy, C. W., 182
Leff, H. S., 176
Legal evidence, 6–7
Lehman, A. F., 176
Lehmann, P., 68
Leslie, D., 2
Letourneau, E. J., 181, 184
Levy, R. L., 3
Lewis, B. Y., 68
Ley, D. J., Jr., 75–76
Liao, J. G., 181, 184
Librarians' Index to the Internet, 114
Library of Congress Classification (LCC), 36–37
Library of Congress Subject Headings (LCSH), 35, 37, 39, 73
Library searches, 63–85
  books, 42, 71–74

dissertations, 42, 74–76
on-line services, 42–43, 71–74, 80–81
organization of resources, 42
professional and scientific journals, 42, 76–81, 86–87
reference works, 42, 64–71
Liebert, R. M., 10
Light, R. J., 162
Littlejohns, P., 121, 167
Llamas, M., 187
Lockwood, A., 119, 176
Logical fallacies, 142–146
Lohr, K. N., 166

Machine-Readable Cataloging (MARC) system, 39
Maciol, K., 68
MacMillan, D. L., 181
MacMillan, H. L., 9
Madison, K., 176
Main, A., 162, 187
Mäkela, M., 121, 167
Mann, T., 50
Manualization, 179–186
Manuals, 71, 72, 179–186
March, J. S., 180
Margolin, G., 10
Markowitz, J. C., 10
Marks, I. M., 176, 187
Marlatt, G. A., 183
Marshall, L. L., 68
Marshall, M., 119, 176
Martin, B. R., 68
Mathews, A. M., 187
Mathews, D. J., 69
Maxwell, C. D., 109
McClennen, J. C., 69
McCue, M. L., 69
McCurry, S., 10, 163, 164
McEvoy, J. P., 180
McGowen, M., 176
McGrew, J. H., 176
McInnis, W. P., 183, 184
McKay, M., 182
McMahon, R. J., 10
McMaster University (Canada), 7–8
McNally, R., 187
Meadows, E. A., 10, 183, 187
Medical evidence, 7–9
Medical Subject Headings (MeSH), 35, 37–39, 73
MEDLINE/PubMed, 37, 38, 52, 88, 89–93
Meichenbaum, D., 10
Meisel, J., 176
Melton, G. B., 181, 184
Mercer, D. E., 182
MeSH (Medical Subject Headings), 35, 37–39, 73
Meta-analyses, 165
Michael, W. B., 151

Miller, A. L., 176
Miller, L. D., 176
Miller, W. R., 182
Mills, L. G., 68
Milrod, B., 187
Mintz, J., 176
Moncher, F. J., 181
Mooney, L. A., 26
Moore, B. N., 142–143
Morbidity rate, 25
Morbidity risk, 25
Morrison-Rodriquez, B., 150–151, 153
Mueser, K. T., 10, 163, 164, 176
Muijen, M., 176
Mullen, E. J., 195
Multisystemic therapy (MST), 181
Murphy, L. L., 30
Murray, R. C., 41, 50
Myers, L. L., 2, 3, 6
Myers, M. A., 184

Nathan, P. E., 10, 155–158, 171, 176
National Alliance for the Mentally Ill
    (NAMI), 2, 5
National Association of Social Workers
    (NASW), 1–2, 12–13
National Clearinghouse on Child Abuse
    and Neglect Information, 104
National Guidelines Clearinghouse
    (NGC), 8–9, 103, 166, 167
National Institute of Mental Health
    (NIMH), 5, 11
National Institute on Alcohol Abuse and
    Alcoholism (NIAAA), 104
National Institutes of Health (NIH), 104
National Library of Medicine (NLM), 88,
    89–91, 104
Nauta, M. C., 187
Nelson, J. P., 68
Netting the Evidence, 8
Nietzel, M. T., 162, 187
Noell, G. H., 181
Nomothetic dimensions of evidence, 4, 18
Norcross, J. C., 10
NORTHERNLIGHT, 97
Note cards
    bibliographic source cards, 55–63, 126
    contents cards, 57–63
Nugent, W. R., 6

Oehrberg, S., 187
Oei, T. P., 187
Oher, J. M., 184
O'Jack, J., 5
O'Leary, K. D., 183
O'Leary, T., 10
Orme, J., 159
Ortiz, E., 167
Orwin, R. G., 184
Osmalov, M., 2
Otto, M. W., 187

OVID Technologies, 88, 95, 101
Oxman, A. D., 164, 172

Page, F. E., 109
Paleg, K., 183
Parker, R., 142–143
Parrillo, V. N., 26
Patterson, G. R., 10
Paul, R., 143
Paulson, R. I., 176
Pearson Research Navigator, 52, 86–91,
    95, 180
Penka, C., 2
Perkinson, R. R., 184
Peterson, L. M., 183
Peterson, R., 187
Petrosino, A., 101, 102
Pickrel, S. G., 181
Plake, B. S., 30
Planning searches, 41–48, 50
Pollack, M. H., 187
Pomeroy, E. C., 122
Popay, J., 119
Pope, K. S., 10, 163, 164
Powers, G. T., 2, 4, 121
Practice Effectiveness Evidence Report
    (PEER), 17, 18, 56–57, 118,
    172–178, 181
    format of, 172–176
    purpose of, 175–176
    sample argument, 176–177
Practice-effectiveness questions, 23–32
    asking about assessment and evaluation
        tools, 30
    asking about services, 30–31
    asking about social problems, 24–27
    asking about special populations, 23–24
    asking about target client groups, 27–29
Practice*Planners*, 183
Practice quality rating (PQR), 168, 169
Practice research networks (PRNs), 181
Prevalence rates, 25
Primary sources, 122
Prinz, R. J., 181
Proctor, E. K., 166
Professional journals, 42, 76–81, 86–87
Pseudo-reasoning, 142–146
Psychological Corporation (PsychCorp),
    183
Psychological evidence, 9–10

Quality, 121
    in classification of evidence, 124–130
    contents rating rubric, 131–142
    practice quality rating rubric (PQR),
        168, 169
    source rating rubric, 126–130
Questioning in EBSW, 15–16, 21–48
    formulating practice-effectiveness ques-
        tion, 23–32
    keyword generation, 32–41

nature of questions, 21–22
planning searches, 41–48, 50
synonym generation, 32–41
Questionnaires, 187

Rabenstein, S., 68
Randomized controlled trials (RCT), 148,
    150–151
Rapee, R. M., 187
Rapp-Paglicci, L. A., 69, 184
Raw, S. D., 6
Reference works, 42, 64–71
    bibliographic, 69, 70–71
    dictionaries, 66
    encyclopedias, 64–69
    other reference works, 67
Reid, J. B., 10
Reid, W. J., 3
Reiss, S., 187
Reliability, 149–151
Rennison, C. M., 108
Research-based evidence, 123, 148–167
    guide for analyzing, 160–161
    practice guidelines, 8–9, 73, 103, 146,
        166–167
    reliability, 149–151
    research papers, 154–161
    research syntheses, 161–165
    validity, 148–154
Research Navigator, 52, 86–91, 95, 180
Research papers, 154–161
    classification of, 155–157, 158
    effect size and, 159–161
    format of, 157–159
    reasons for rejection, 154–155
Research syntheses, 161–165
    hierarchical scheme for, 162–163
    meta-analyses, 165
reSearchWeb, 103
Resick, P. A., 182
Resnick, S. G., 176, 188
Richardson, W. S., 20n
Richey, C. A., 2, 166
Roberts, A. R., 68, 69, 70
Robinson, E. A. R., 5
Rodgers, A. Y., 188
Roffman, R. A., 166
Rosen, A., 166
Rosen, G. M., 181
Rosen, P., 176
Rosenberg, G., 6
Rosenberg, W., 20n
Rosenblum, S., 181
Rosenthal, R., 159
Rosnow, R. L., 159
Roth, A., 148, 151
Rothbaum, B. O., 183
Rothman, J., 118, 162
Rothstein, H., 165
Rounsaville, B. J., 10
Rowland, M. D., 181, 188

Royse, D., 151, 153
Rubin, A., 122, 151, 153
Rubin, D. B., 159
Ruesink, B., 187
Rush, A. J., 10
Rusin, M. J., 184

Sackett, D. L., 20n, 121, 155, 162, 163, 172, 176
Salkovskis, P. M., 10
Salyers, M. P., 176, 184
Sanders, M. R., 10
Sanderson, W. C., 10, 163, 164
Santos, A. B., 176
Saunders, D. G., 68
Schacht, C., 26
Schaedle, R., 176
Scheifler, P. L., 180
Scherer, D. G., 181, 184
Schinke, S. P., 6
Schnicke, M. K., 182
Schoenwald, S. K., 181, 184, 188
Scientific journals, 42, 76–81, 86–87
Scott, J. E., 176
Searching in EBSW, 16–17, 49–117
    basics, 51–63
    Boolean logic and, 52–55
    databases and, 51–52, 53, 85–100
    documenting search activities, 50, 55–63
    evidence-based collaborations, 101–112
    government resources, 101–112
    keywords in, 16, 32–41
    library searches, 63–85
    planning searches, 41–48, 50
    synonyms in, 16, 32–41
    World Wide Web, 43, 50, 112–117
Secondary sources, 122–123
Severin, B., 187
Shapiro, D. A., 181
Shaw, B. F., 10
Sheafer, B. W., 74
Sheldon, B., 2
Sheldon, T. A., 162, 164
Shenassa, E., 118, 162
Shermer, M., 142
Shoham, V., 10, 163, 164
Siegel, D., 3
Silver, N., 10
Simes, R. J., 162
Sinclair, J. C., 121, 155, 162, 163, 172, 176
Singer, M. l., 34
Slaggert, K., 184
Slavin, R. E., 118
Smeenk, S., 187
Smyth, L., 182
Social problems
    formulating questions about, 24–27
    list of contemporary, 26
    nature of, 25
Social services

formulating questions about, 30–31
    Social Services Citations Index, 93–95
Social work
    evidence in, 11–14
Social Work Abstracts (SWABS), 87, 91–93
Social Work Research Development Centers (SWRDC), 11–12
Society for Social Work and Research (SSWR), 12
Society for the Psychological Study of Social Issues (SPSSI), 27
Society for the Study of Social Problems (SSSP), 27
Society of Clinical Psychology, 163–164
Soegaard, J., 187
Song, F., 162, 164
Source of evidence
    contents versus, 131
    evaluating, 121–130
    source cards for, 55–63, 126
Special populations
    formulating questions about, 23–24
    nature of, 23–24
Spinhoven, P., 186, 187
Standards, practice, 73
Stanley, J. C., 13, 151, 153
Startup, M., 181
Steer, R. A., 187
Stein, L. I., 176
Steinwachs, D. M., 176
Steketee, G. S., 10, 166, 182
Stern, J. M., 162
Stickle, T., 10, 163, 164
Stout, C. E., 184
Straus, M. A., 68
Straus, S. E., 20n
Strean, H. S., 6
Style guides, 57–62
Sugarman, D. B., 68
Sullivan, K. O. C., 184
Sutton, A. J., 162, 164
Synonyms, 16
    generating, 32–34
    planning searches based on, 41–48, 50
Synthesizing evidence, 172–178

Target client groups
    formulating questions about, 27–29
    identifying, 15–16, 28–29
Taylor, M. E., 5
Teague, G. B., 184, 188
Teare, R., 74
TherapyWorks, 183
Thorpe, G. L., 10
Thyer, B. A., 2, 3, 6
Torrey, W. C., 176
Toulmin, S., 57, 143
True negative, 120
True positive, 120
Trull, T. J., 162, 187

Turabian, K. L., 57
Turk, C. L., 10, 183
Turk, D. C., 10
Turner, S. M., 10
Turning Research Into Practice (TRIP), 8, 103
Turpin-Petrosino, C., 101, 102
Tutty, L., 2

Ulrich's Periodical Directory, 81
United States Government Printing Office (GPO), 109
University Microfilms International (UMI), 74–76

Validity, 148–154
    external, 151, 153–154
    internal, 151–153
van Balkom, A. J., 186, 187
Vandiver, V. L., 166
van Dyck, R., 186
Van Hasselt, V. B., 180, 182
Videka-Sherman, L., 162
Vogler, K. M., 184, 188

Walker, R. J., 122
Wambach, K. G., 166
Ward, R. S., 176
Wasmer, D., 176
Watkins, P. L., 187
Watts, V., 176
Webb, J., 176
Weiberg, N., 6
Weinbach, R. W., 150–151, 153, 159
Weissman, M. M., 10, 183
Welchans, S., 108
White, B. W., 166
White, J. R., 182
White, R. J., 114–115
Williams, C., 187
Williams, D. A., 10, 163, 164
Williams, J., 184
Williams, J. B. W., 166
Wilson, G. T., 10, 181
Wilson, K. J., 69
Winkelstern, J. A., 184
Witheridge, T. F., 176
Witkin, S. L., 6
Wodarski, J. S., 3, 69, 184
Woody, G. E., 182
Woody, S. R., 10, 163, 164
Woolf, S., 167
World Wide Web
    search engines, 50, 113
    searching, 43, 112–117

YAHOO, 97
Yegidis, B. L., 150–151, 153, 159

Zuercher-White, E., 182, 187